Adrian Raeside
The World According to
DOGS
AN OWNER'S MANUAL

Adrian Raeside

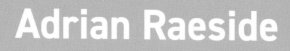

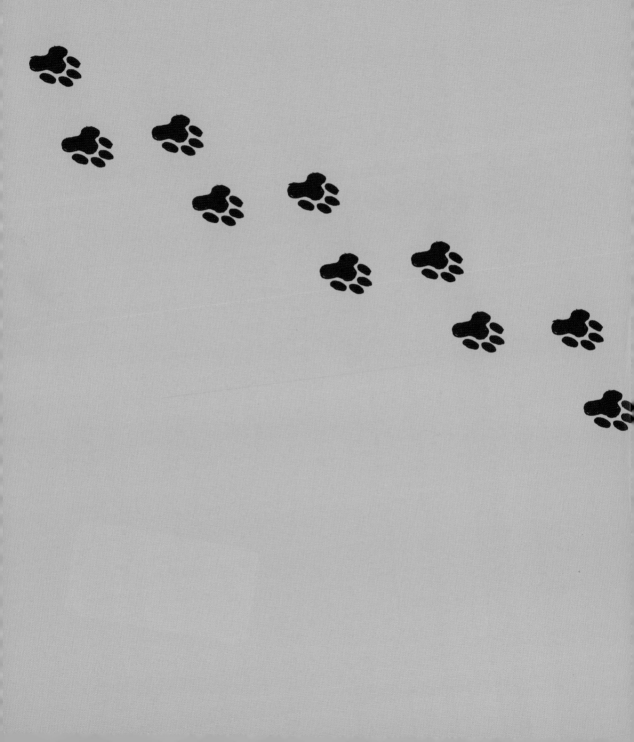

The World
According to Dogs

An Owner's Manual

HARBOUR
PUBLISHING

For those who have rescued a dog.

2 3 4 5 6 — 26 25 24 23 22

Harbour Publishing Co. Ltd.
P.O. Box 219, Madeira Park, BC, V0N 2H0
www.harbourpublishing.com

Cover design by Shed Simas / Onça Design
Text design by Teresa Karbashewski & Shed Simas / Onça Design
Printed and bound in South Korea

Canada | British Columbia Arts Council | British Columbia | Canada Council for the Arts | Conseil des arts du Canada

Harbour Publishing acknowledges the support of the Canada Council for the Arts, the Government of Canada, and the Province of British Columbia through the BC Arts Council.

Library and Archives Canada Cataloguing in Publication

Title: The world according to dogs : an owner's manual / Adrian Raeside.
Names: Raeside, Adrian, 1957- author, artist.
Identifiers: Canadiana (print) 20210238240 | Canadiana (ebook) 20210238267 | ISBN 9781550179699 (softcover) | ISBN 9781550179705 (EPUB)
Subjects: LCSH: Dogs—Caricatures and cartoons. | LCSH: Canadian wit and humor, Pictorial. | LCGFT: Comics (Graphic works)
Classification: LCC NC1449.R34 A4 2021 | DDC 741.5/6971—dc23

CONTENTS

INTRODUCTION

There are libraries full of books written about dogs: dog behaviour, dog breeding, dog grooming, dog showing and so on. But they've all been written by people. Why haven't there been any books written about dogs from a dog's perspective? You already treat us like small, hairy people anyway, so it stands to reason we should be able to put paw to paper and compile a book about us, by us.

The World According to Dogs: An Owners Manual is about how we like to be treated, what we like and dislike, repairs and maintenance, how to deal with a puppy, how to tell what we're thinking, and what the world would be like if dogs ran it, along with a few interesting facts about dogs thrown in occasionally.

We've been observing you for generations and we've pretty much got you figured out. But sometimes we wonder if you've really figured us out…

So, whether you're a new dog owner who is wondering what makes us tick, or someone who is lucky enough to have had dogs all your life, *The World According to Dogs* has something for everyone.

—A Dog

DOG

This is a book about dogs, not cats. As you can see, there are subtle differences between a dog and a cat...

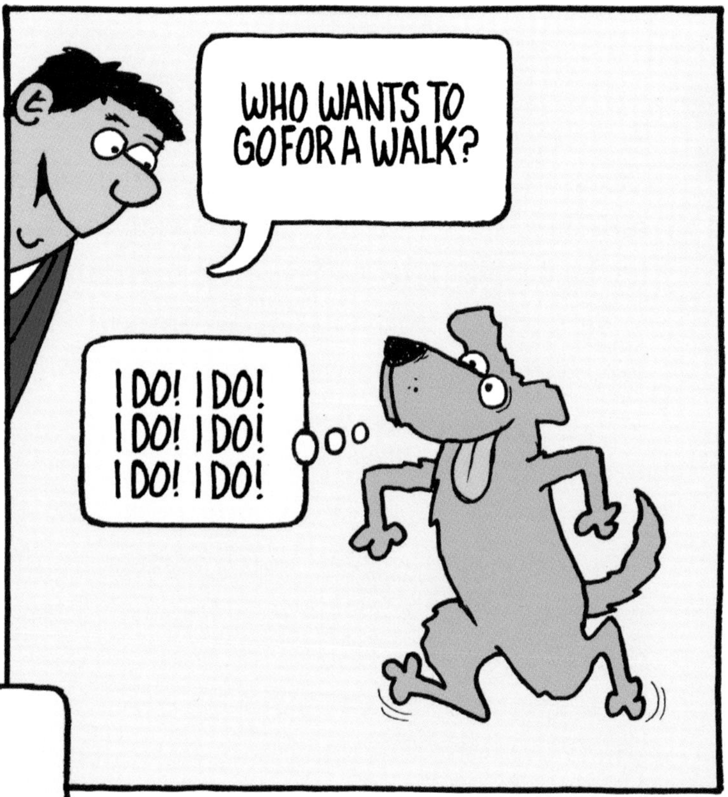
WHO WANTS TO GO FOR A WALK?
I DO! I DO! I DO! I DO! I DO! I DO!

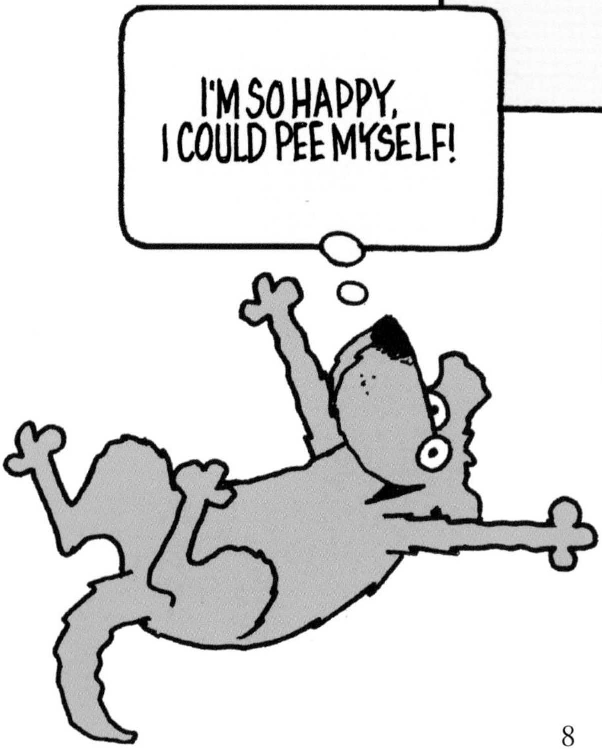
I'M SO HAPPY, I COULD PEE MYSELF!

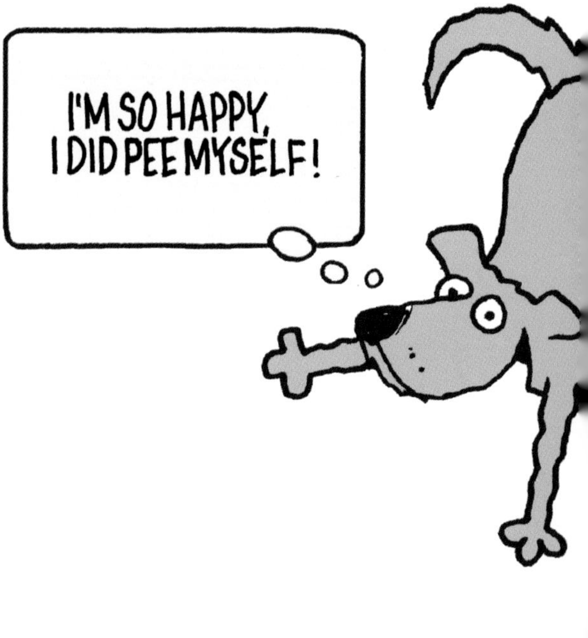
I'M SO HAPPY, I DID PEE MYSELF!

CaT

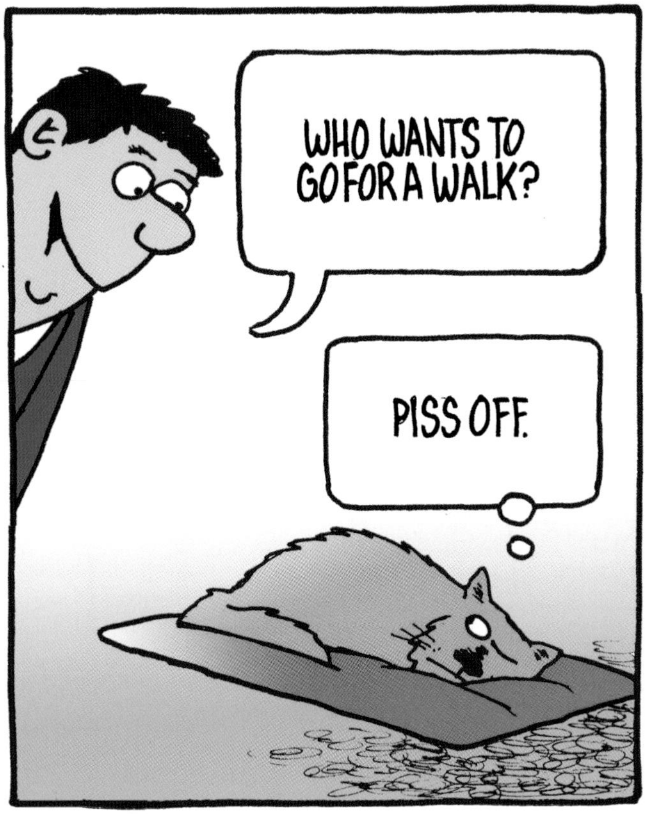
WHO WANTS TO GO FOR A WALK?
PISS OFF.

There are numerous references to dogs in the bible...

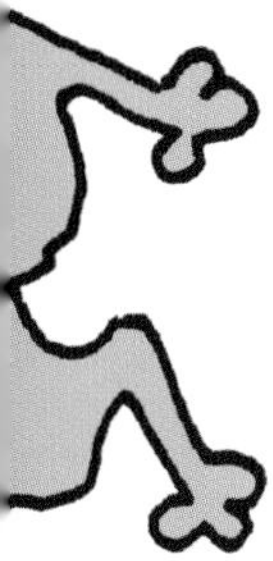

... there are no references to cats.

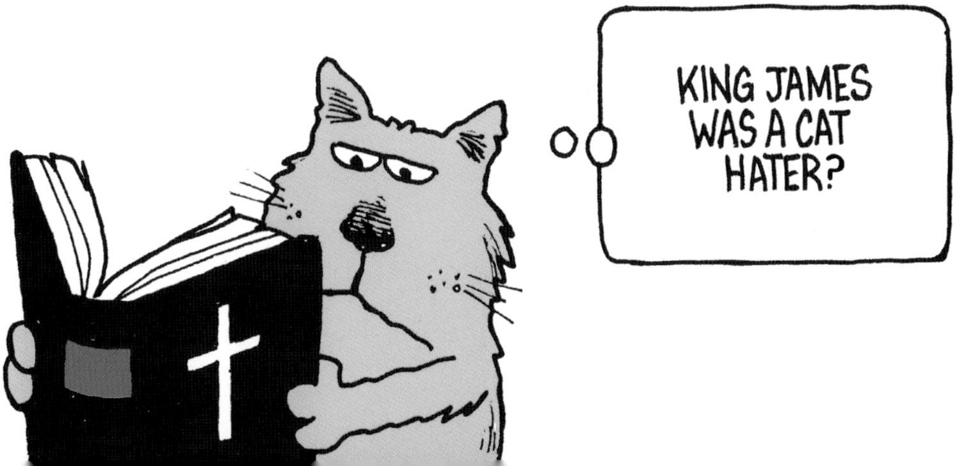
KING JAMES WAS A CAT HATER?

TO DO LIST FOR DOGS

RUN AROUND THE HOUSE
GO FOR A LONG WALK
CHASE SQUIRRELS
FIND PERFECT STICK
PEE ON A LOT OF TREES
DIG IN THE GARDEN
ROLL IN SOMETHING SMELLY
GO FOR A CAR RIDE AND HANG
HEAD OUT WINDOW
BEG FOR TABLE SCRAPS
SNEAK ONTO COUCH
BARK
SCARF DOWN SOMETHING FOUND
ON THE SIDEWALK
THROW UP ON THE RUG
FART
GAZE ADORINGLY AT MOM & DAD

FOR CATS

EAT
SLEEP
KILL A BIRD

DID YOU KNOW...?

It is estimated there are around 78,000,000 dogs in the USA and Canada.

...AND ONLY 77,999,999 BUTTS LEFT TO SNIFF.

When it comes to literature, ***WE RULE!***
There are more books written
about dogs than cats.

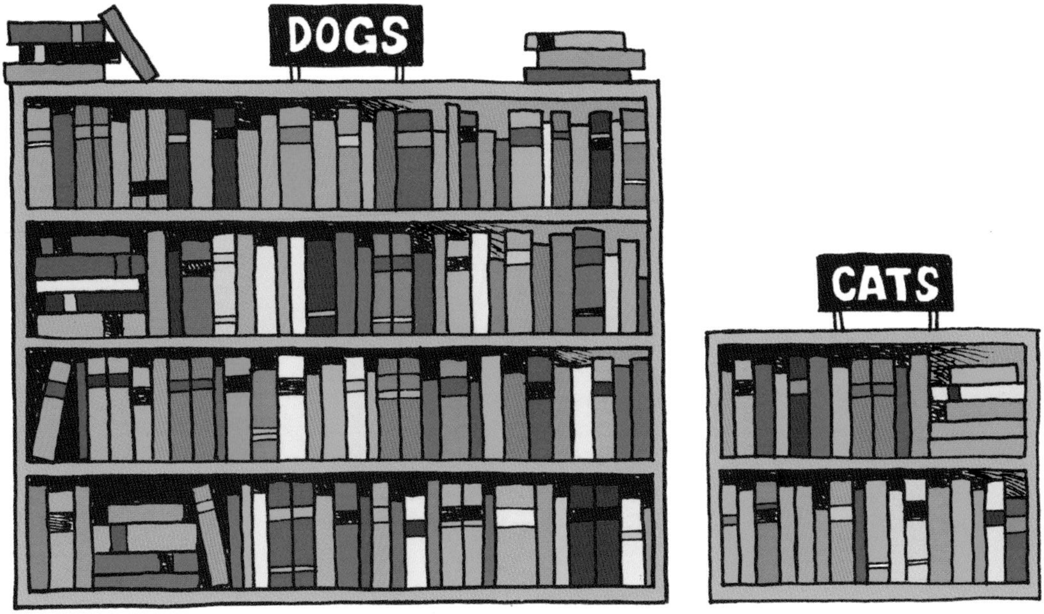
DOGS
CATS

But there are more cat videos than dog videos.

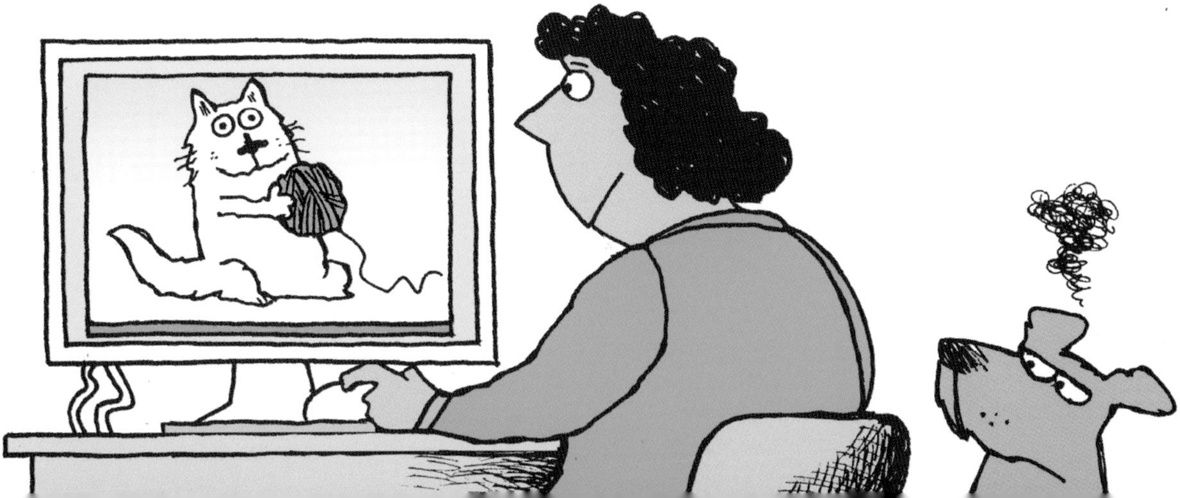

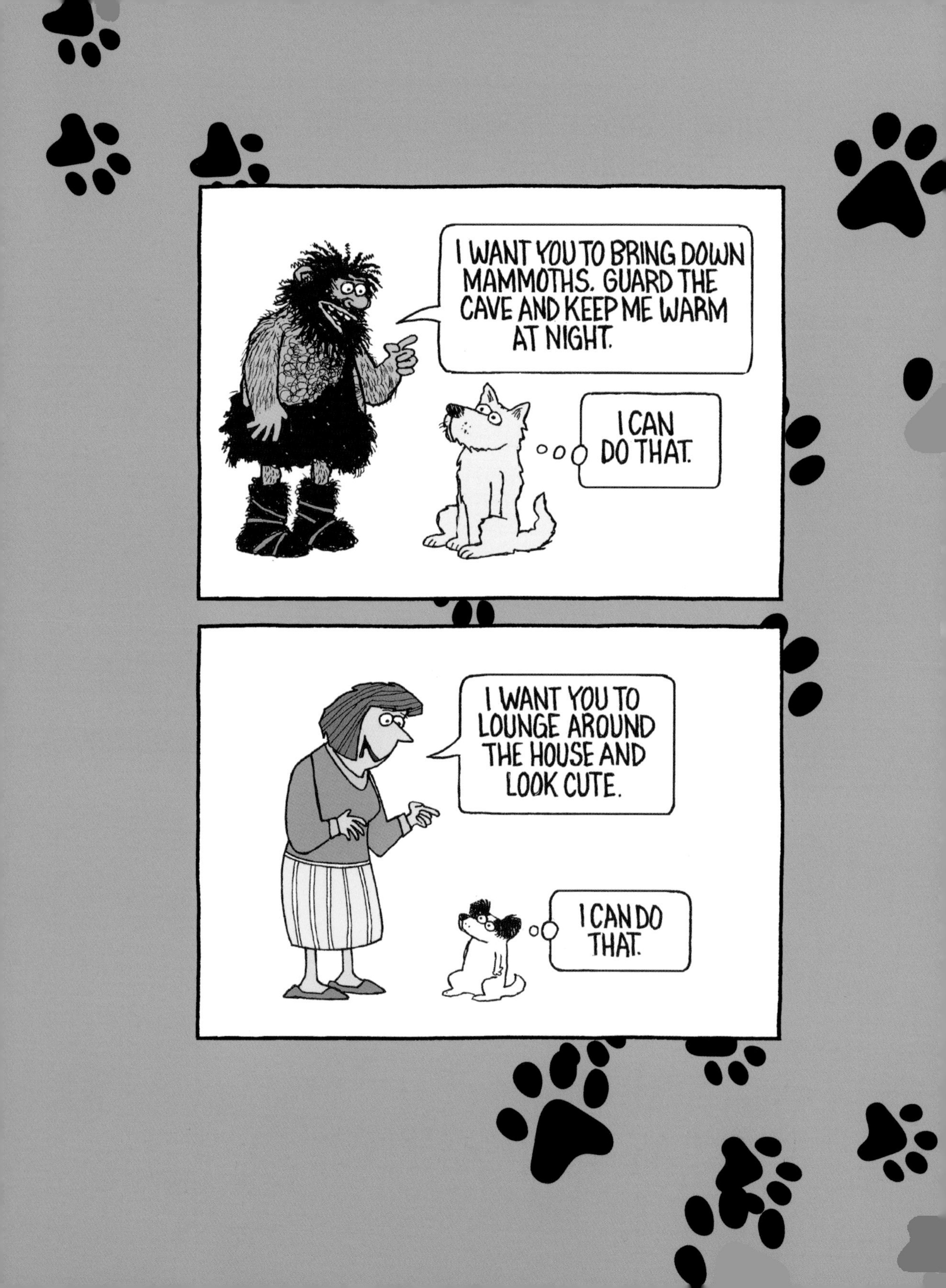
I WANT YOU TO BRING DOWN MAMMOTHS. GUARD THE CAVE AND KEEP ME WARM AT NIGHT.
I CAN DO THAT.
I WANT YOU TO LOUNGE AROUND THE HOUSE AND LOOK CUTE.
I CAN DO THAT.

THE EVOLUTION OF DOGS

We've been around for a while in the form of Eurasian Grey Wolves. (That's the human name; the dog name is "Mighty Lords of All We Survey.") We were quite happy on our own, doing what comes naturally to wolves—namely, hunting prey in packs. But then around fifteen thousand years ago we started competing for food with a group of not-so-hairy two-legged creatures who, it turned out, were also pretty good at hunting. Some of us (we call them the "lazy lords of all they survey") thought it would be preferable to hang around with the two-legged hunters. Why chase after prey when someone else would do it for you? All the lazy lords had to do in return was guard the cave, which wasn't hard because there was nothing much to guard except some mud and sticks, and keep the hunters warm at night.

Since those humble beginnings, we've gone through a remarkably rapid evolution, from helping with the hunt to helping ourselves off the kitchen counter. Even though we were "domesticated," i.e., not savaging and eating our two-legged companions, we were still relegated to hanging around outside your dwellings. However, by what you call the Victorian Period, people realized they rather liked having us inside, especially to keep them warm in cold, drafty houses. We were also pretty good at getting rid of rats and chewing the leg off the occasional burglar. This arrangement suited us just fine, as the outside had become pretty horrible by then. Instead of just dodging wild animals, we were dodging horses, carts and even trains. So we moved indoors, climbed onto the most comfortable piece of furniture available, and have stayed there ever since.

IN THE BEGINNING...

Our ancestors were natural hunters but they noticed man was getting pretty good at it too.

It soon became obvious that there wasn't much point in spending the day chasing after your dinner when there was someone else to do it for you.

All it took was a little teamwork.

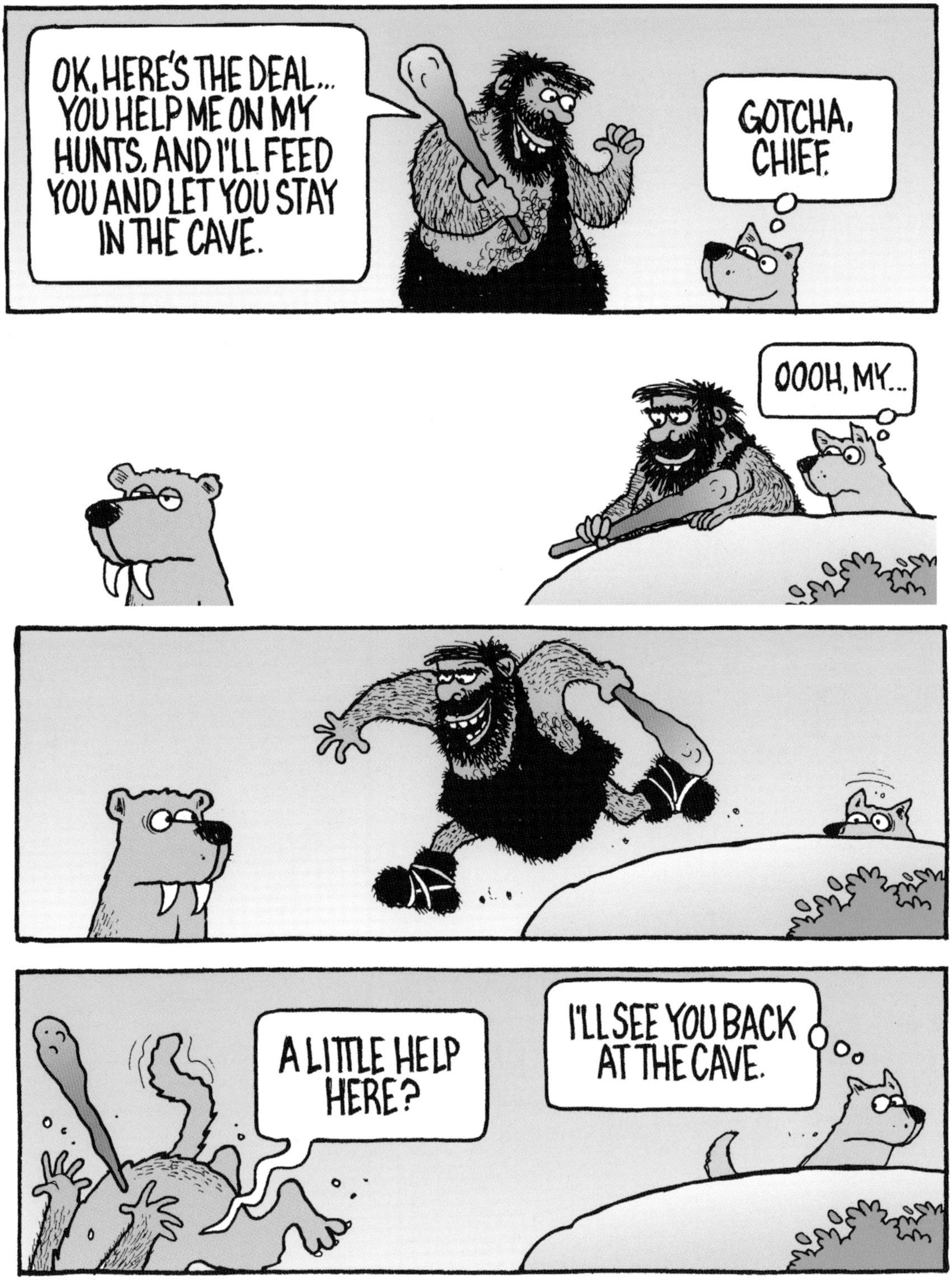

OK, HERE'S THE DEAL... YOU HELP ME ON MY HUNTS, AND I'LL FEED YOU AND LET YOU STAY IN THE CAVE.
GOTCHA, CHIEF.
OOOH, MY...
A LITTLE HELP HERE?
I'LL SEE YOU BACK AT THE CAVE.

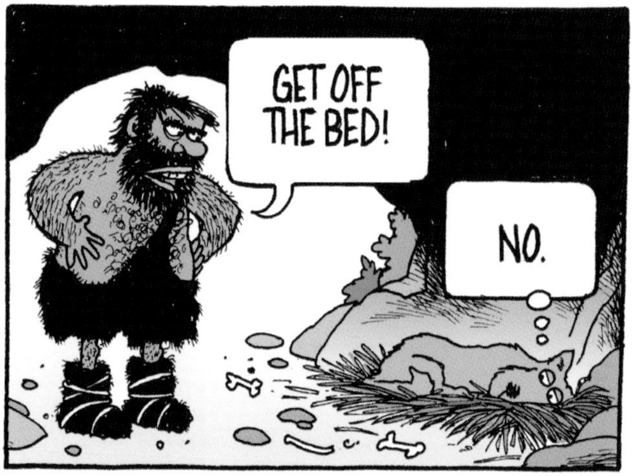
GET OFF THE BED!
NO.

Before long, we realized even if we didn't go out into the cold and wet to hunt we'd still get our dinner.

And so began the evolution from wild wolf to house pet.

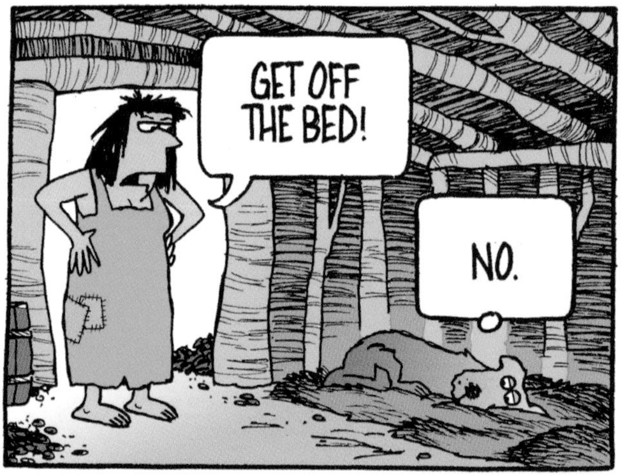
GET OFF THE BED!
NO.

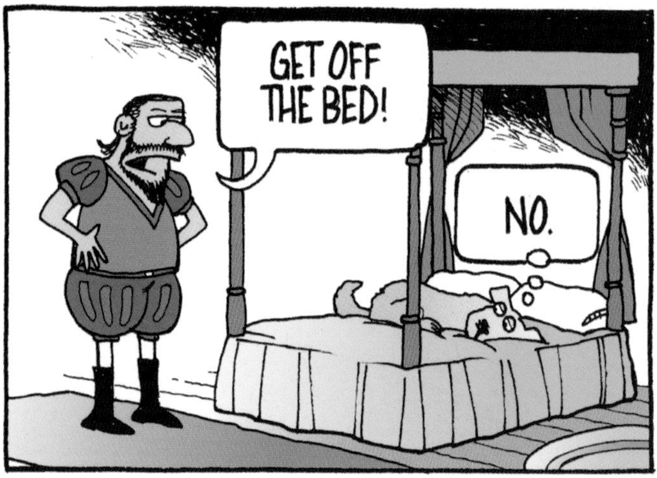
GET OFF THE BED!
NO.

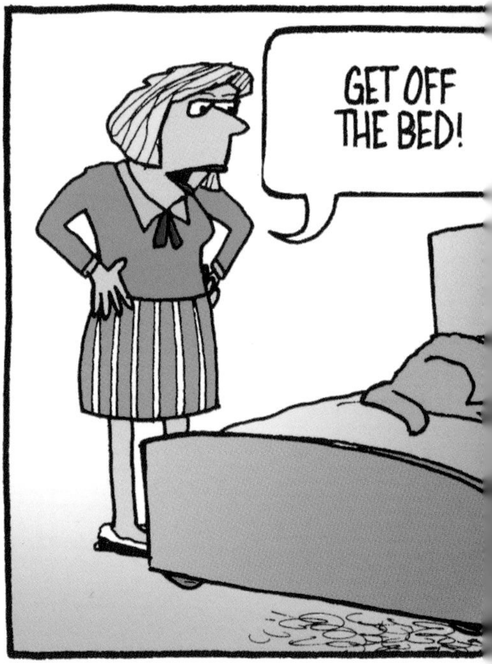
GET OFF THE BED!

THE TRANSITION FROM HUNTER TO PET:

OH, GREAT. RAT BREATH.
OH, GREAT. CANNED DOG FOOD BREATH.

NO.

DID YOU KNOW...?

70 percent of dog owners allow their dog to sleep on the bed.

100 percent of dogs fart on the bed.

Cool fact: We first appeared in prehistoric cave art roughly 8,000 years ago...

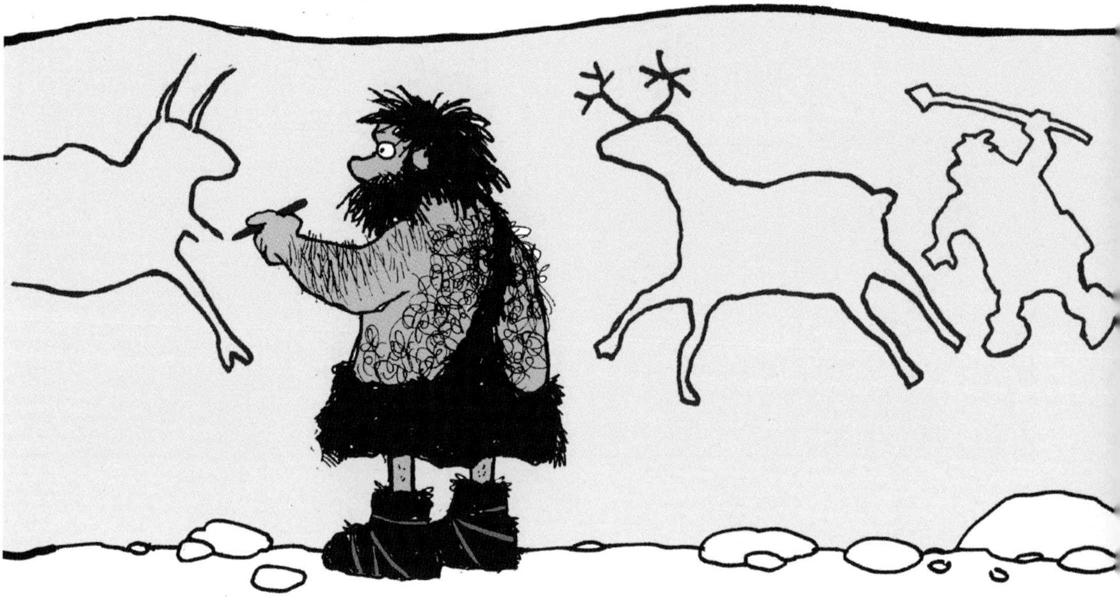

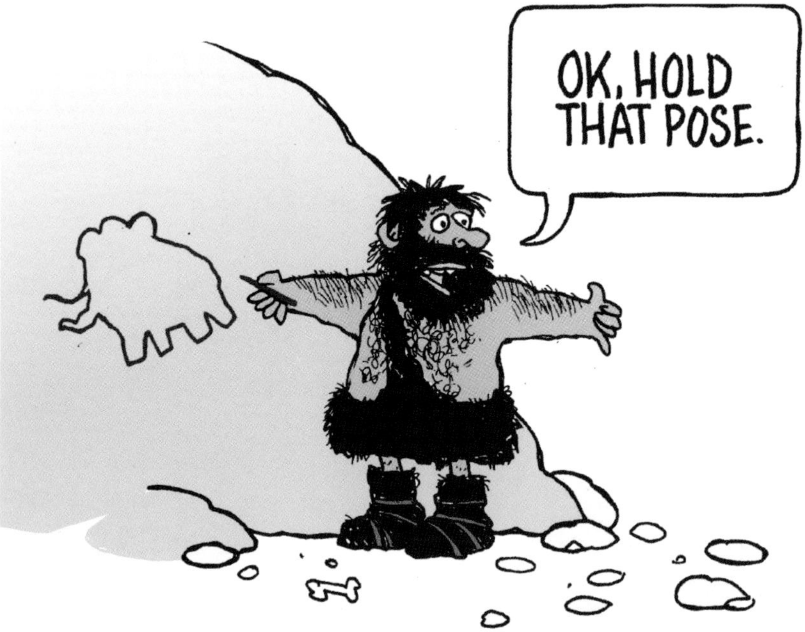
OK, HOLD THAT POSE.

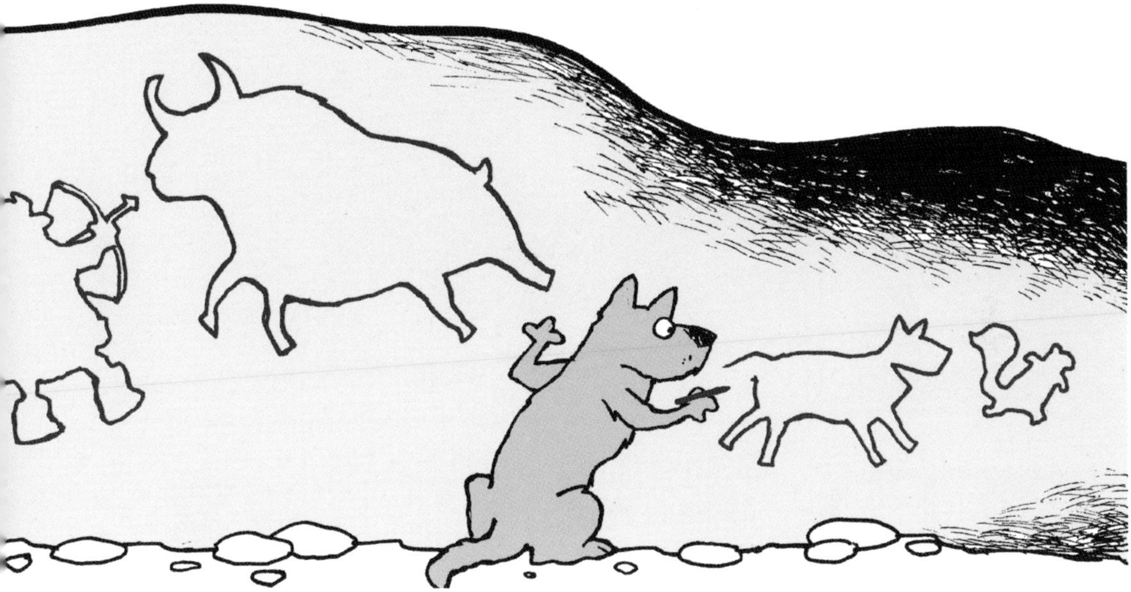

... and we've
been dominating
art ever since.

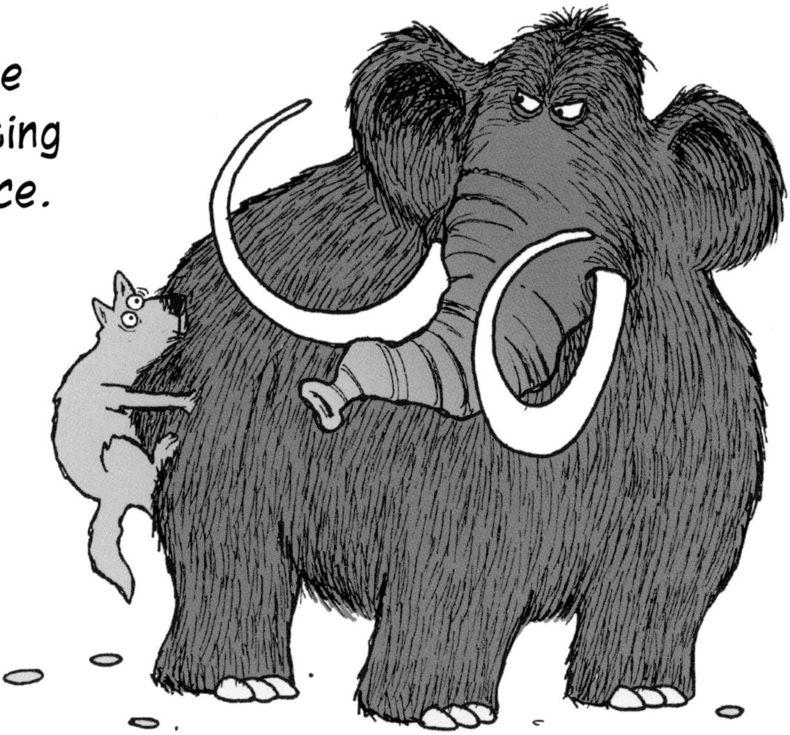

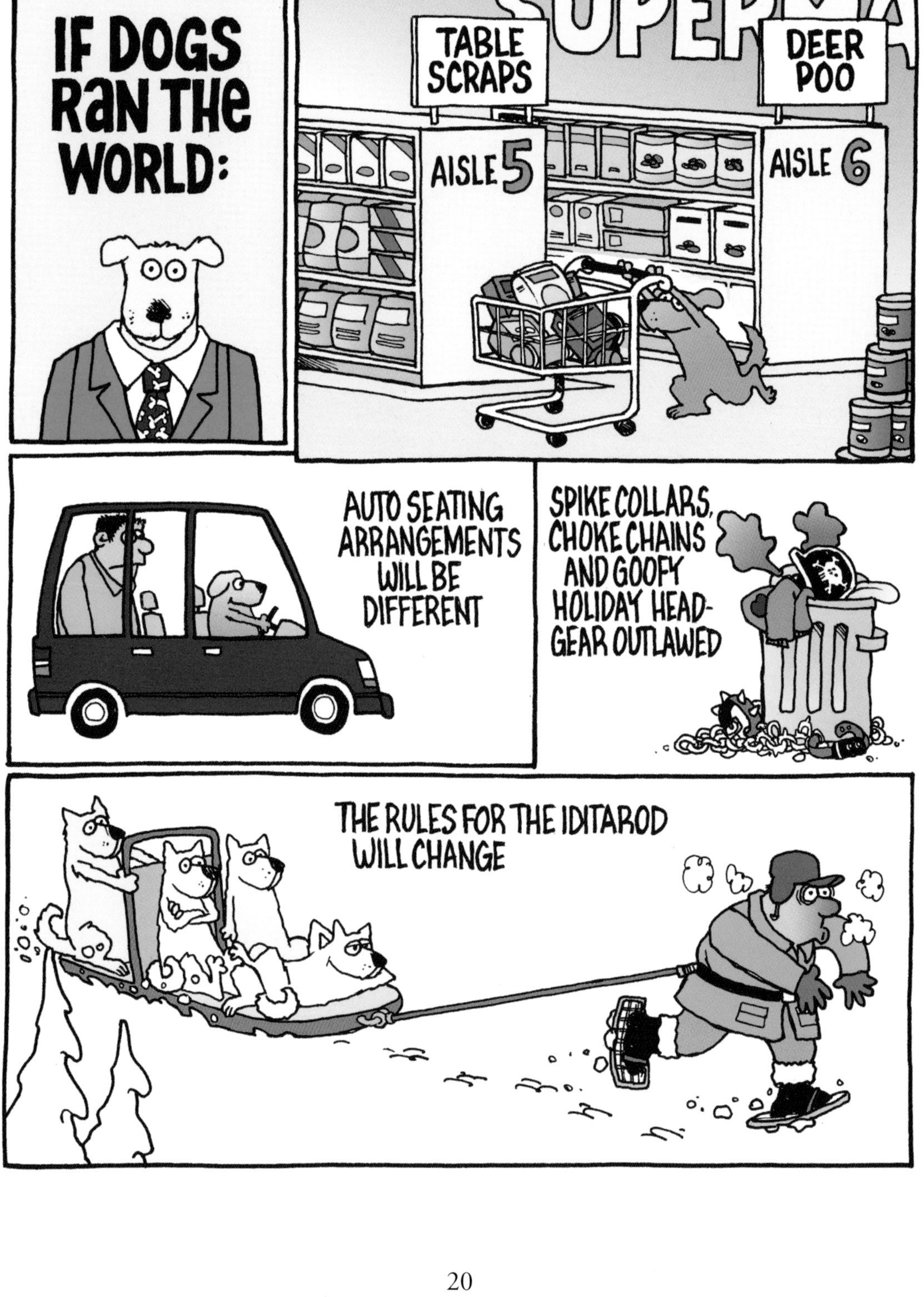
IF DOGS RaN THE WORLD:
SUPERMA
TABLE SCRAPS
DEER POO
AISLE 5
AISLE 6
AUTO SEATING ARRANGEMENTS WILL BE DIFFERENT
SPIKE COLLARS, CHOKE CHAINS AND GOOFY HOLIDAY HEAD-GEAR OUTLAWED
THE RULES FOR THE IDITAROD WILL CHANGE

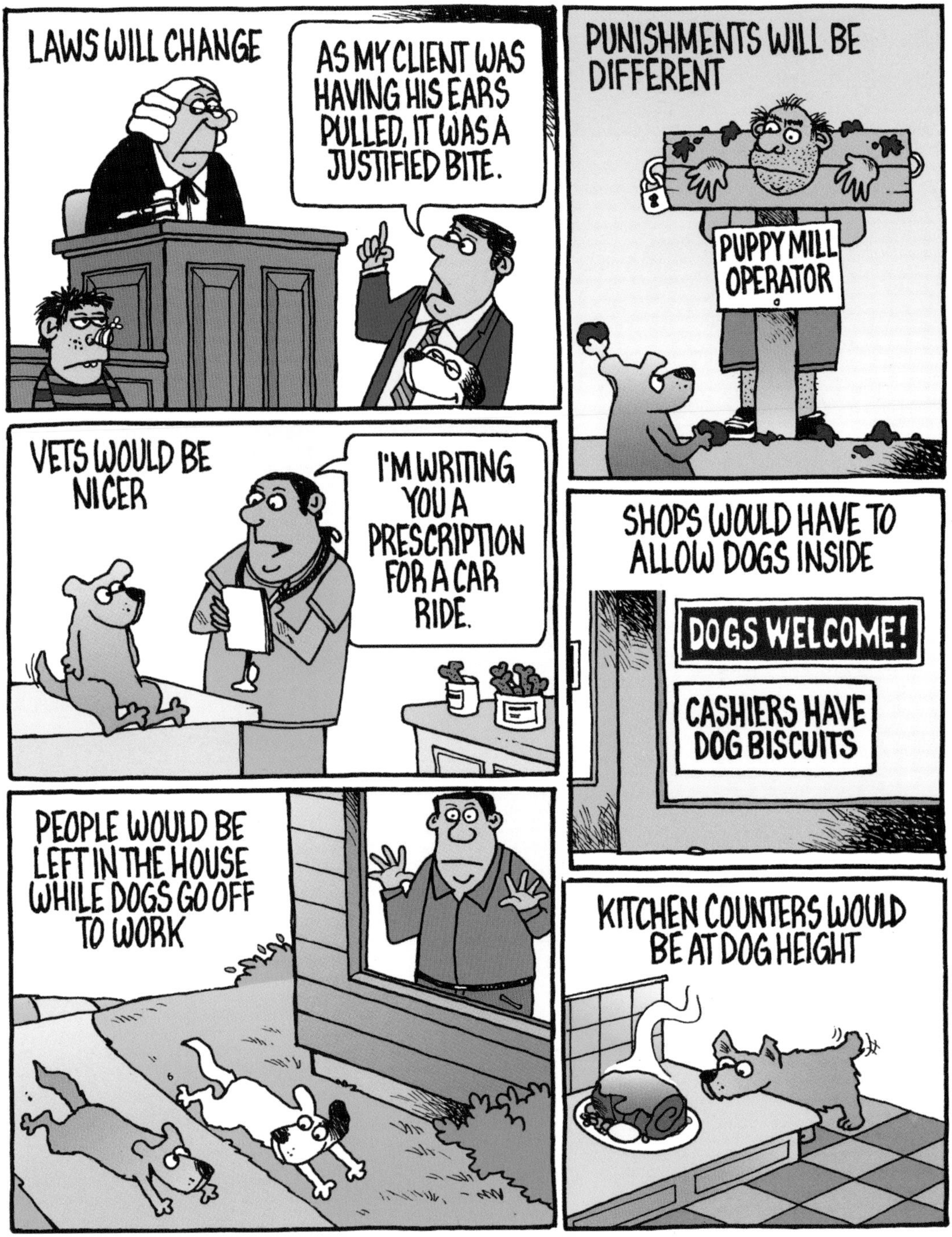
LAWS WILL CHANGE
AS MY CLIENT WAS HAVING HIS EARS PULLED, IT WAS A JUSTIFIED BITE.
PUNISHMENTS WILL BE DIFFERENT
PUPPY MILL OPERATOR
VETS WOULD BE NICER
I'M WRITING YOU A PRESCRIPTION FOR A CAR RIDE.
SHOPS WOULD HAVE TO ALLOW DOGS INSIDE
DOGS WELCOME!
CASHIERS HAVE DOG BISCUITS
PEOPLE WOULD BE LEFT IN THE HOUSE WHILE DOGS GO OFF TO WORK
KITCHEN COUNTERS WOULD BE AT DOG HEIGHT

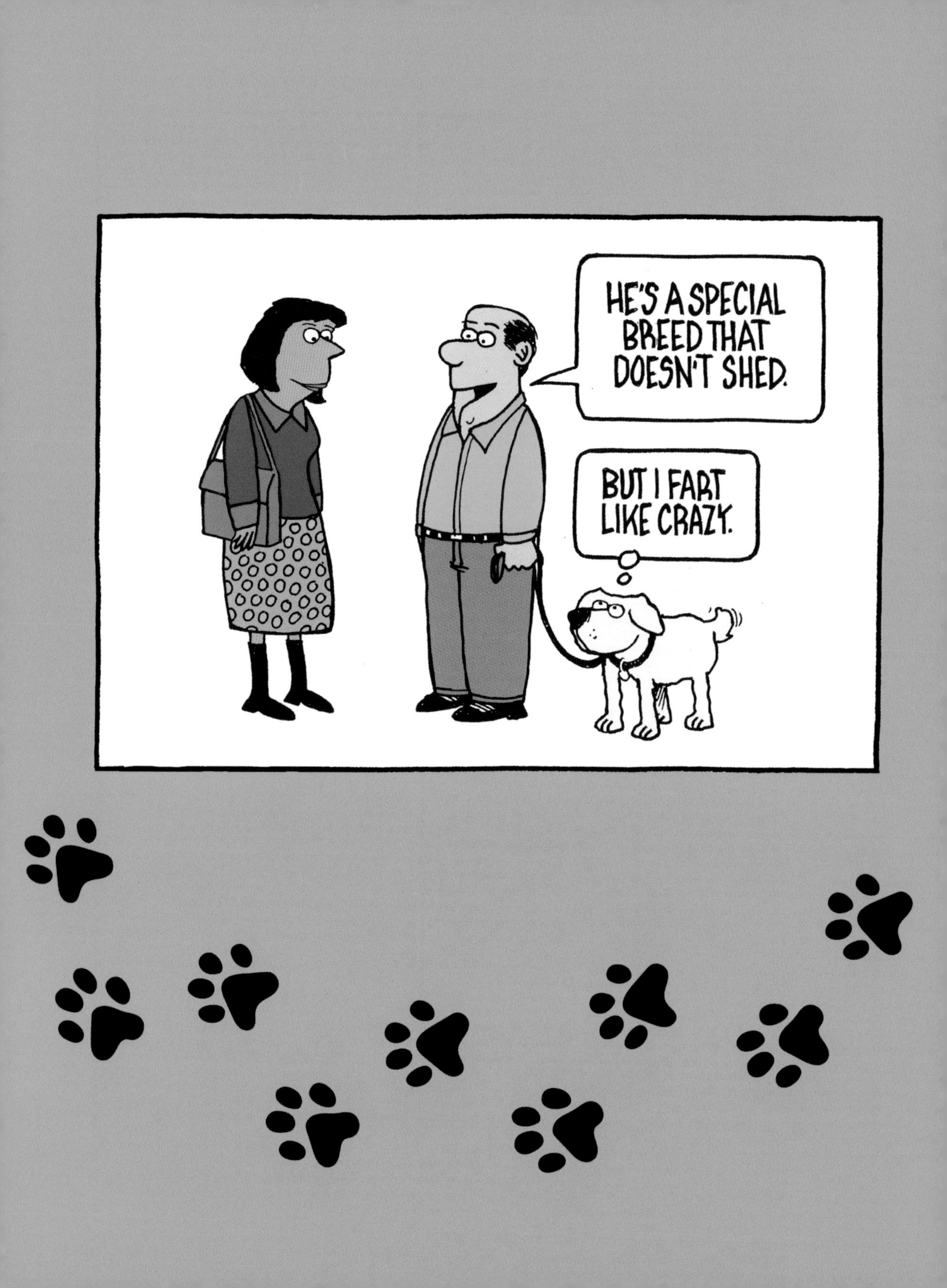
HE'S A SPECIAL BREED THAT DOESN'T SHED.
BUT I FART LIKE CRAZY.

BREEDS

We're everything from a teacup Chihuahua (doomed to never experience the joy of scrounging a roast off a kitchen counter) to a Great Dane, where everything in the house can be scrounged.

We'd have been quite content to stay wolf-sized, but your ancestors had other ideas. Rather than fit the task to us, you fitted us to the task. With the lack of mammoths to hunt, we were bred to go after smaller quarry like badgers, rats, ducks—in fact, anything you wanted to eat (and probably didn't share). We were even bred to not hunt game, like sheep and cattle, but to keep an eye on them. But don't think we don't occasionally dream of lamb chops as we gaze upon our charges…

And for those of you who didn't hunt or keep sheep, you wanted "companion" dogs to keep you company and warm at night. And to be fair, a fluffy Pomeranian makes a better pillow companion than a wolf with bad breath.

Not content with your basic one-size-fits-all dog, you started cross-breeding more for show, although we draw the line at a Doberman that can fit in a purse… This process has been going on for many hundreds of years and still continues to this day—Labradoodles, Dorgis. Fortunately for you, we're not fussy over who we sleep with.

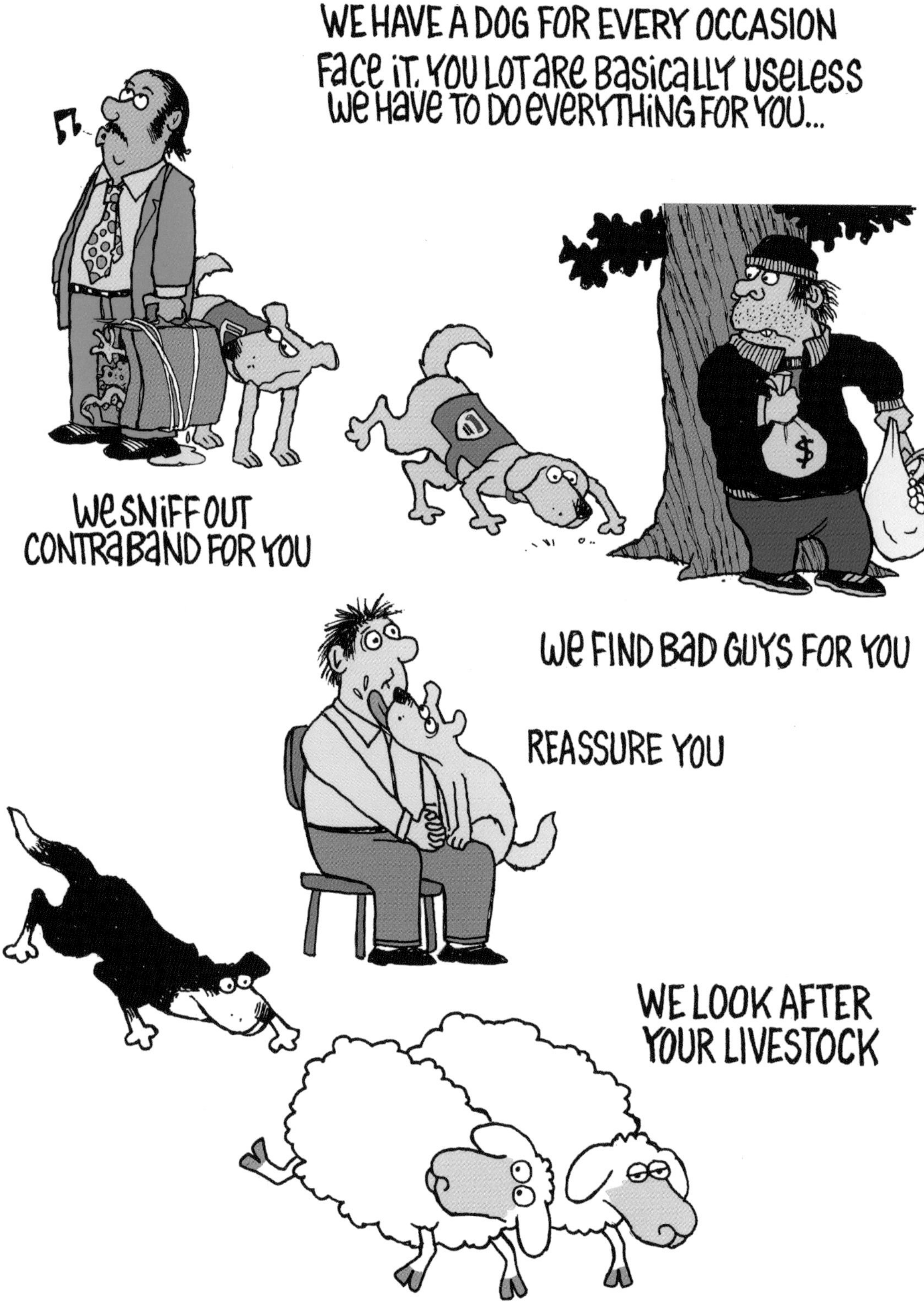
WE HAVE A DOG FOR EVERY OCCASION
FACE IT, YOU LOT ARE BASICALLY USELESS
WE HAVE TO DO EVERYTHING FOR YOU...
WE SNIFF OUT CONTRABAND FOR YOU
WE FIND BAD GUYS FOR YOU
REASSURE YOU
WE LOOK AFTER YOUR LIVESTOCK

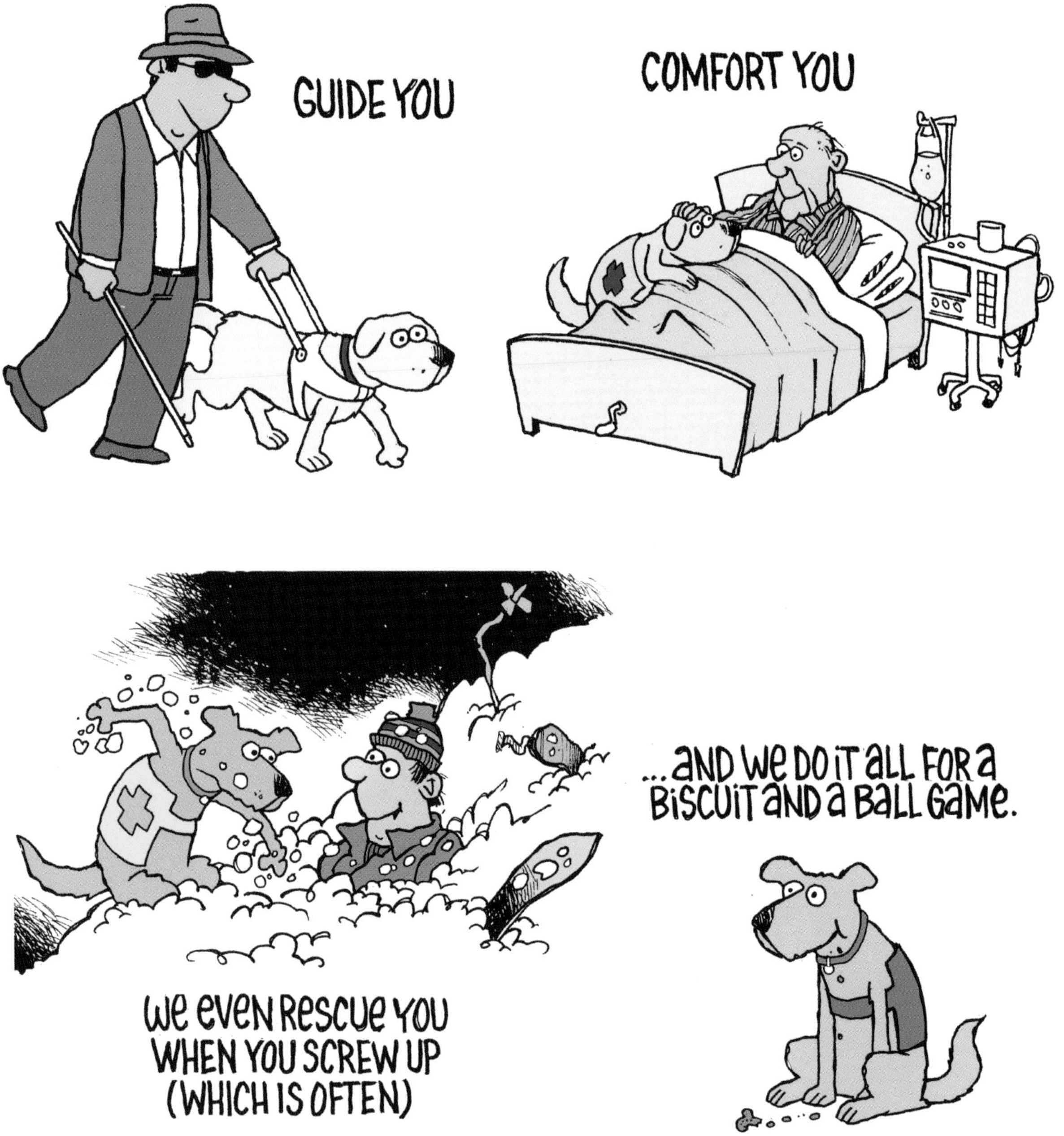
GUIDE YOU
COMFORT YOU
WE EVEN RESCUE YOU WHEN YOU SCREW UP (WHICH IS OFTEN)
...AND WE DO IT ALL FOR A BISCUIT AND A BALL GAME.
WE'RE A HECKOVA DEAL!

PUREBRED FAMILY TREE

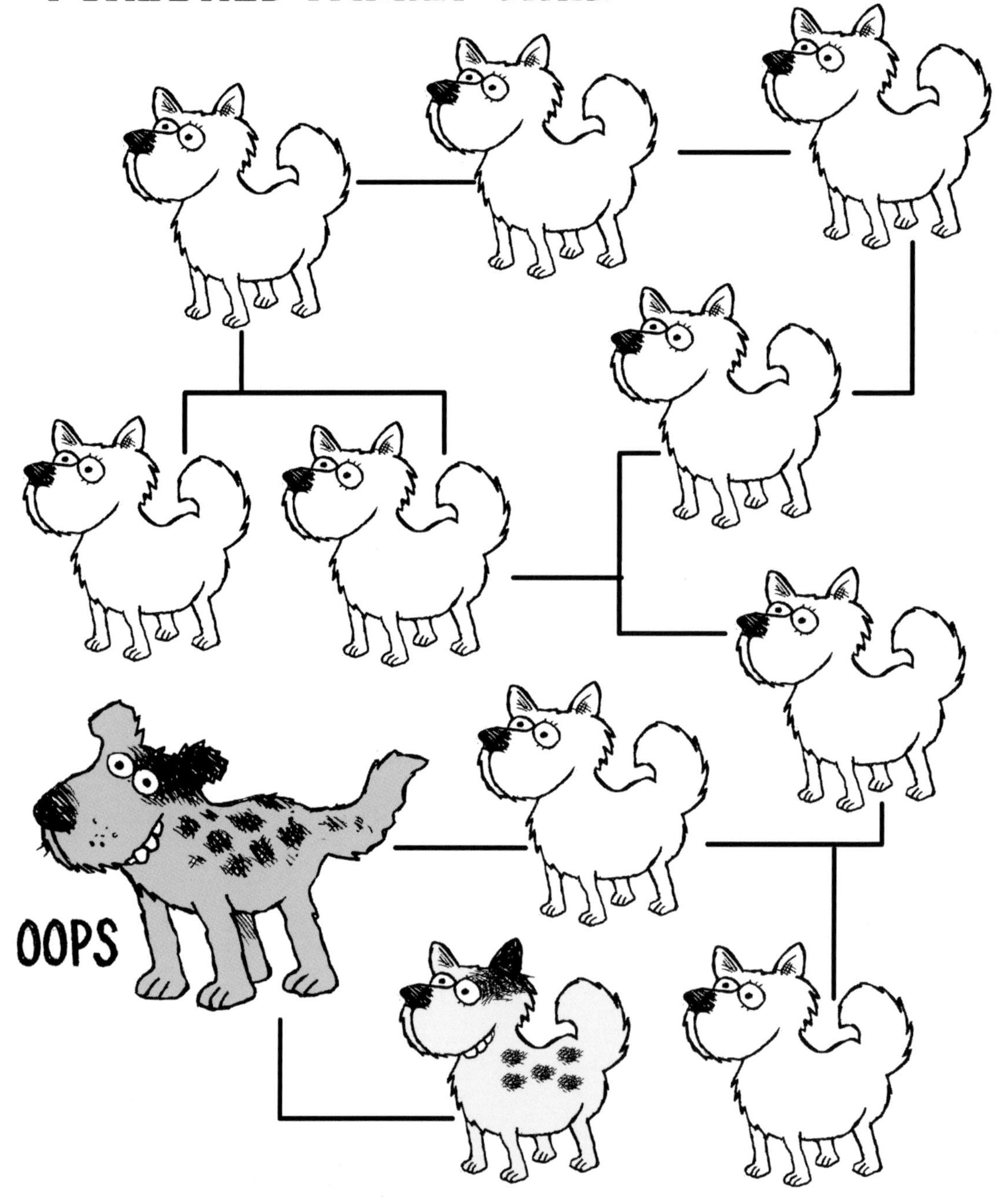
OOPS

MUTT FAMILY TREE

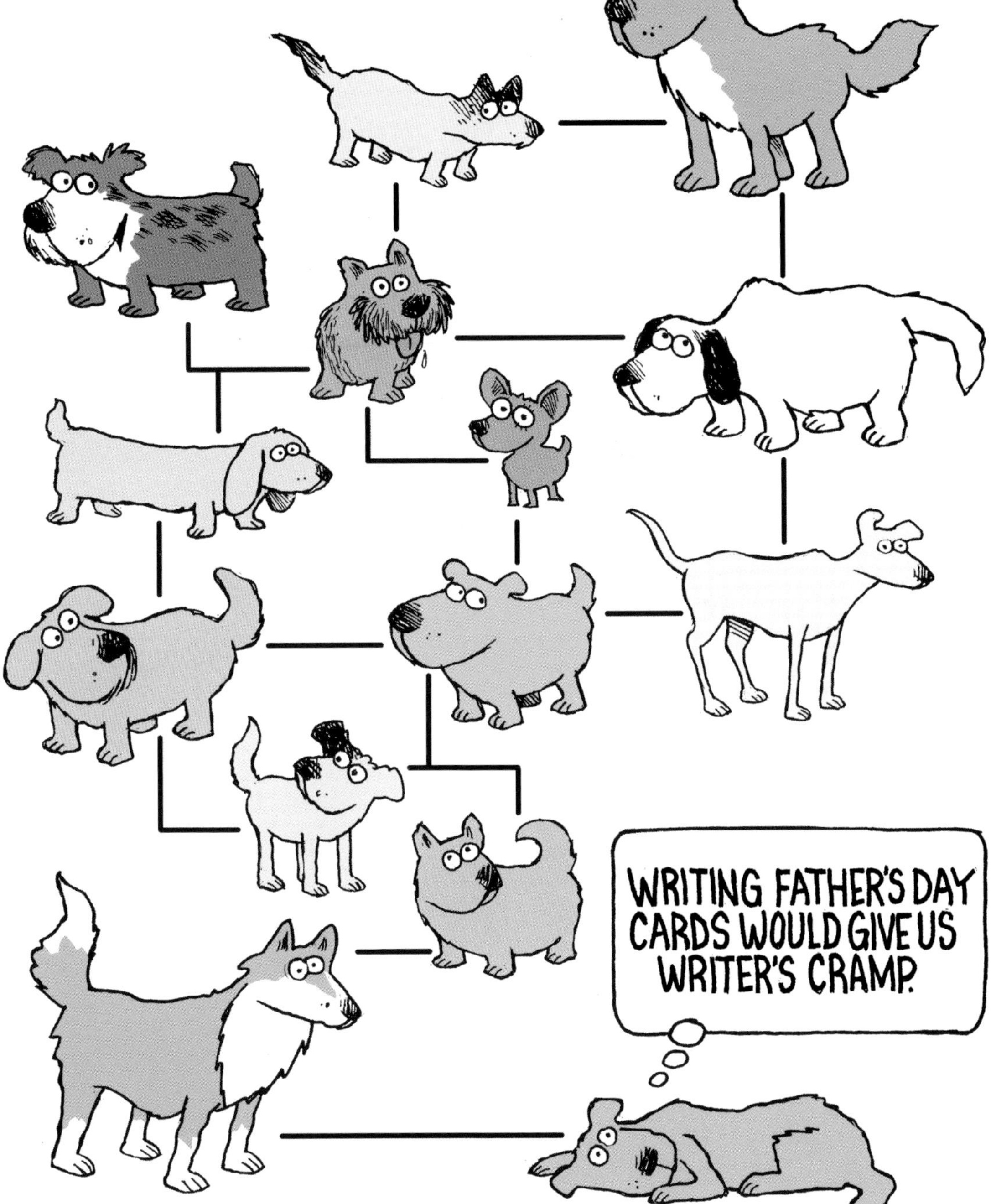
WRITING FATHER'S DAY CARDS WOULD GIVE US WRITER'S CRAMP.

We think your mating habits are painfully complicated dramas that usually end badly.

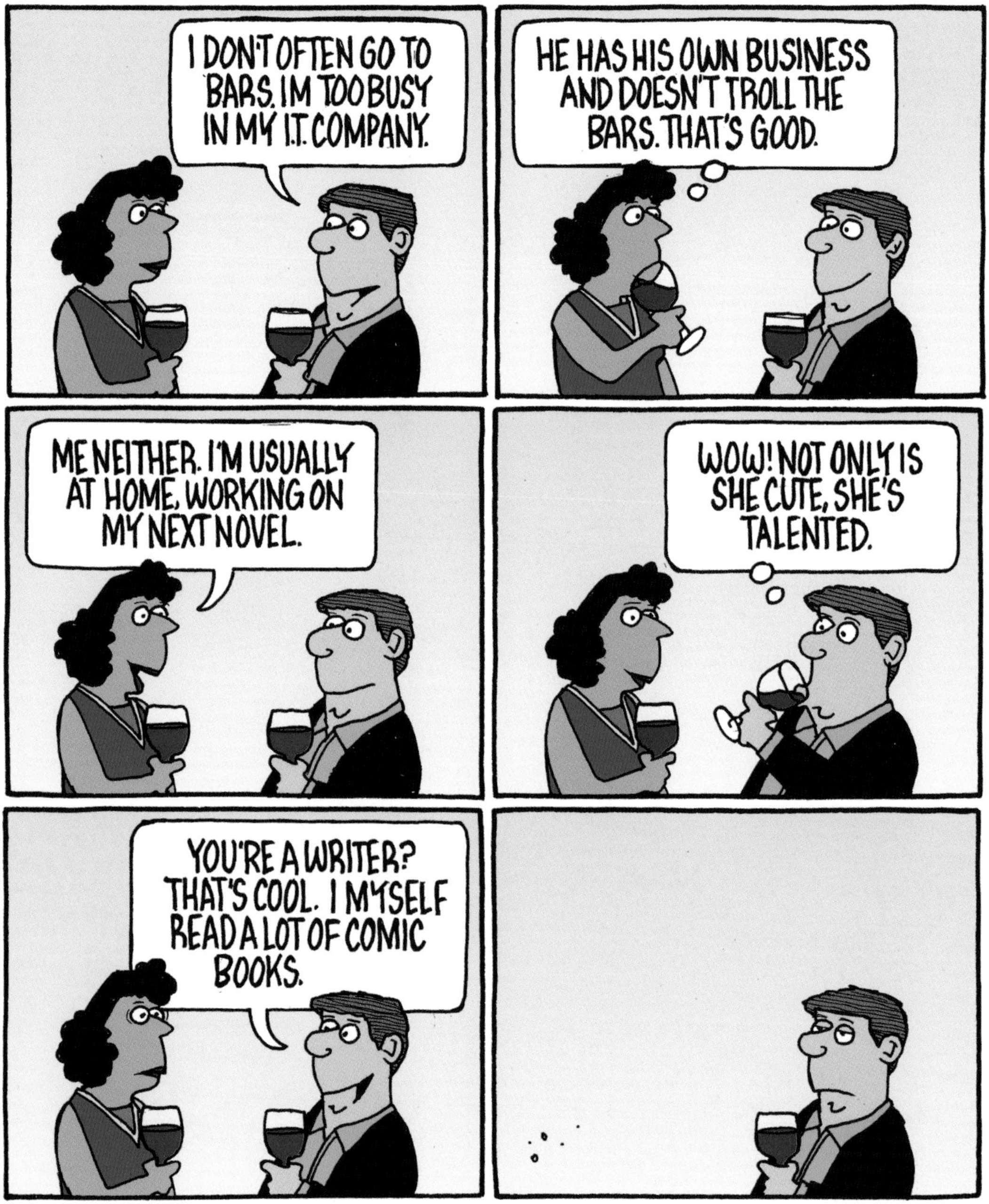
I DON'T OFTEN GO TO BARS. IM TOO BUSY IN MY I.T. COMPANY.
HE HAS HIS OWN BUSINESS AND DOESN'T TROLL THE BARS. THAT'S GOOD.
ME NEITHER. I'M USUALLY AT HOME, WORKING ON MY NEXT NOVEL.
WOW! NOT ONLY IS SHE CUTE, SHE'S TALENTED.
YOU'RE A WRITER? THAT'S COOL. I MYSELF READ A LOT OF COMIC BOOKS.

Ours, on the other hand, are simpler and less complicated.

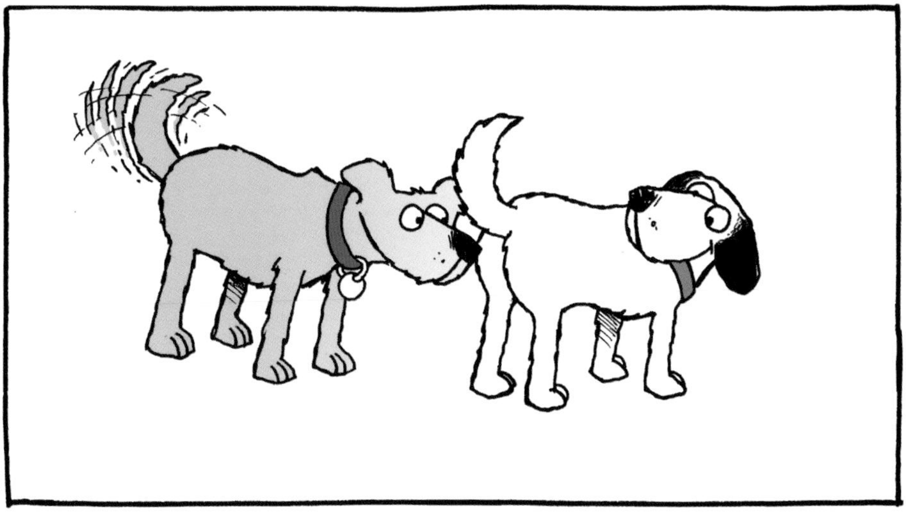

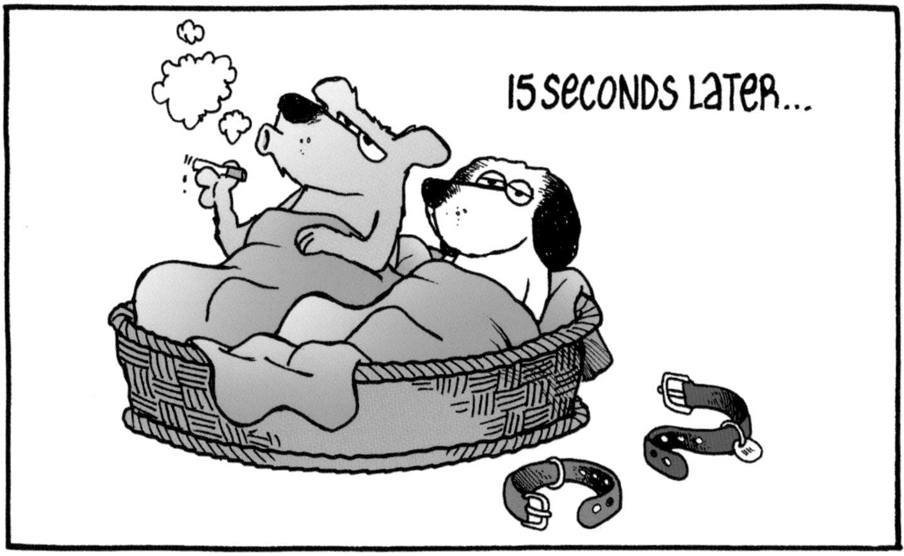
15 SECONDS LATER...

So if you have a dog in heat, keep her home. A dog park is our version of a singles bar.

Our concept of size is different from yours.

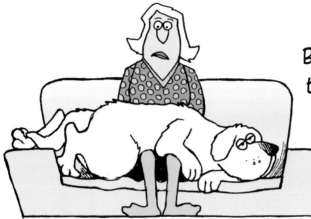

Big dogs think they're small dogs...

... and small dogs think they're big dogs.

QUIZ TIME!

Which dog is the show dog?

A

B

Answer: B
(never judge a dog by its collar)

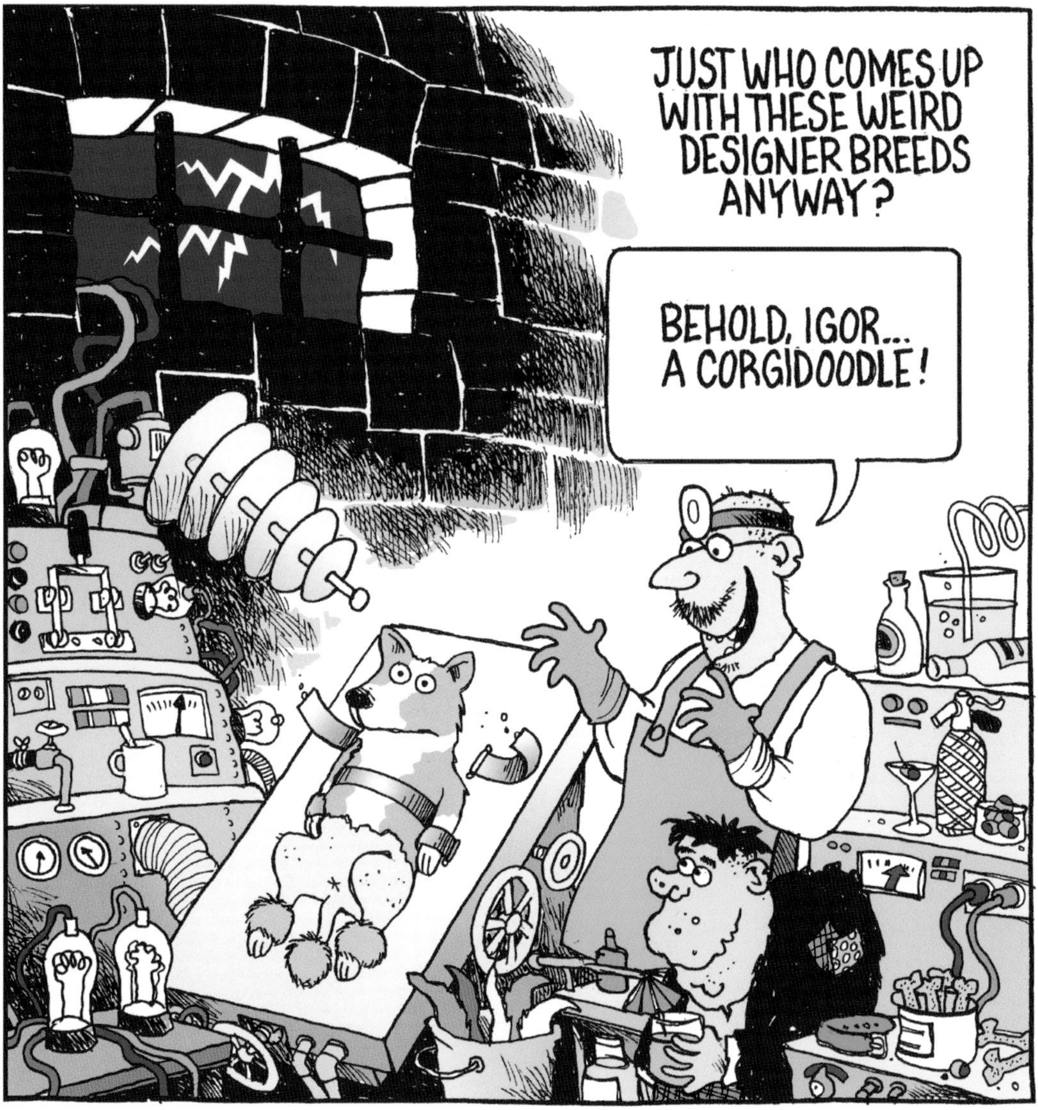
JUST WHO COMES UP WITH THESE WEIRD DESIGNER BREEDS ANYWAY?
BEHOLD, IGOR... A CORGIDOODLE!

...LEAVE THE CROSSBREEDING TO US. WE DO IT NATURALLY.

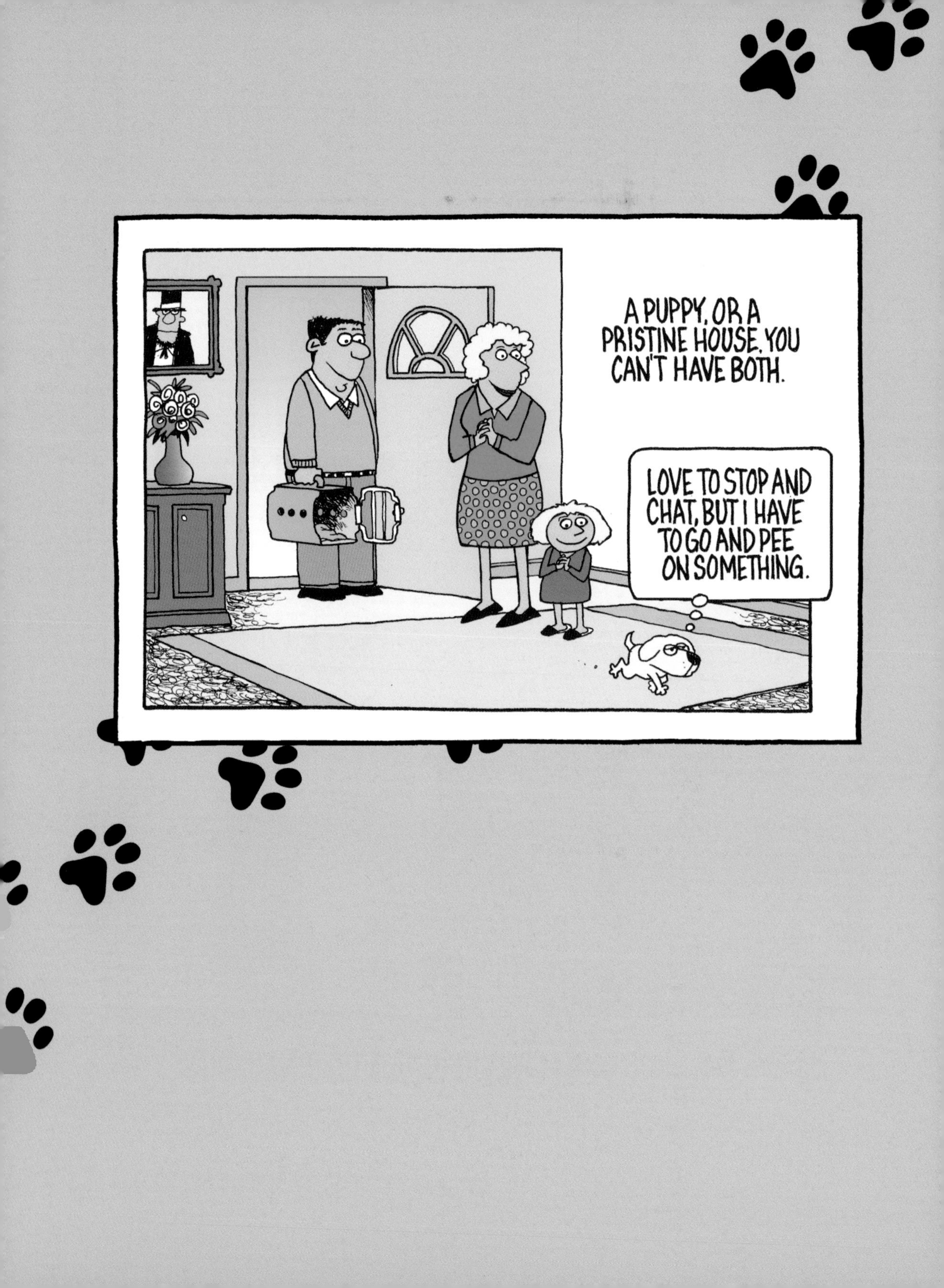
A PUPPY, OR A PRISTINE HOUSE. YOU CAN'T HAVE BOTH.
LOVE TO STOP AND CHAT, BUT I HAVE TO GO AND PEE ON SOMETHING.

CHAPTER 3

THE NEW DOG

If you don't already have a dog, what are you waiting for? You bought this book (or are cheap and just standing in the bookstore reading it), so it's obvious you're interested in us. If you're thinking of getting a dog—and we highly recommend it—you have two options: you can buy one from a breeder, or rescue a dog from a shelter.

From a canine's perspective, rescuing a dog is by far the best option. There are thousands of us waiting in shelters across the country. But if you're set on getting a puppy from a breeder or a pet store, beware of puppy mills. Do your research first. Buying from a puppy mill just means they stay in business longer.

Regardless of whether it's a puppy from a breeder or a rescue dog, once we step across the threshold, your house will change forever. Puppies will pee on everything, and some rescue dogs come with emotional baggage from a previous life and may need some time to adjust to a normal life. But with a little patience and (a lot of) dog treats, we will eventually become the most important member of your family.

It is an appalling fact that hundreds of thousands of homeless and stray dogs are euthanized every year in North America!

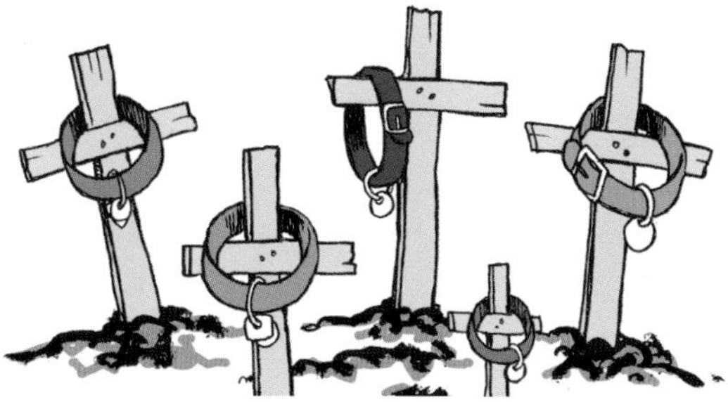

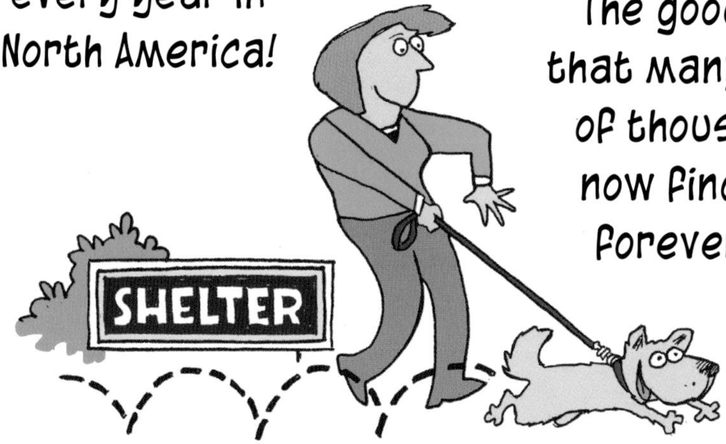
SHELTER

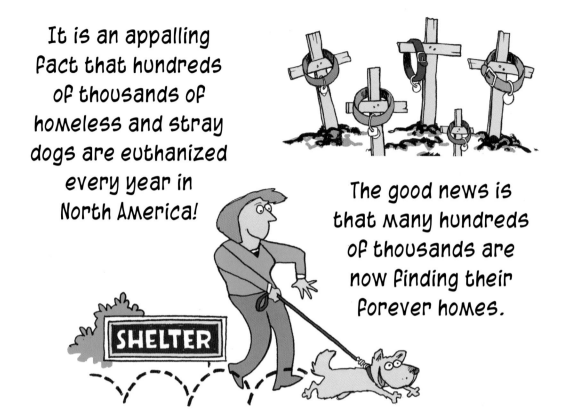

The good news is that many hundreds of thousands are now finding their forever homes.

DID YOU KNOW...?

Dogs can reduce your stress, anxiety, depression and improve your cardiovascular health.

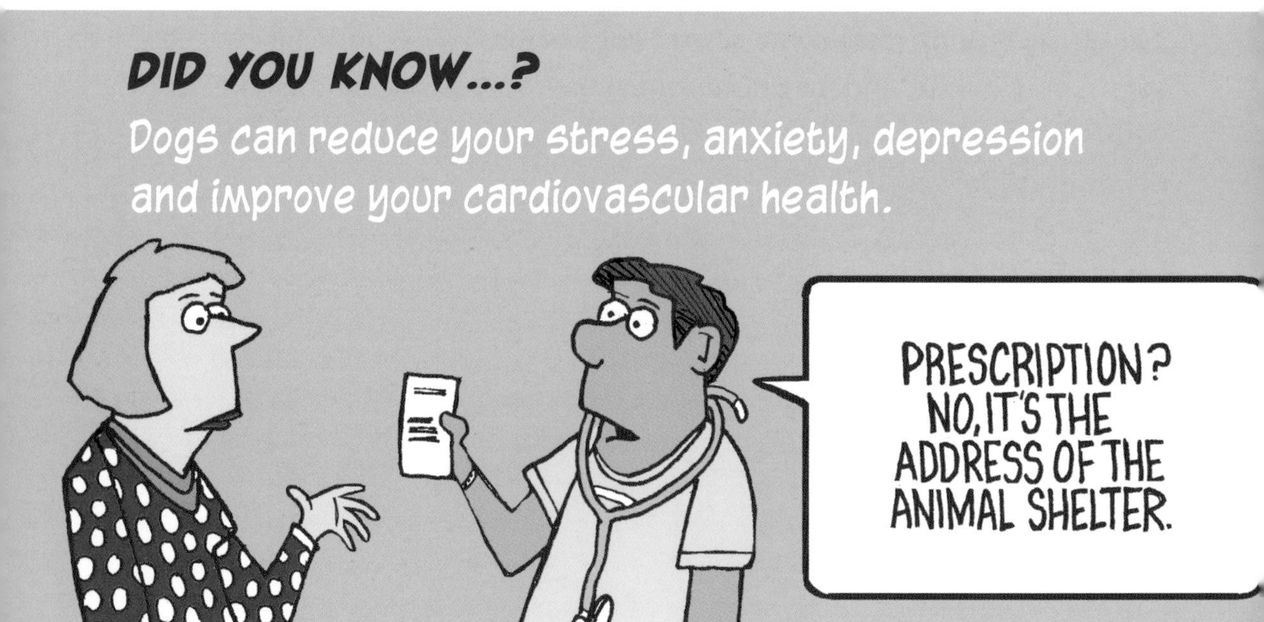
PRESCRIPTION? NO, IT'S THE ADDRESS OF THE ANIMAL SHELTER.

If you're looking for a dog, a good place to start is online. There are lots of reputable breeders out there if you want a puppy.

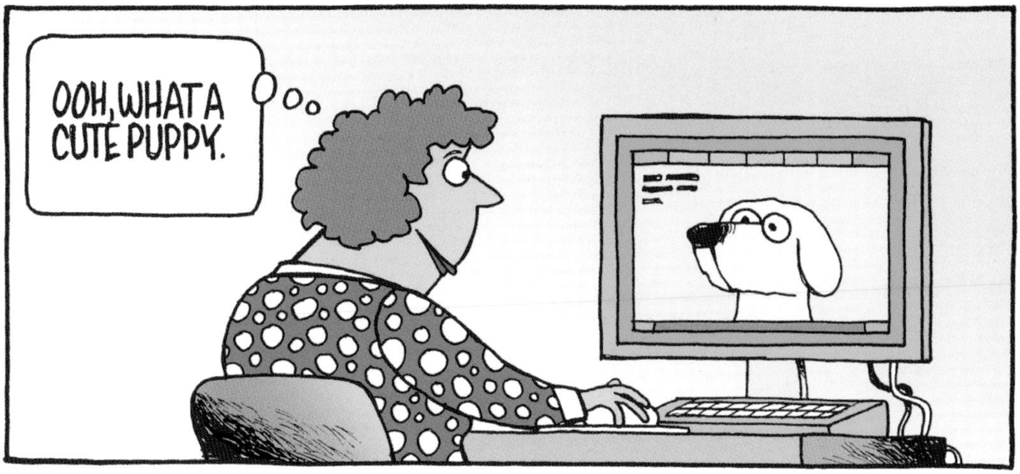
OOH, WHAT A CUTE PUPPY.

But there is an evil that lurks on the internet...

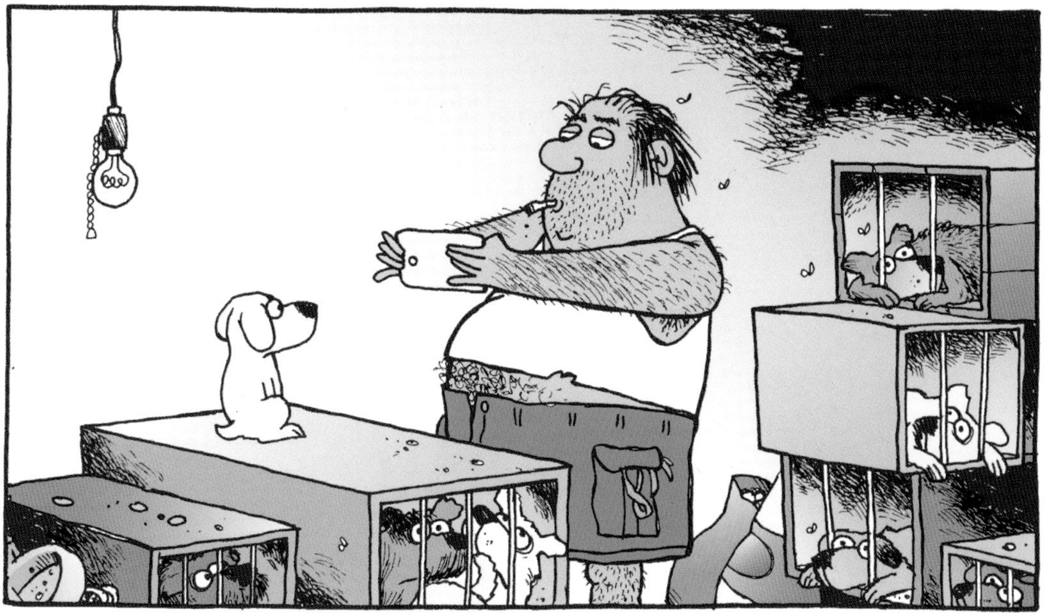

... puppy mills, where unspeakable horrors take place all to make a quick buck.

The best place to find a dog is at your local animal shelter. They have big dogs, small dogs, hairy dogs, smooth dogs, fat dogs, thin dogs, young dogs, old dogs, slobbery dogs...

So chances are good there is exactly the right dog there waiting for you.

A rescued dog knows you've rescued them and will always be most grateful. And in so many cases, we've rescued you.

Some rescued dogs might still be getting over the abuse they suffered in their previous life, so something seemingly innocent can trigger unpleasant memories.
It's doggy PTSD.

HOT TIP!

If you want a friend for life, scratch that hard-to-get-to spot at the base of our tails... but ask the dog first!

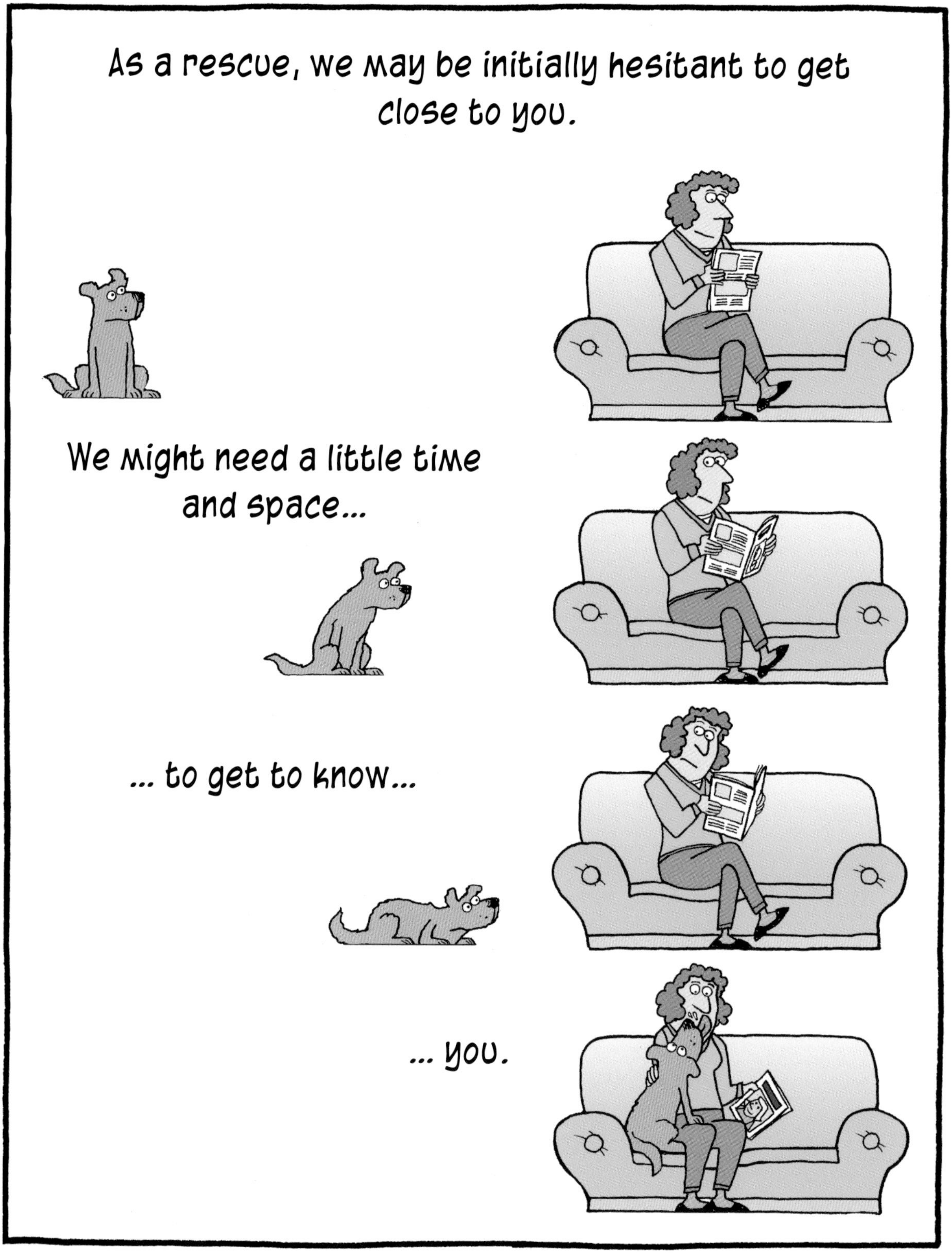
As a rescue, we may be initially hesitant to get close to you.
We might need a little time and space...
... to get to know...
... you.

You don't pick us. We pick you.

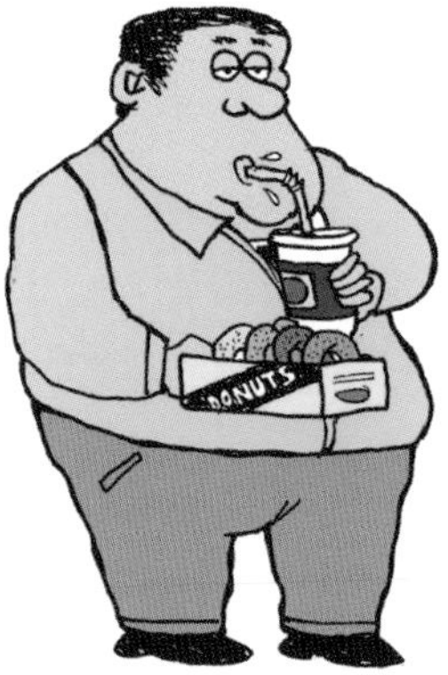
DONUTS

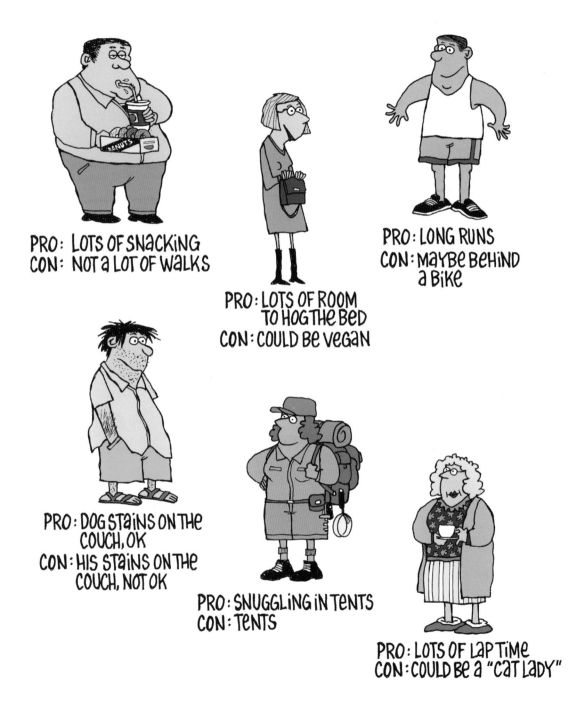

PRO: LOTS OF SNACKING
CON: NOT A LOT OF WALKS

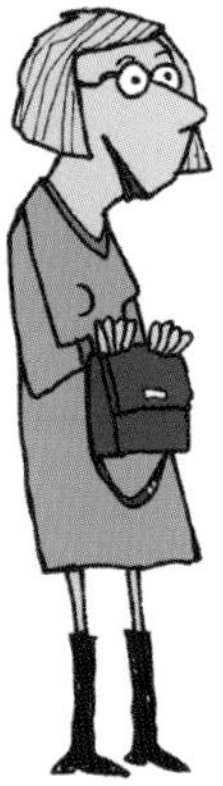

PRO: LOTS OF ROOM TO HOG THE BED
CON: COULD BE VEGAN

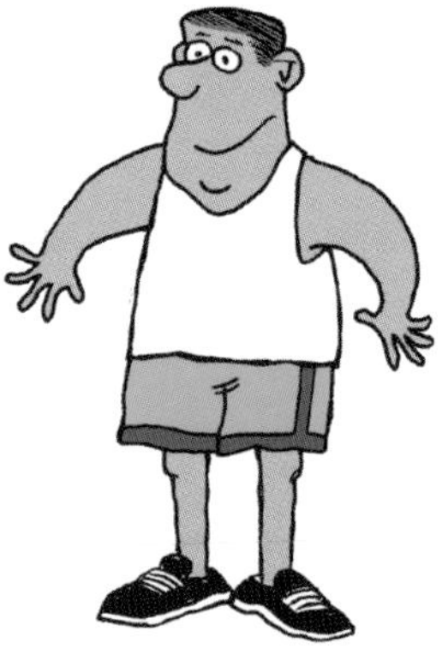

PRO: LONG RUNS
CON: MAYBE BEHIND A BIKE

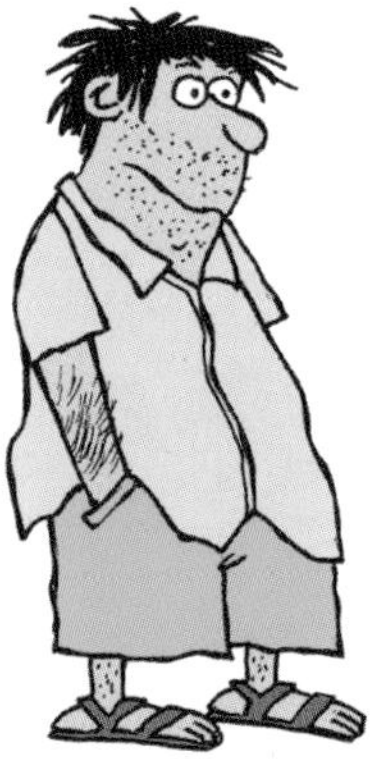

PRO: DOG STAINS ON THE COUCH, OK
CON: HIS STAINS ON THE COUCH, NOT OK

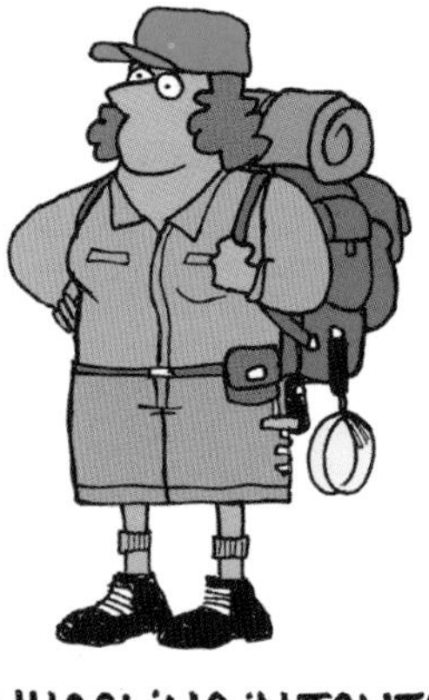

PRO: SNUGGLING IN TENTS
CON: TENTS

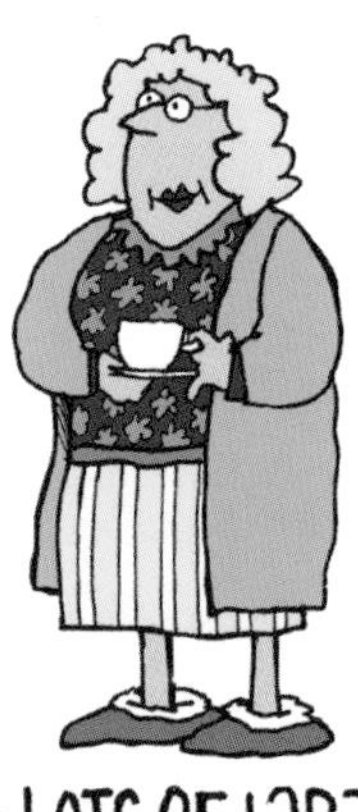

PRO: LOTS OF LAP TIME
CON: COULD BE A "CAT LADY"

Although you may be delighted with your new puppy, not all of us are so enamoured. Introduce a dog into the house slowly.

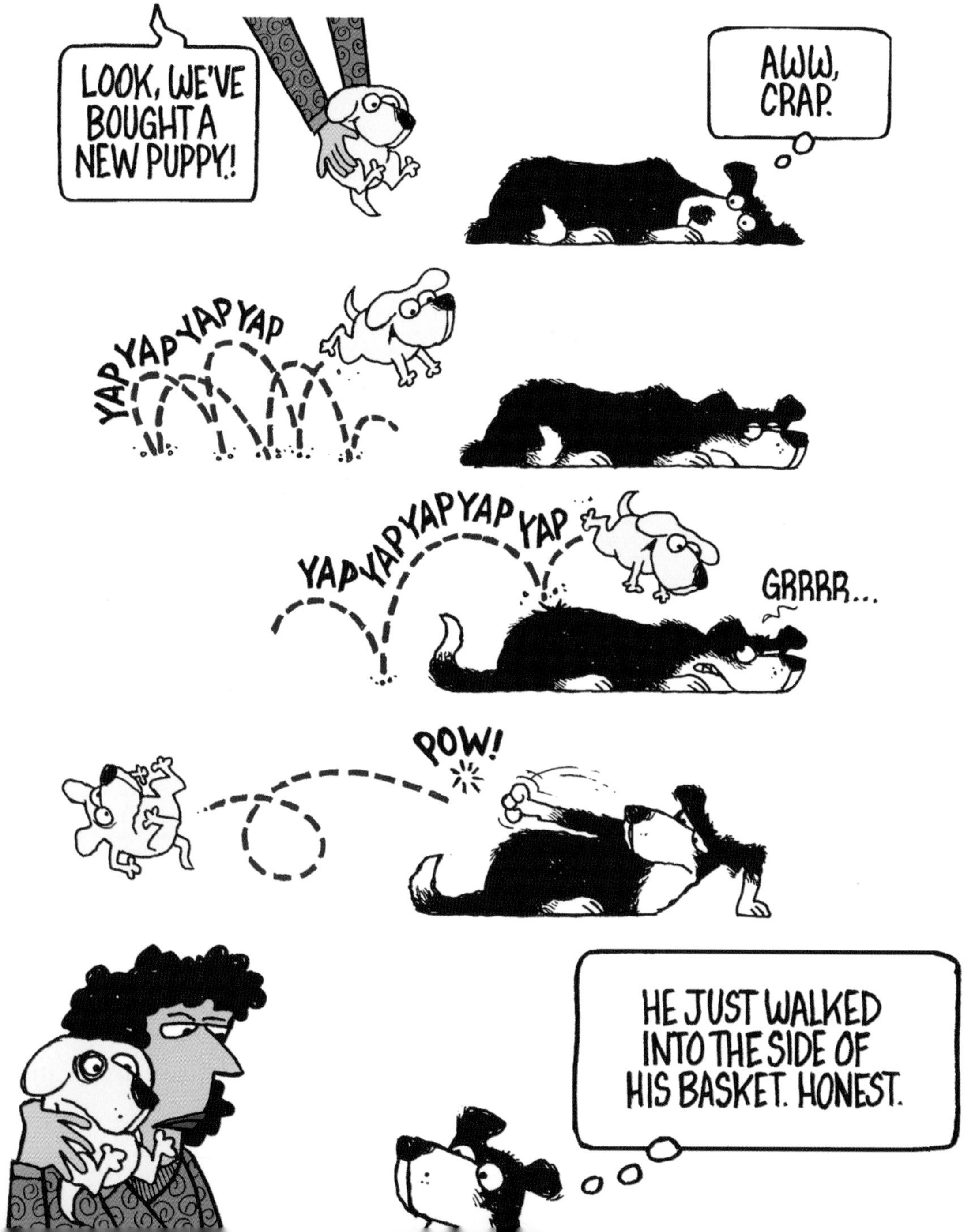
LOOK, WE'VE BOUGHT A NEW PUPPY!
AWW, CRAP.
YAP YAP YAP YAP
YAP YAP YAP YAP YAP
GRRRR...
POW!
HE JUST WALKED INTO THE SIDE OF HIS BASKET. HONEST.

If we're used to being the official "house dog," having another dog muscle in on our gig will ***NOT*** be appreciated.

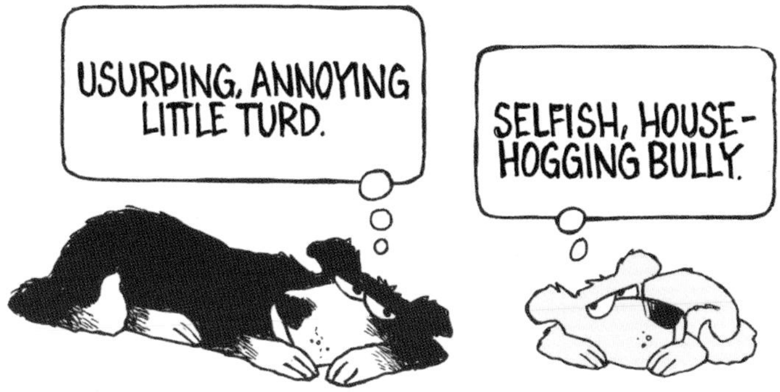
USURPING, ANNOYING LITTLE TURD.
SELFISH, HOUSE-HOGGING BULLY.

How would you like it if your spouse brought someone new into the relationship, potentially replacing you?

But, over time, chances are we will discover we have some things in common.

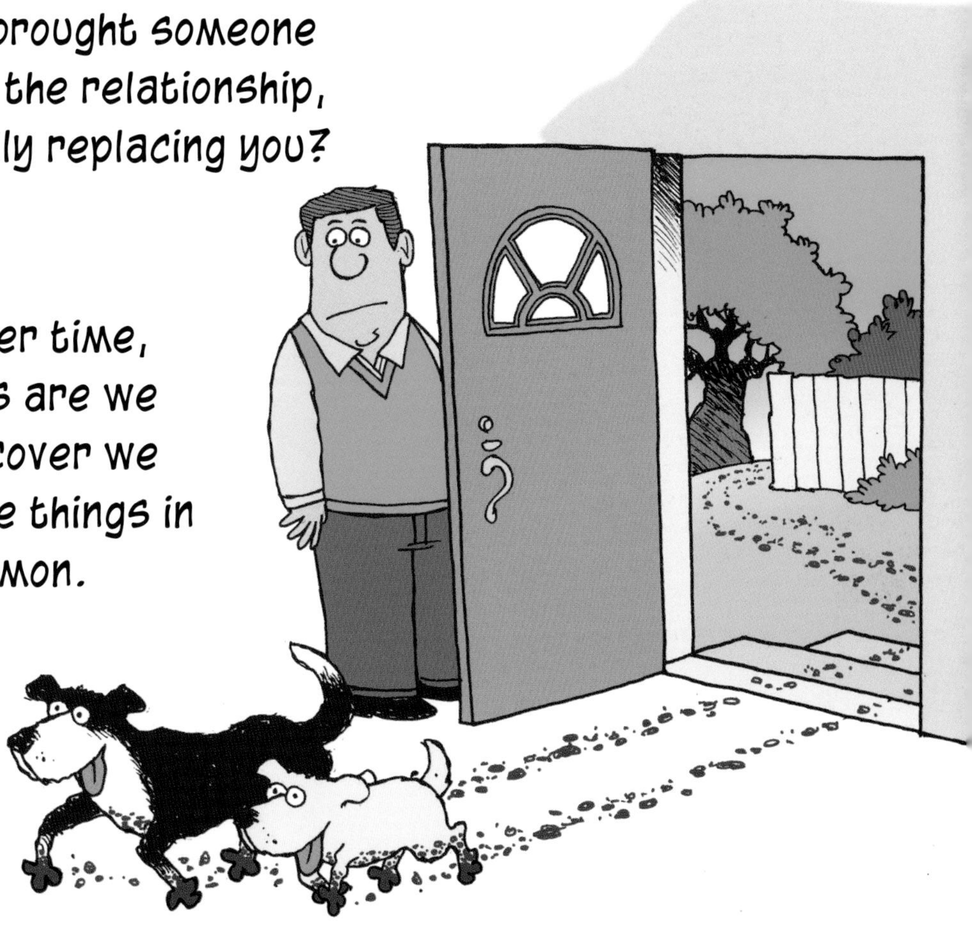

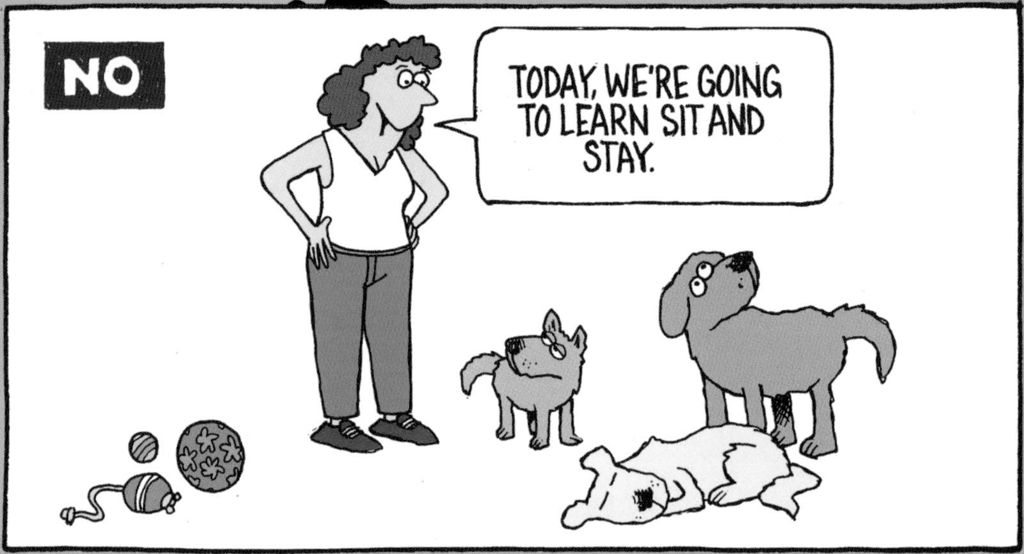
NO
TODAY, WE'RE GOING TO LEARN SIT AND STAY.

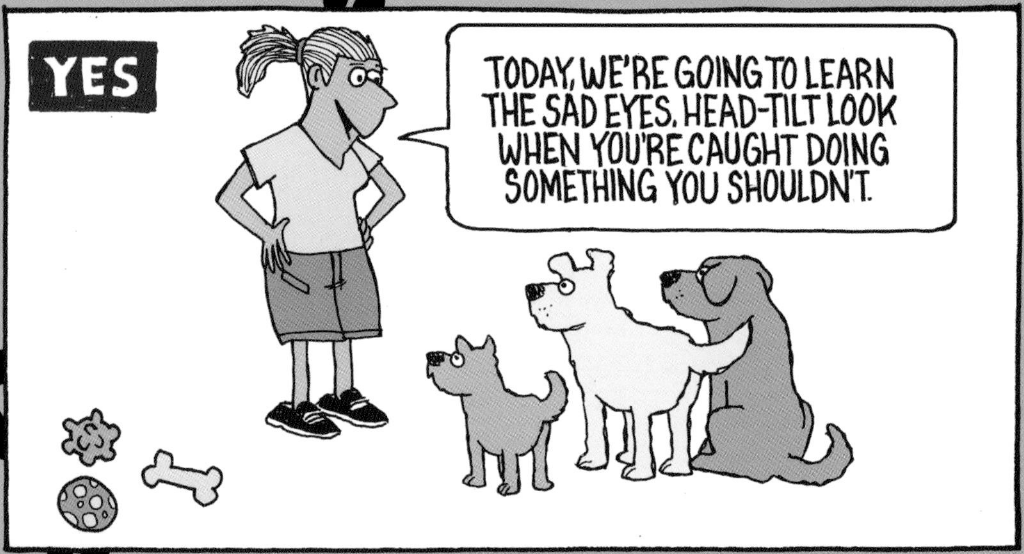
YES
TODAY, WE'RE GOING TO LEARN THE SAD EYES, HEAD-TILT LOOK WHEN YOU'RE CAUGHT DOING SOMETHING YOU SHOULDN'T.

TRAINING AND DECODING A DOG

Actually, this is about training you. You probably don't realize it but little by little (and through books like this) you're starting to understand us: what our eyes tell you, or the different tones to our barks. We strongly recommend you get to know the difference between the "my dinner is late" bark and the "I really need to go outside to pee, no kidding!" bark.

We know that training us with a biscuit is just bribery, but we don't care. If having to sit still for a few seconds gets us a snack, that's no sweat off our snouts. Although it does bother us if we just get a "Good dog!" and a head pat instead of a biscuit.

There are extreme cases where working dogs have to go for hours performing heroic tasks and only get a treat at the end of the day. Don't think we're not dreaming of that biscuit as we pull another earthquake victim from the rubble, or sniff out a pound of heroin from a suitcase filled with dirty underwear and socks.

Oh, and don't waste your time trying to train us not to climb onto the bed or couch. We have all the time in the world to wear you down and will climb back on as soon as your back is turned. (It's good to not have guilt.) Resistance is futile.

Then there is our secret weapon: the "sad eyes" look. It can melt any resolve to not feed us scraps from the kitchen table, or boot us off the bed. Again, resistance is futile.

Training a puppy may be frustrating at times but always remember: everything goes better with a biscuit.

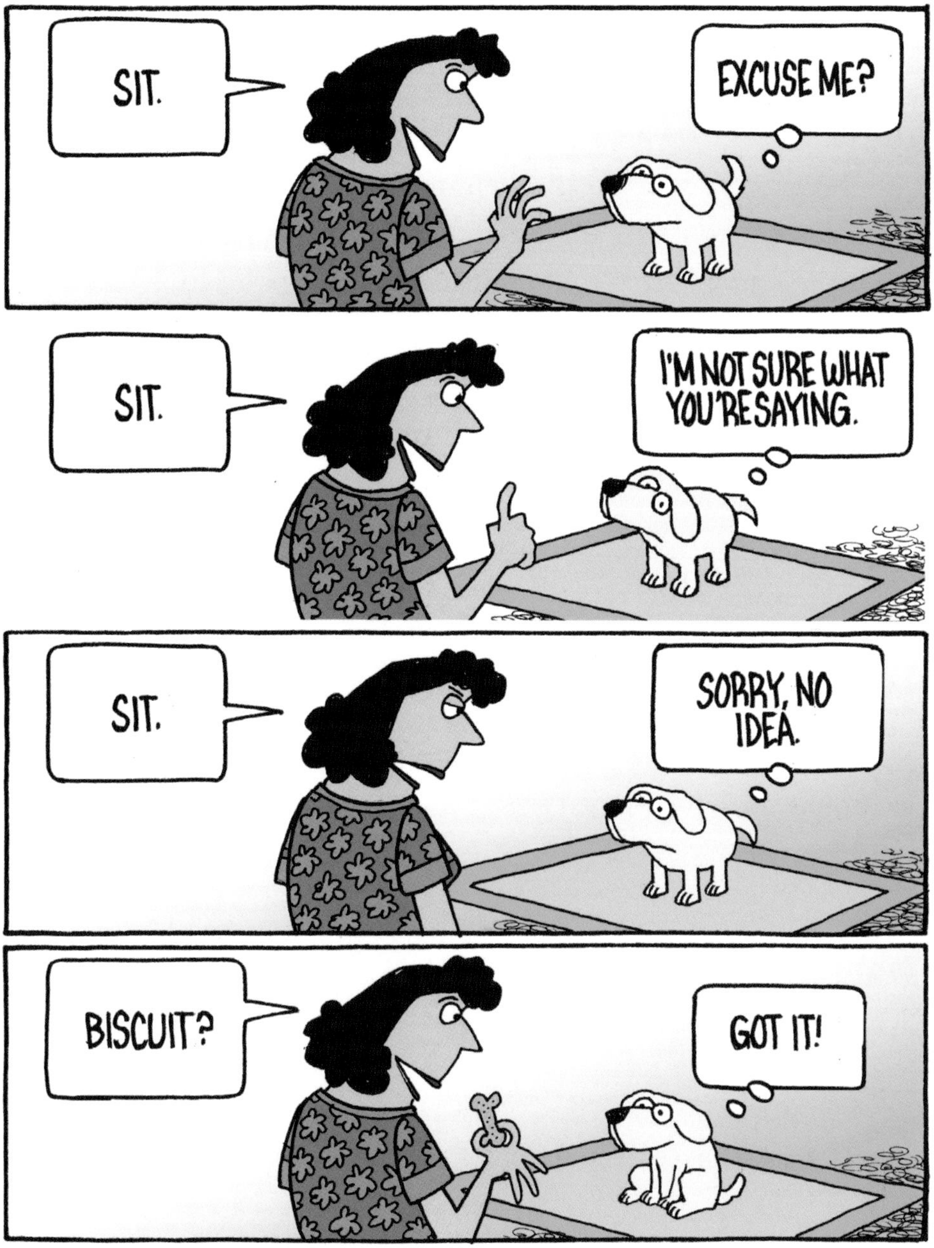
SIT.
EXCUSE ME?
SIT.
I'M NOT SURE WHAT YOU'RE SAYING.
SIT.
SORRY, NO IDEA.
BISCUIT?
GOT IT!

It takes us a bit of time to figure out where you want us to do our business. Some of us get it quickly...

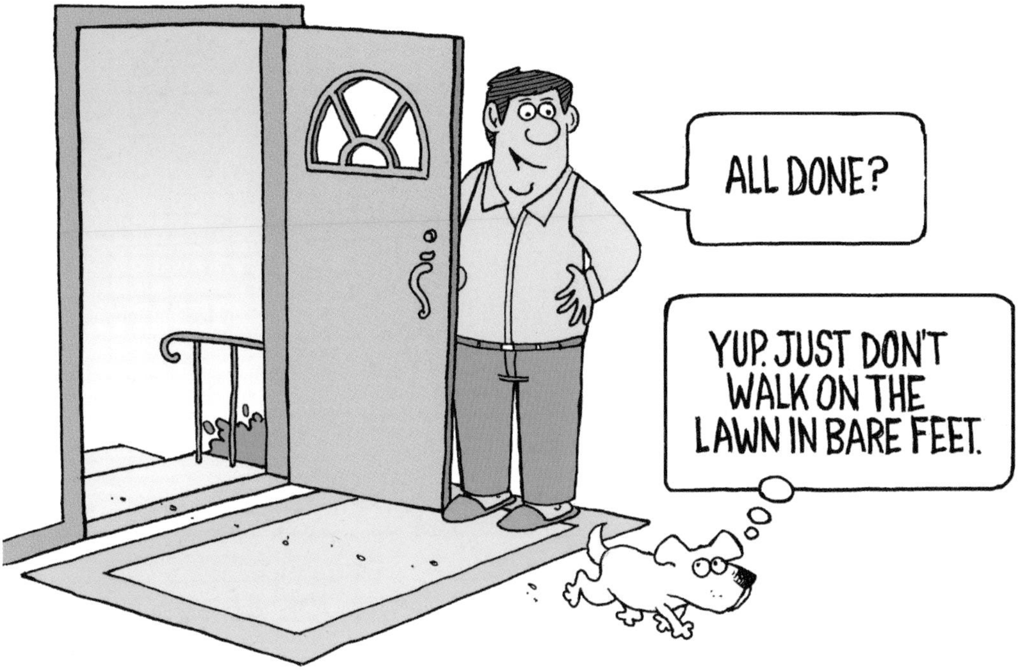
ALL DONE?
YUP. JUST DON'T WALK ON THE LAWN IN BARE FEET.

... and some of us require a little more time.

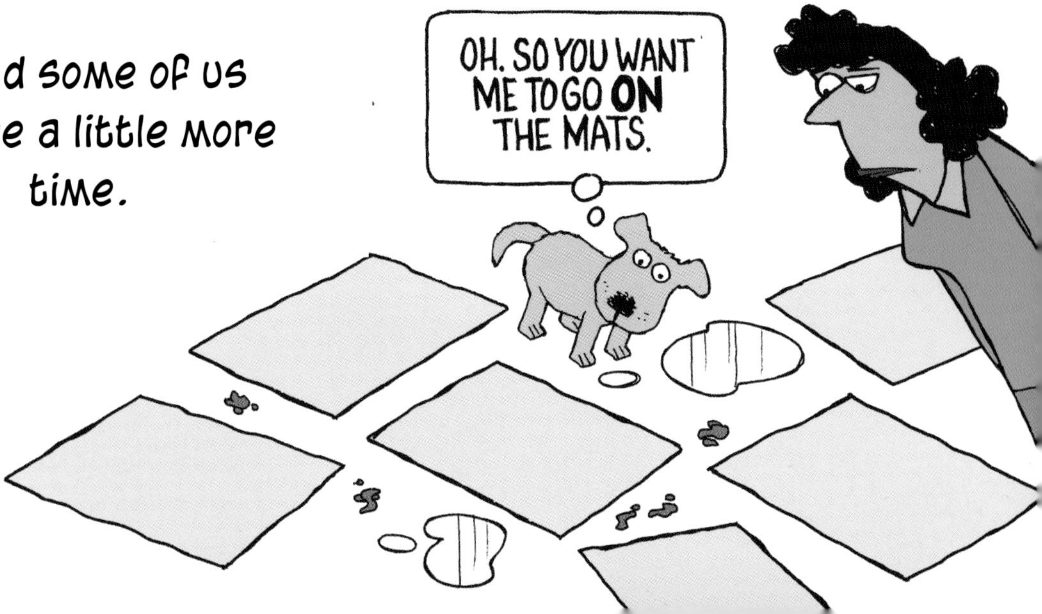
OH. SO YOU WANT ME TO GO **ON** THE MATS.

We can be trained to detect diseases and disorders like cancer, low blood sugar, migraines and seizures.

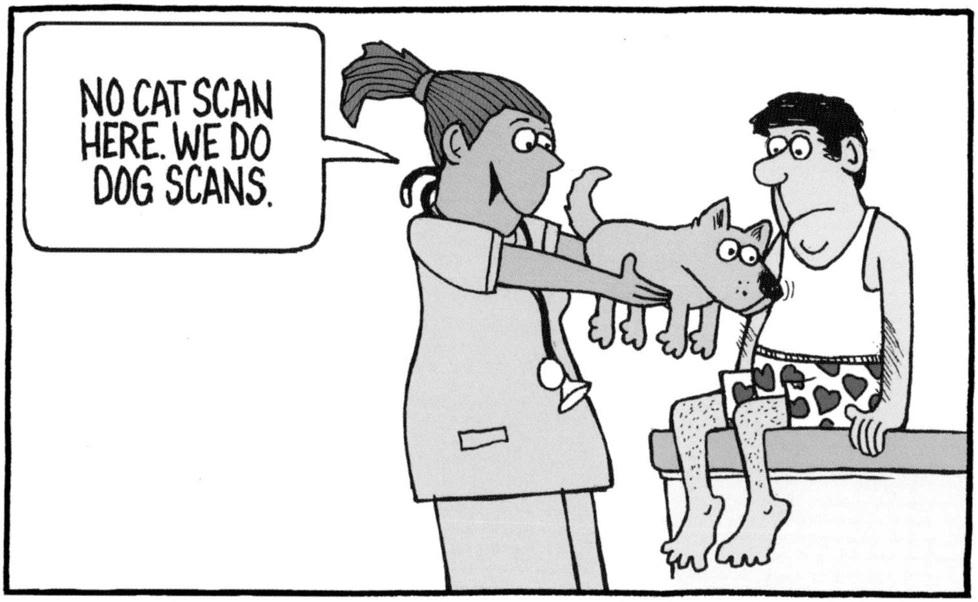
NO CAT SCAN HERE. WE DO DOG SCANS.

Just one sniff, and we can tell a lot about you. We're nature's lie detectors.

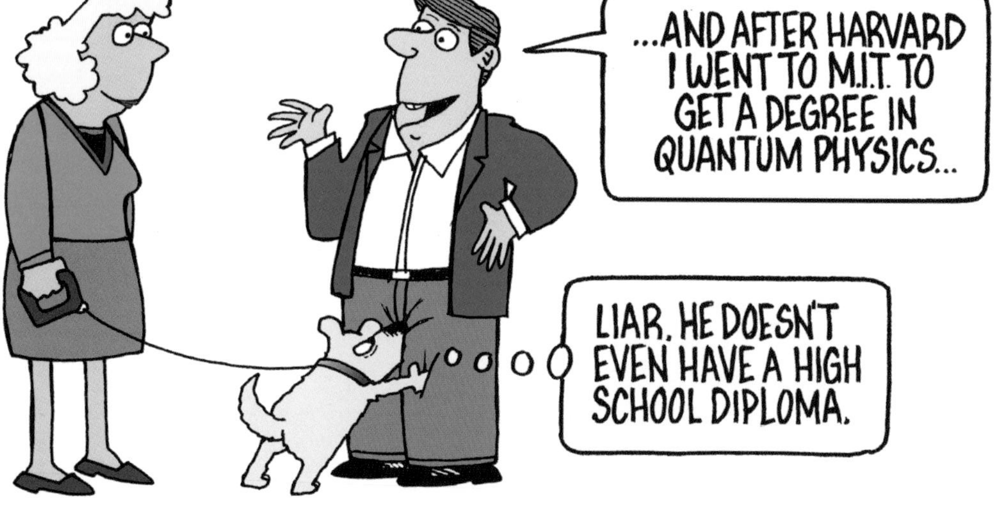
...AND AFTER HARVARD I WENT TO M.I.T. TO GET A DEGREE IN QUANTUM PHYSICS...
LIAR. HE DOESN'T EVEN HAVE A HIGH SCHOOL DIPLOMA.

It may be embarrassing to you but we like to sniff crotches

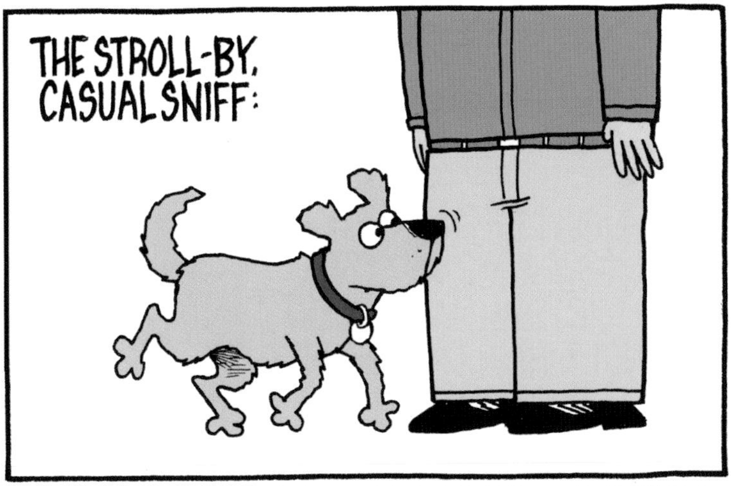
THE STROLL-BY, CASUAL SNIFF:

We can learn a lot about you from a good crotch sniff.

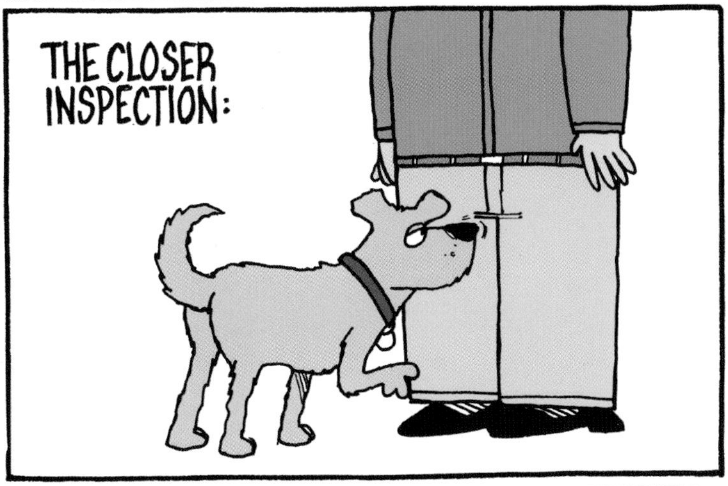
THE CLOSER INSPECTION:

Besides, you should be flattered we're so interested in you.

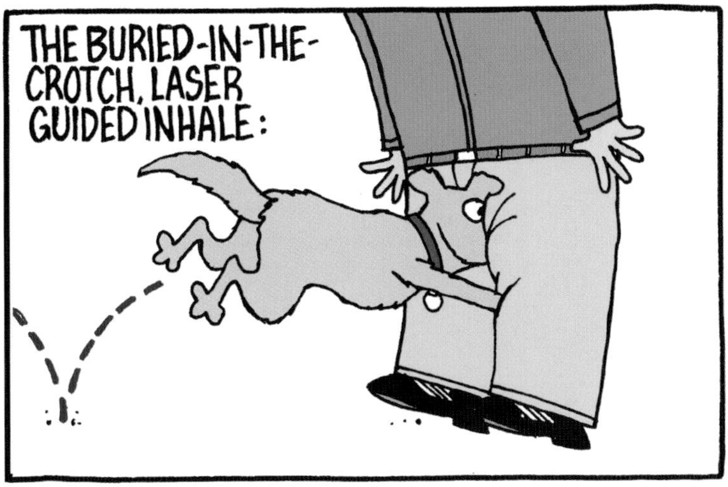
THE BURIED-IN-THE-CROTCH, LASER GUIDED INHALE:

You think we understand around 200 words,
however, we have selective hearing.

NOW LISTEN, BUSTER,
NEXT TIME WE GO TO
THE PARK, PLEASE DO
NOT FIND A DEAD RABBIT
AND ROLL IN IT.

GO TO PARK.
FIND DEAD
RABBIT.
ROLL IN IT.

DID YOU KNOW...?

We measure distance not in miles,
but in window slobber.

WINDOW COVERED......FIVE MILES

SEAT COVERED........TEN MILES

YOU MAY WANT
TO STOP AT A
CAR WASH....TWENTY MILES

Unlike you, we don't have a vast vocabulary of words to tell you what we're thinking. But we can express a lot just through our eyes.

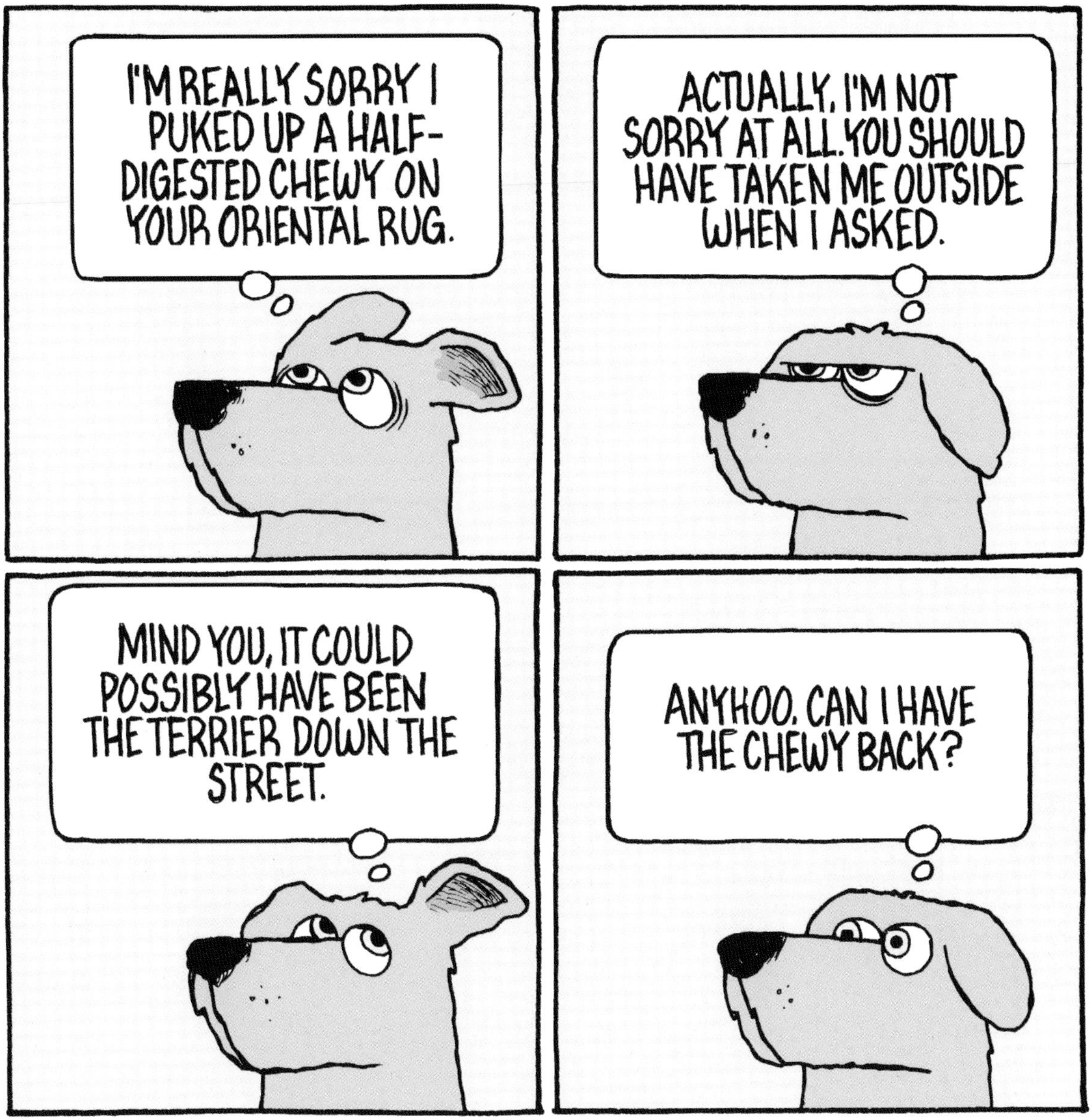

I'M REALLY SORRY I PUKED UP A HALF-DIGESTED CHEWY ON YOUR ORIENTAL RUG.
ACTUALLY, I'M NOT SORRY AT ALL. YOU SHOULD HAVE TAKEN ME OUTSIDE WHEN I ASKED.
MIND YOU, IT COULD POSSIBLY HAVE BEEN THE TERRIER DOWN THE STREET.
ANYHOO. CAN I HAVE THE CHEWY BACK?

Our tails are also a good indicator of what we're thinking.

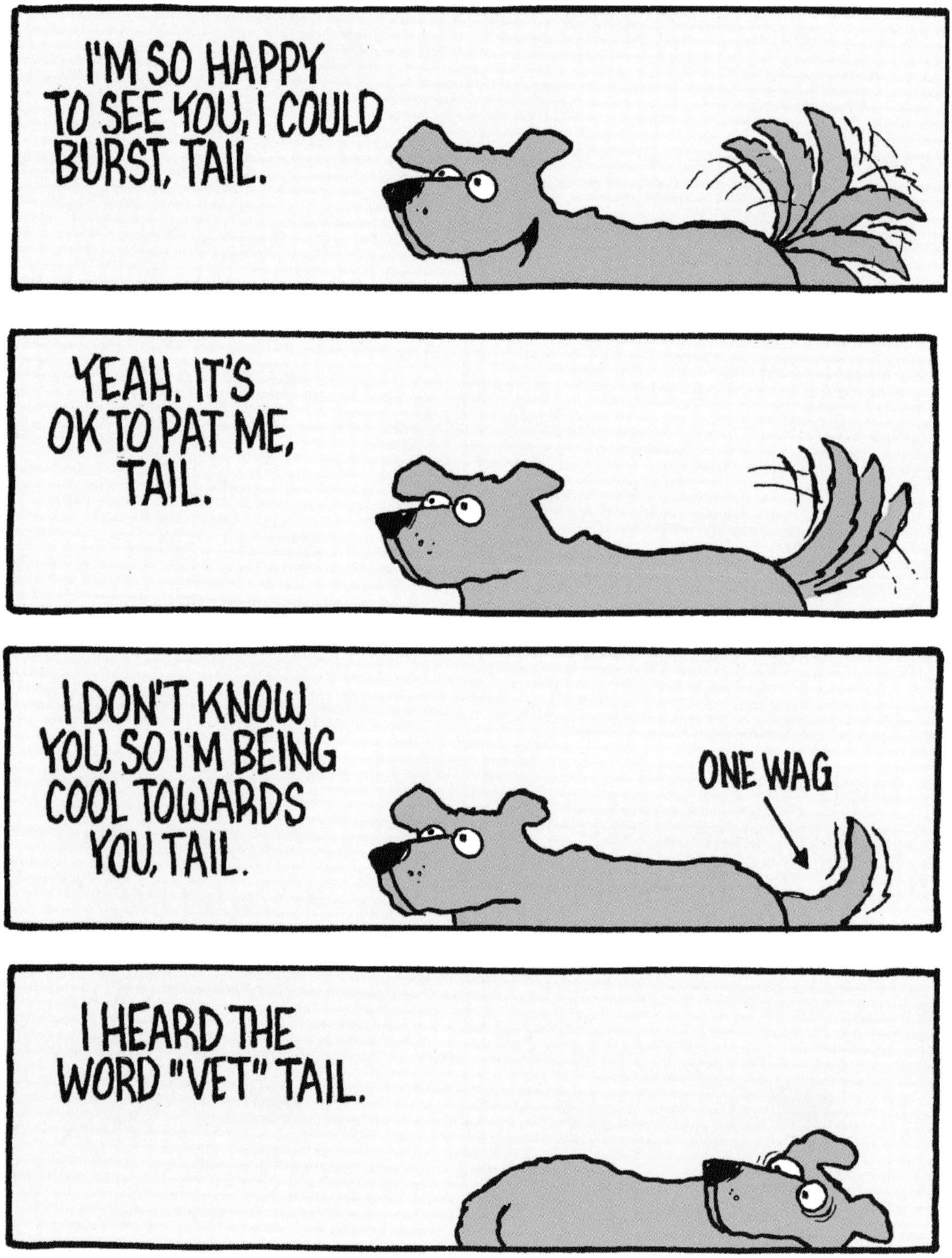

I'M SO HAPPY TO SEE YOU, I COULD BURST, TAIL.
YEAH. IT'S OK TO PAT ME, TAIL.
I DON'T KNOW YOU, SO I'M BEING COOL TOWARDS YOU, TAIL.
ONE WAG
I HEARD THE WORD "VET" TAIL.

You think you train us but, actually, we train you.

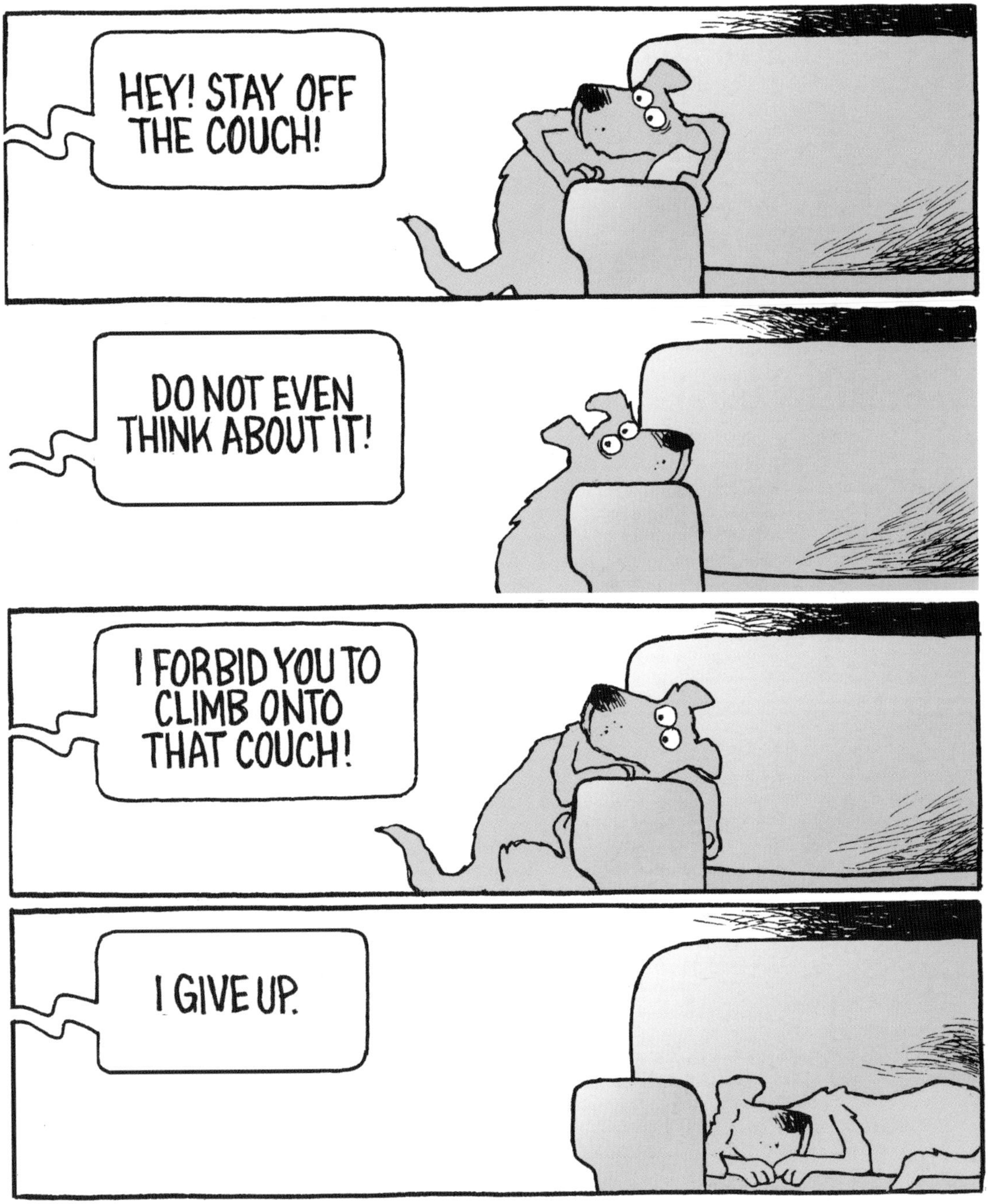
HEY! STAY OFF THE COUCH!
DO NOT EVEN THINK ABOUT IT!
I FORBID YOU TO CLIMB ONTO THAT COUCH!
I GIVE UP.

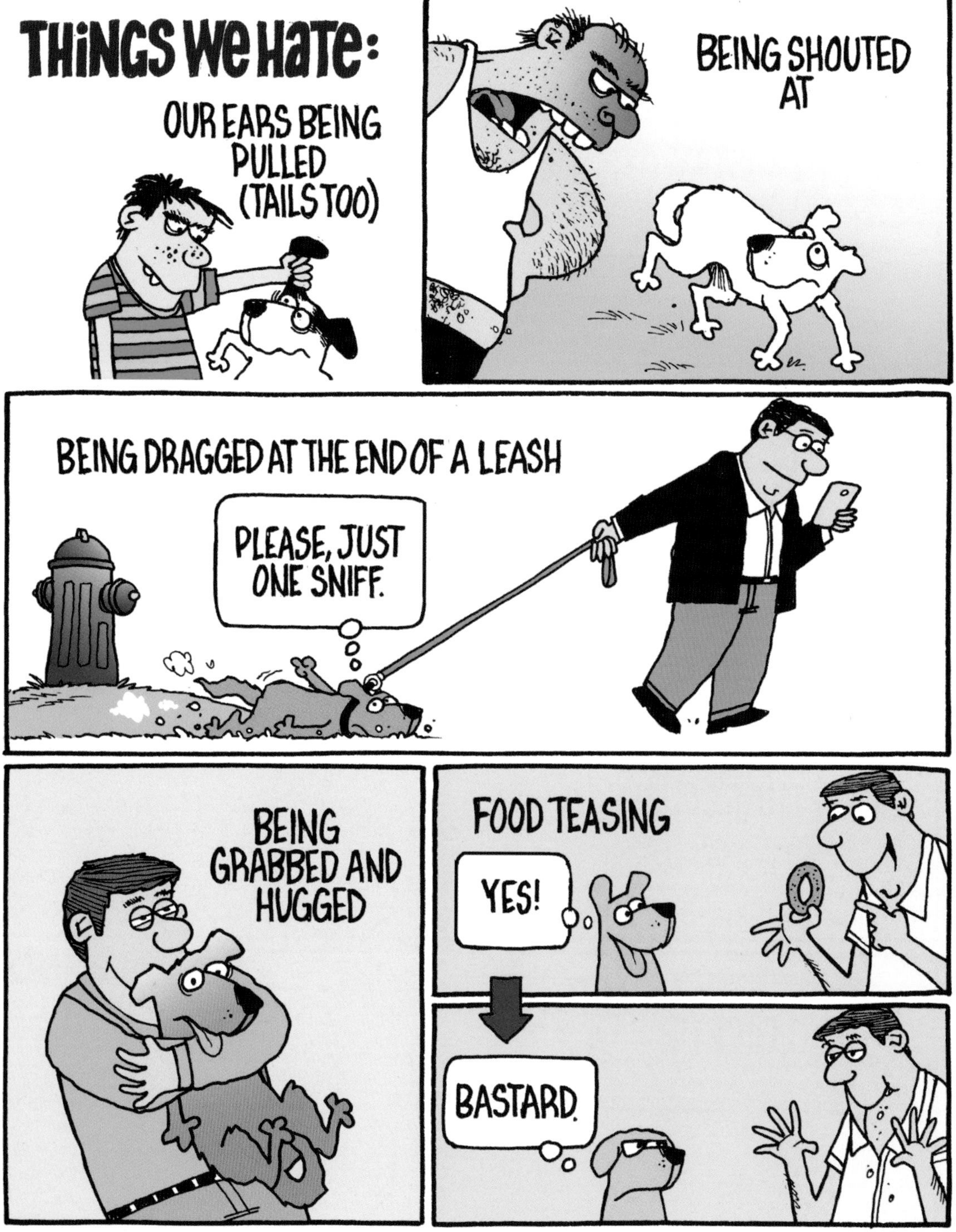
THINGS WE HATE:
OUR EARS BEING PULLED (TAILS TOO)
BEING SHOUTED AT
BEING DRAGGED AT THE END OF A LEASH
PLEASE, JUST ONE SNIFF.
BEING GRABBED AND HUGGED
FOOD TEASING
YES!
BASTARD.

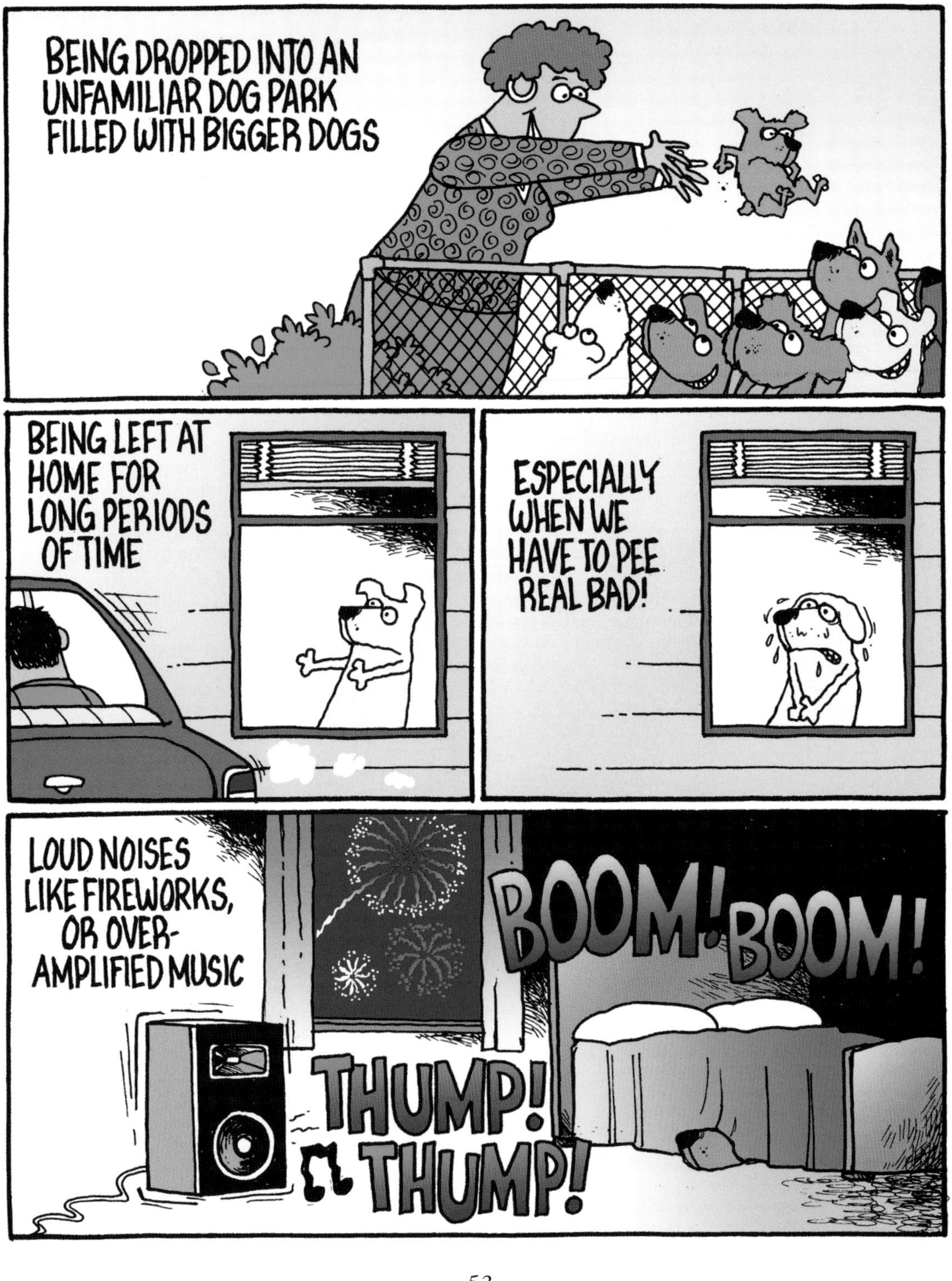
BEING DROPPED INTO AN UNFAMILIAR DOG PARK FILLED WITH BIGGER DOGS
BEING LEFT AT HOME FOR LONG PERIODS OF TIME
ESPECIALLY WHEN WE HAVE TO PEE REAL BAD!
LOUD NOISES LIKE FIREWORKS, OR OVER-AMPLIFIED MUSIC
BOOM! BOOM!
THUMP! THUMP!

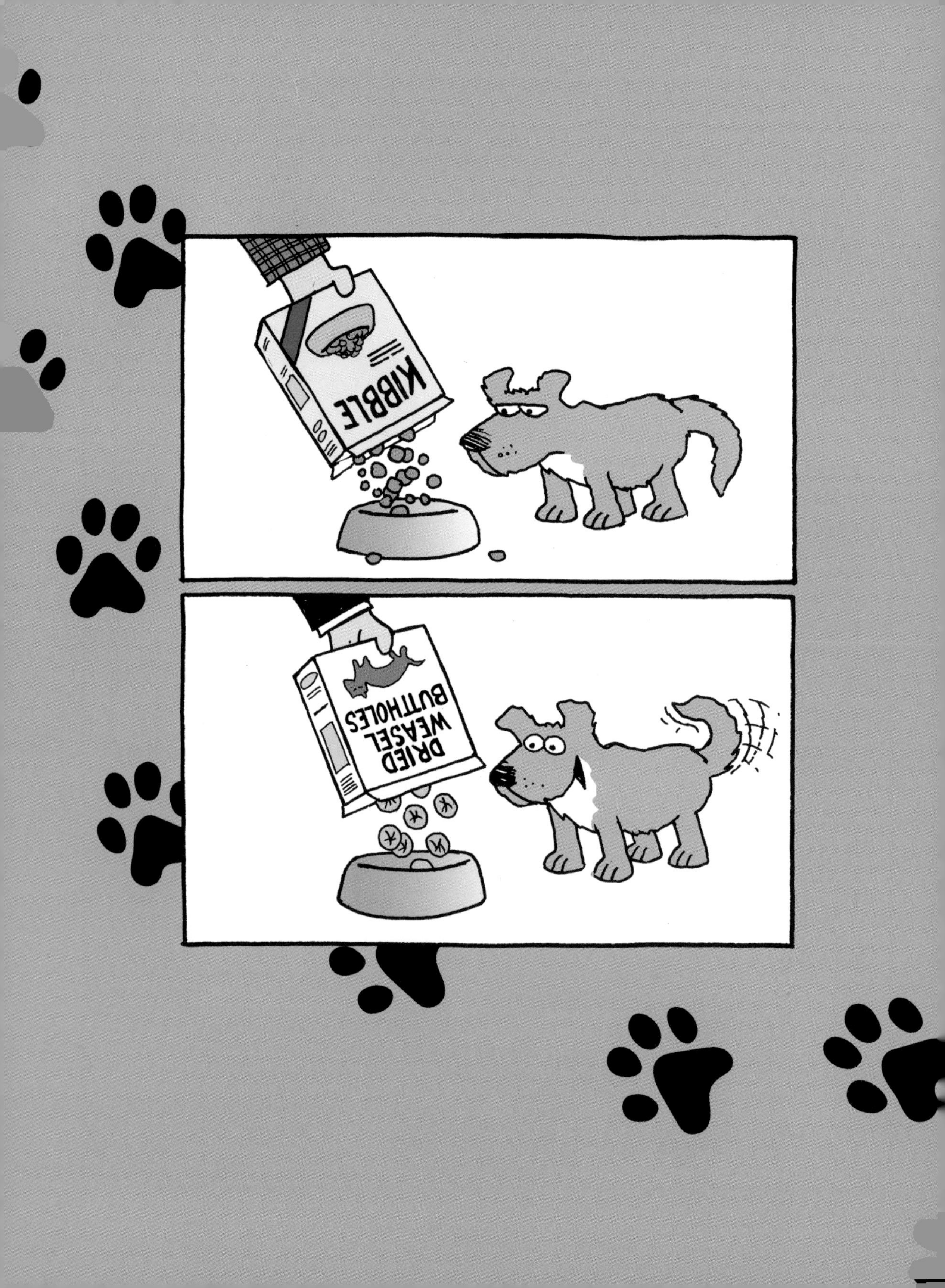
KIBBLE
DRIED WEASEL BUTTHOLES

CHAPTER 5

FEEDING

We've been called "hairy garbage cans." And in the past, that's basically what we were, living on stuff you threw out. Okay, we're still happy to eat leftovers, but like you, our tastes have been refined over the years. Rather than scrabble in the dirt hunting for a burnt piece of mammoth testicle, we've become rather used to finding our dinner in a bowl. At the exact same time every day.

As for what you put in the bowl, there are roughly a thousand different types of commercial dog food available, all of them featuring a cute dog on the package and most of them "vet recommended." Really? You're telling us vets eat this crud? And just because we wolf it down, doesn't mean to say we prefer it over something scrounged off the dinner table. You say you consider us family, so why don't we get a chair at the table?

There is a simple reason why we gobble our food: Other dogs.

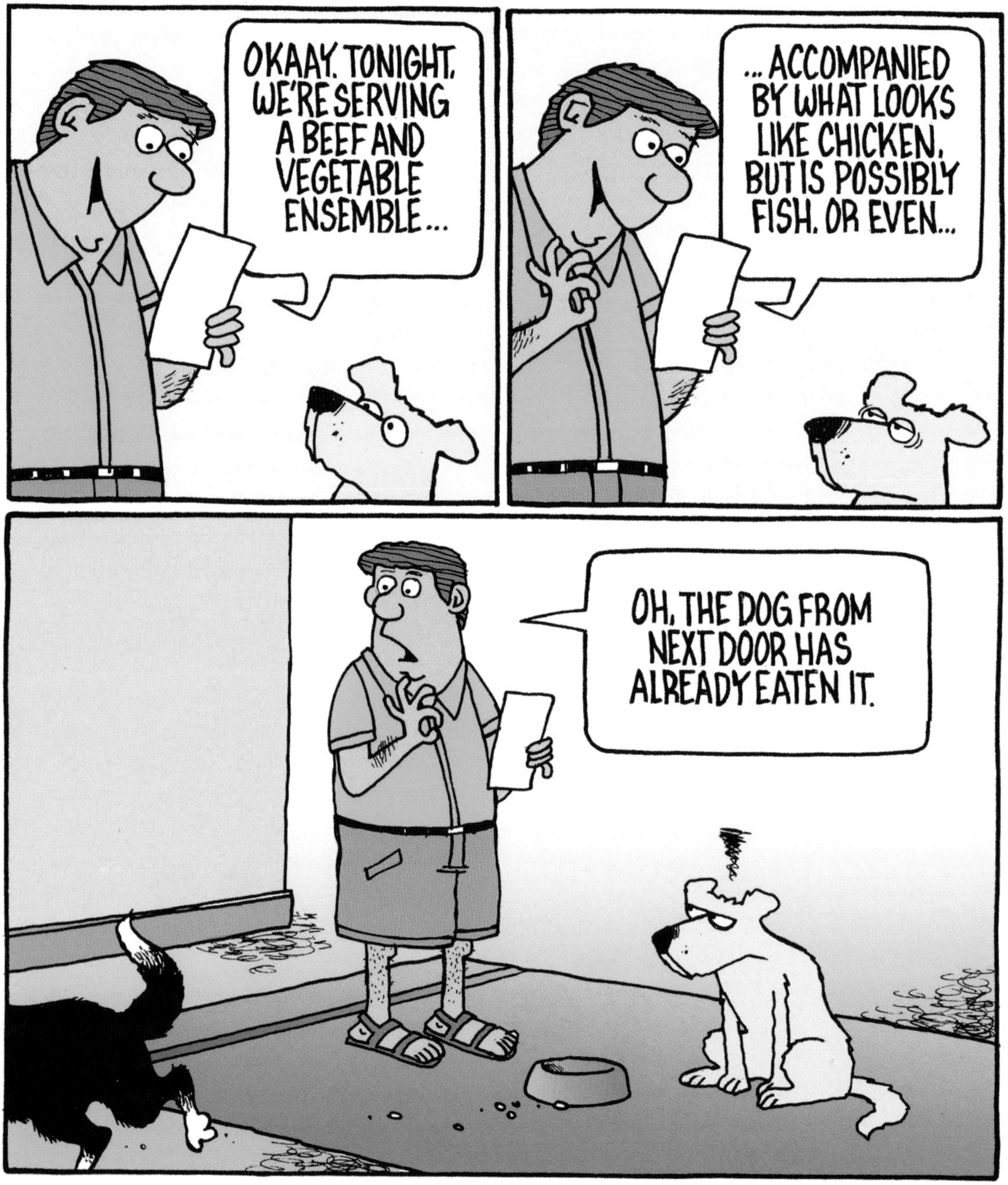
OKAAY. TONIGHT, WE'RE SERVING A BEEF AND VEGETABLE ENSEMBLE...
...ACCOMPANIED BY WHAT LOOKS LIKE CHICKEN, BUT IS POSSIBLY FISH. OR EVEN...
OH, THE DOG FROM NEXT DOOR HAS ALREADY EATEN IT.

We learned to do this thousands of years ago when the longer we took on a juicy piece of mammoth meat meant more time for a bigger dog to turn up, beat us up, and take our dinner from us. If we ate like you, we'd starve.

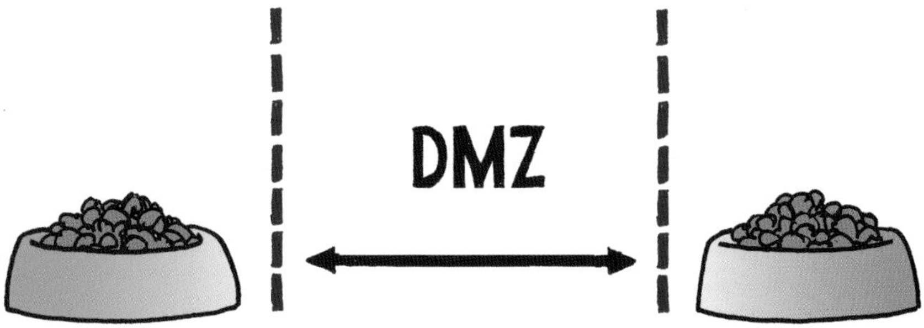
DMZ

No matter how well we get along with each other, if there are two dogs in the house and you want to avoid an unexpected vet bill, keep the dinner bowls a respectable distance apart... preferably in different provinces or states.

DID YOU KNOW...?

A dog's sense of smell is thousands of times more sensitive than that of humans... so of course we can find where you've hidden the treats.

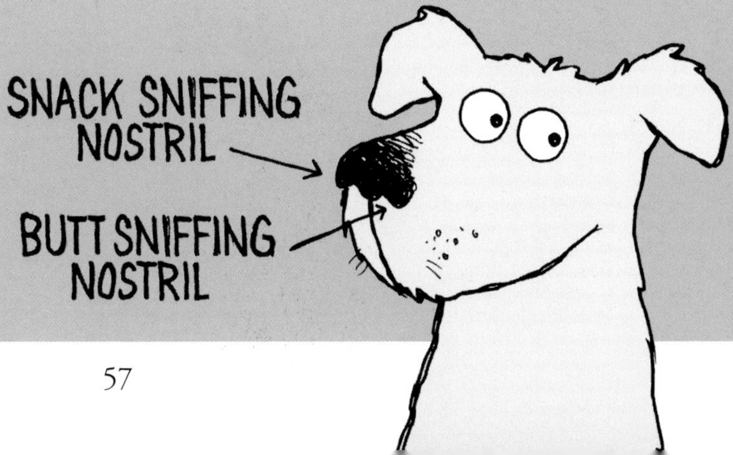
SNACK SNIFFING NOSTRIL
BUTT SNIFFING NOSTRIL

If we can't get a biscuit, we'll eat other things.

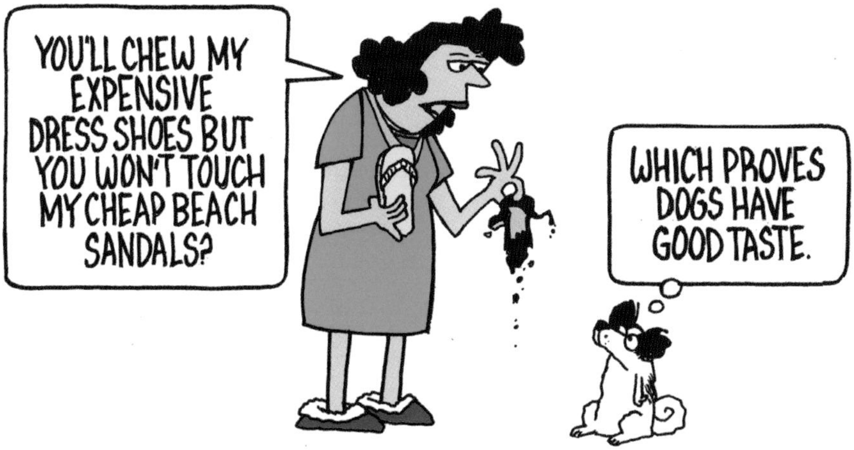
YOU'LL CHEW MY EXPENSIVE DRESS SHOES BUT YOU WON'T TOUCH MY CHEAP BEACH SANDALS?
WHICH PROVES DOGS HAVE GOOD TASTE.

In fact, puppies will eat pretty much anything.

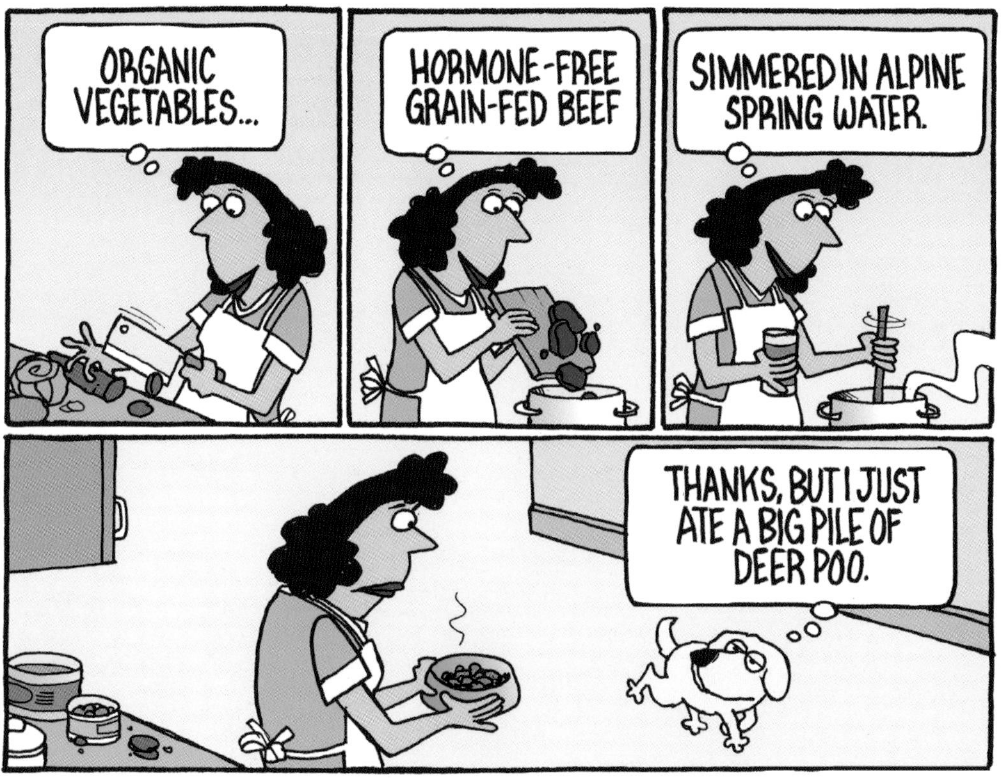
ORGANIC VEGETABLES...
HORMONE-FREE GRAIN-FED BEEF
SIMMERED IN ALPINE SPRING WATER.
THANKS, BUT I JUST ATE A BIG PILE OF DEER POO.

We're experts at scrounging food when you're not looking. It's your own fault, of course. If you leave food out, we will find it.

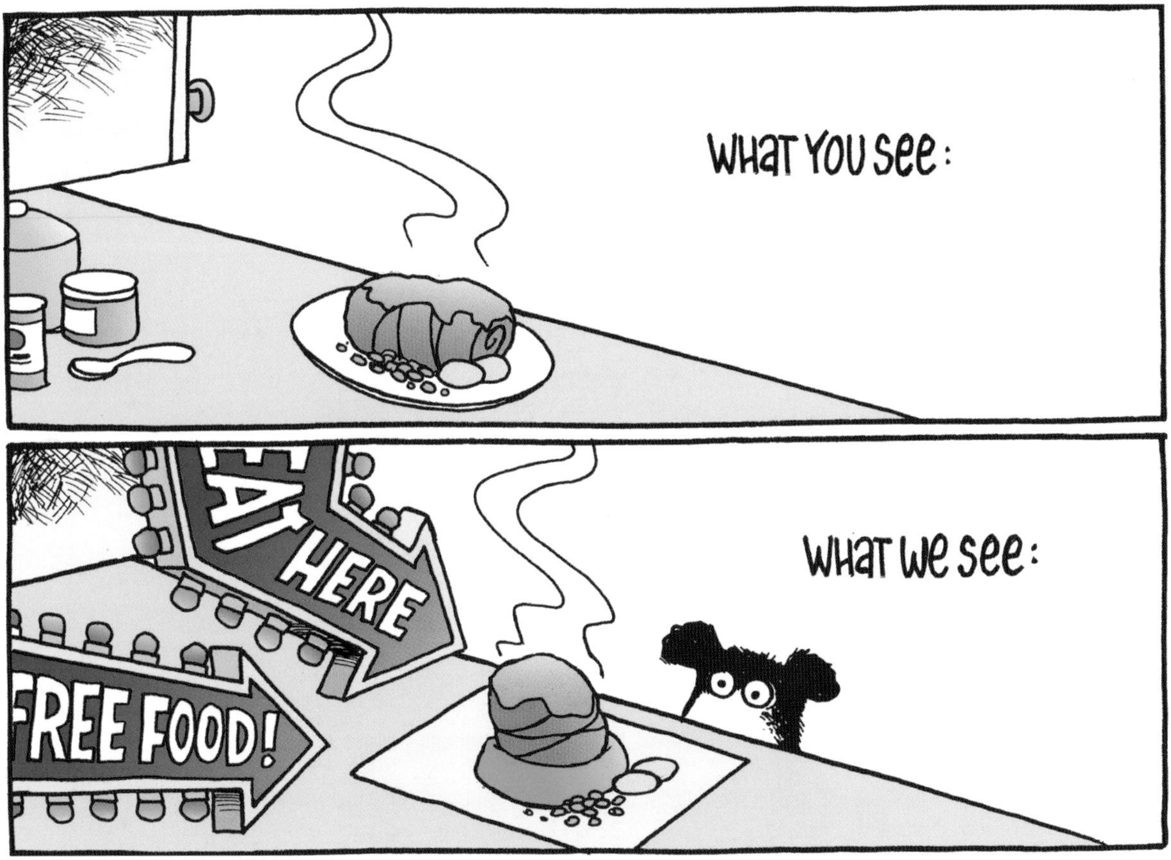
WHAT YOU SEE:
WHAT WE SEE:
EAT HERE
FREE FOOD!

Besides the obvious pilfering-the-roast-beef-off-the-kitchen-counter scrounge, there are other, more subtle ways we get our paws on your food...

... the coffee-table-tail-sweep scrounge...

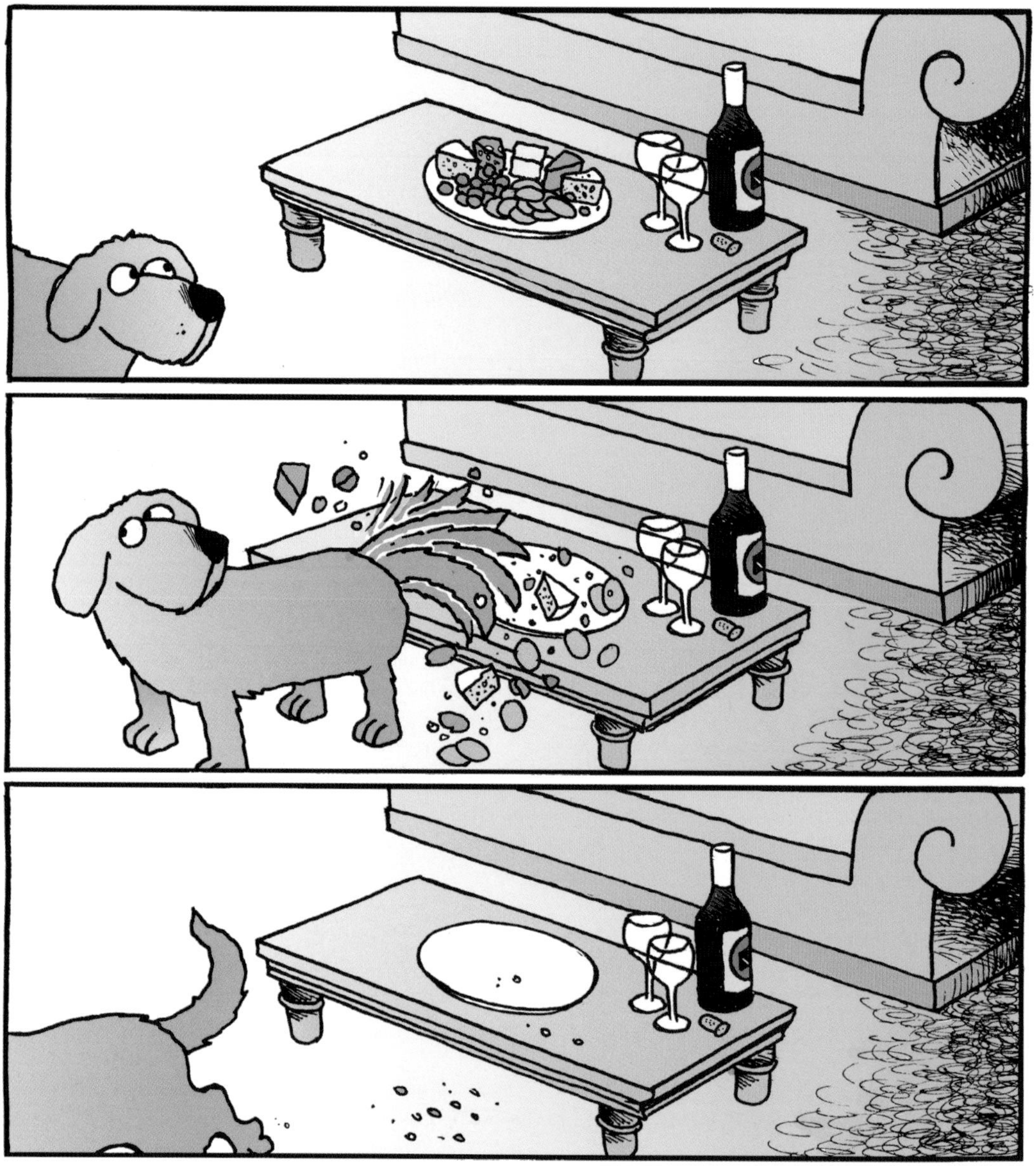

... and, of course, the classic
tried-and-true-dinner-table scrounge...

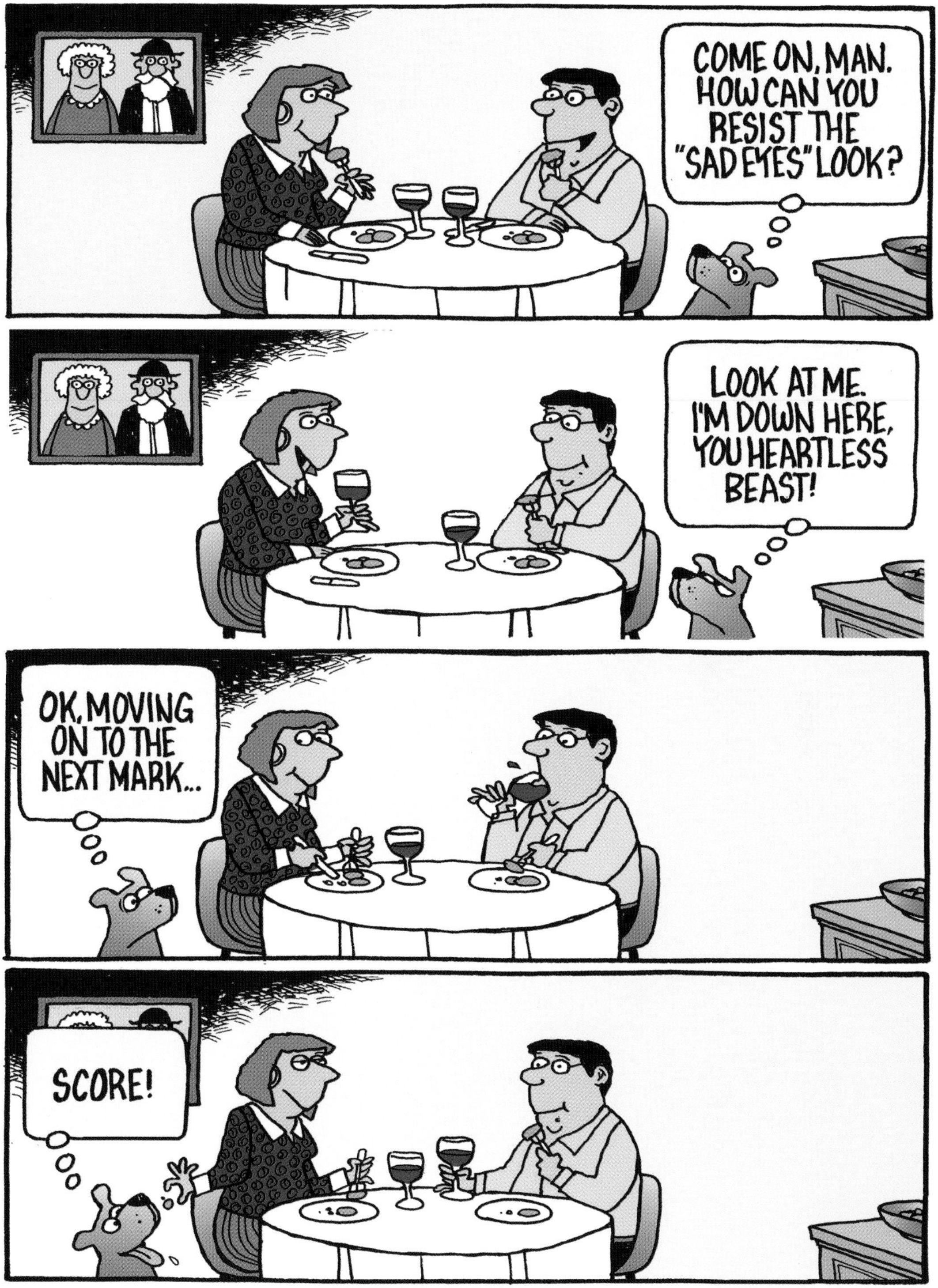
COME ON, MAN. HOW CAN YOU RESIST THE "SAD EYES" LOOK?
LOOK AT ME. I'M DOWN HERE, YOU HEARTLESS BEAST!
OK, MOVING ON TO THE NEXT MARK...
SCORE!

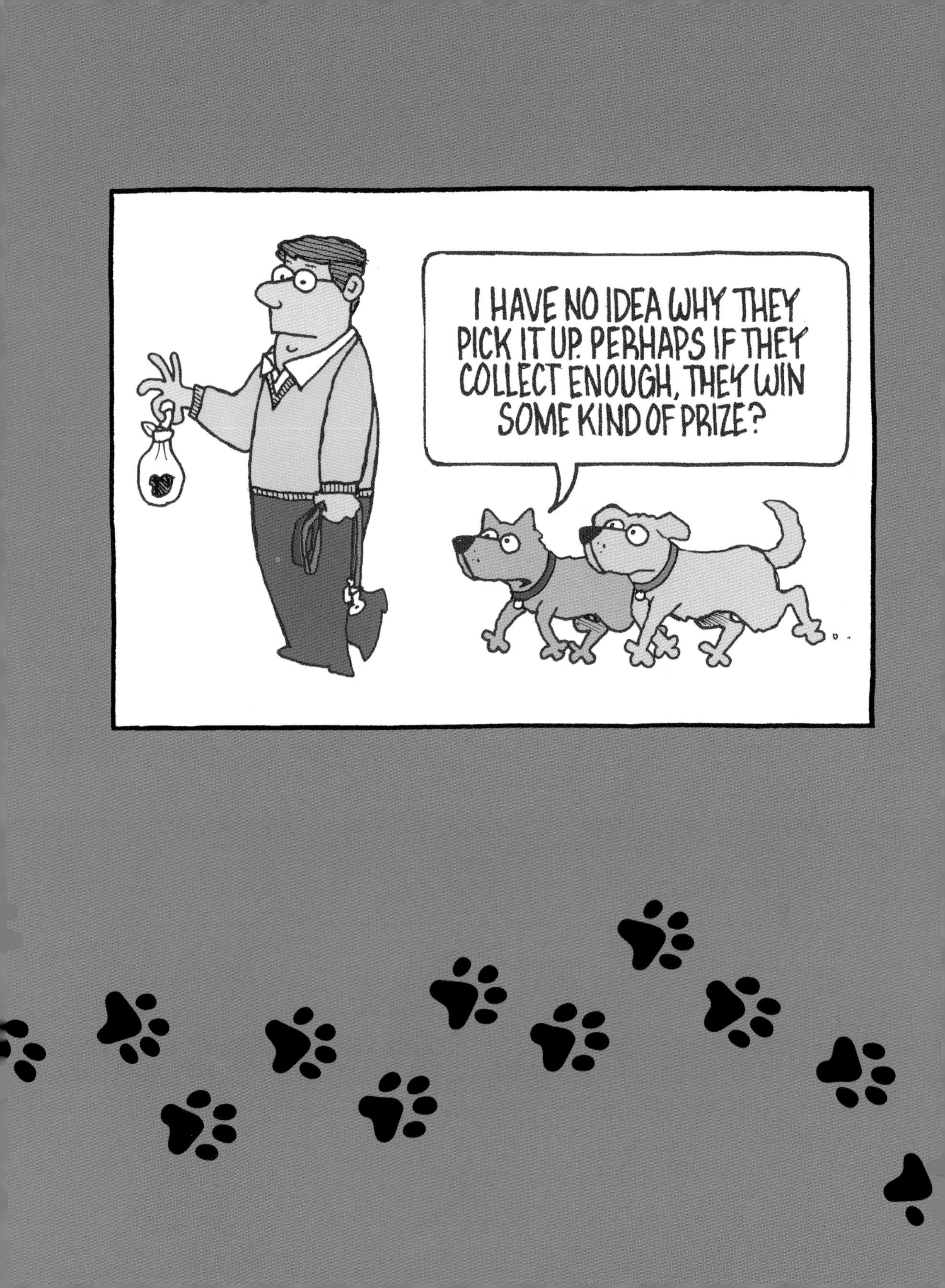
I HAVE NO IDEA WHY THEY PICK IT UP. PERHAPS IF THEY COLLECT ENOUGH, THEY WIN SOME KIND OF PRIZE?

BATHROOM HABITS

Unlike cats, we like to go outside. Not only is it an excuse to get out of the house and sniff things, it's also our way of marking our territory.

There is that first morning "I have to go out to pee so bad, my back teeth are afloat" pee, to the "hanging around by the door looking hopeful someone will open it because I feel like sniffing something" pee. And regardless of how long our walk is, we will never ever run out of pee to mark things.

Pooping is a different matter. Pooping is "doggie dark art." There is a system to it. You think it is pointless and frustrating standing around waiting for us to go, but finding the right place to poop is like you looking for the perfect parking spot. Time consuming, but so satisfying when we find that exact right spot.

You can try, but you cannot make us poop on command. We will go where we want, when we want.

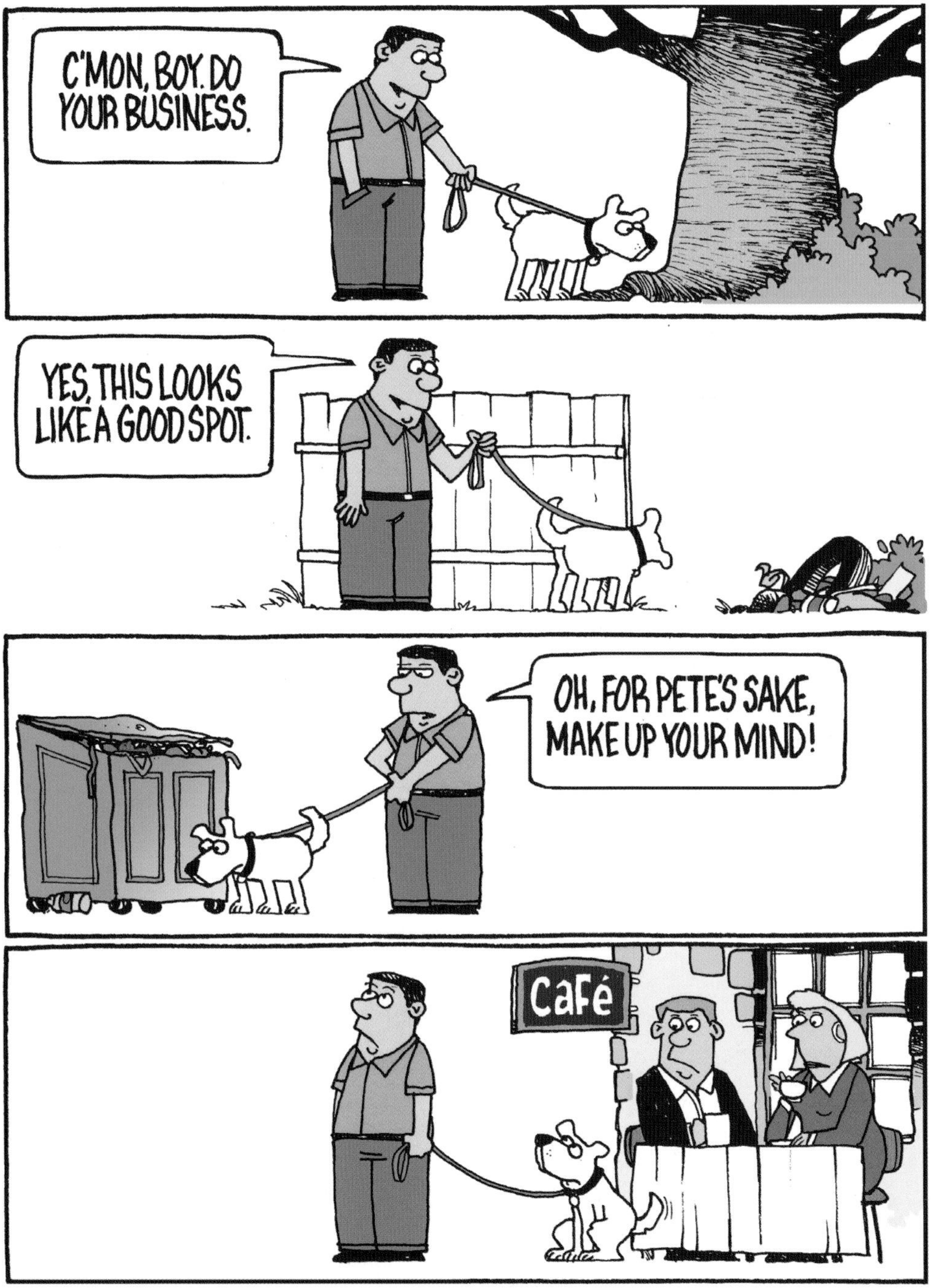
C'MON, BOY. DO YOUR BUSINESS.
YES, THIS LOOKS LIKE A GOOD SPOT.
OH, FOR PETE'S SAKE, MAKE UP YOUR MIND!
CaFé

We know you like to pick up our poop so we go out of our way to make it exciting for you.

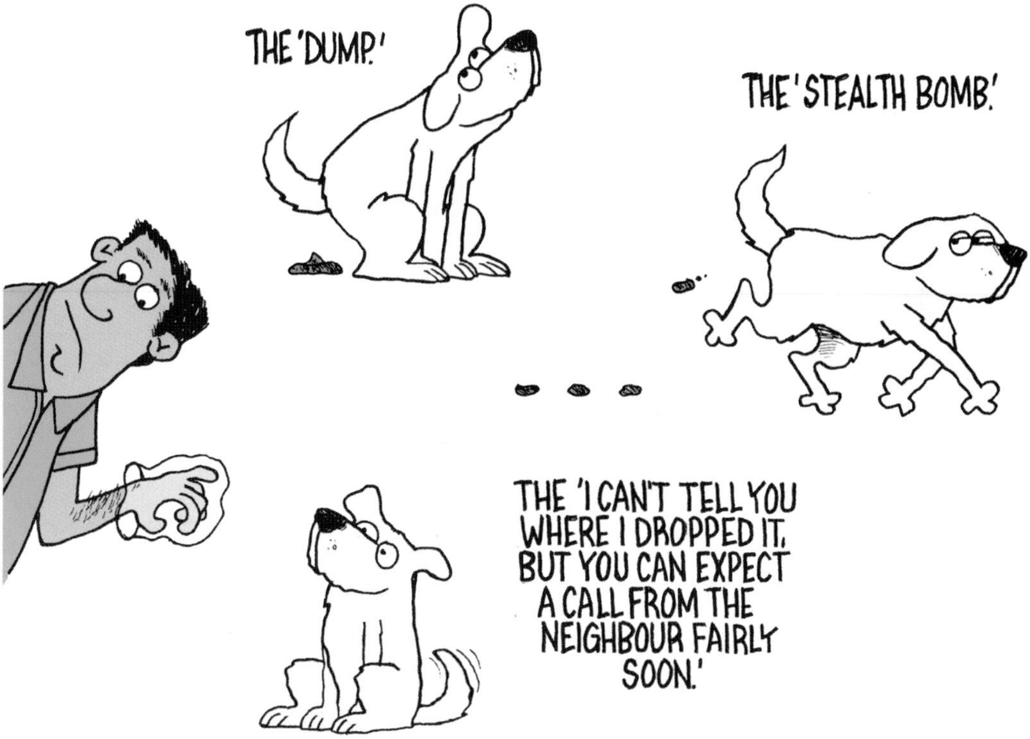

THE 'DUMP.'
THE 'STEALTH BOMB.'
THE 'I CAN'T TELL YOU WHERE I DROPPED IT, BUT YOU CAN EXPECT A CALL FROM THE NEIGHBOUR FAIRLY SOON.'

DID YOU KNOW...?

In the USA, dogs dump approximately 40,000 tons of poop per day. That's equivalent to the weight of 180 blue whales.

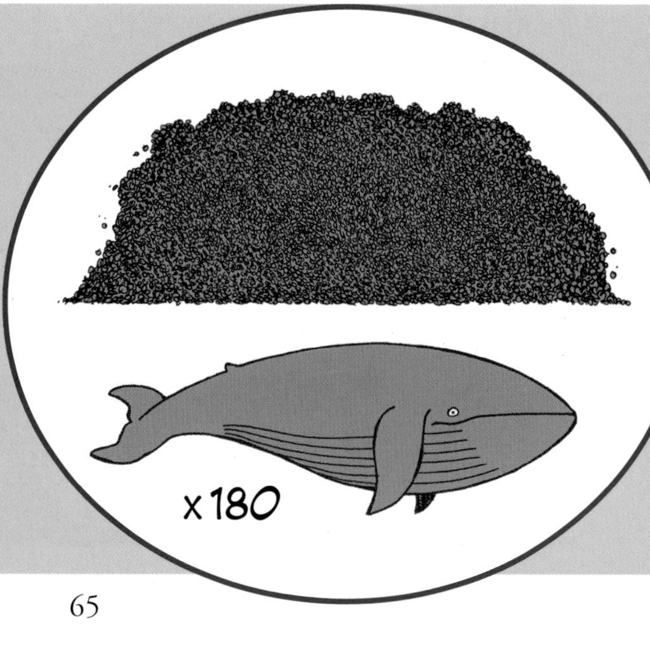

x180

Dogs have a robust digestive system and we're happy to share with you what we ate during the day.

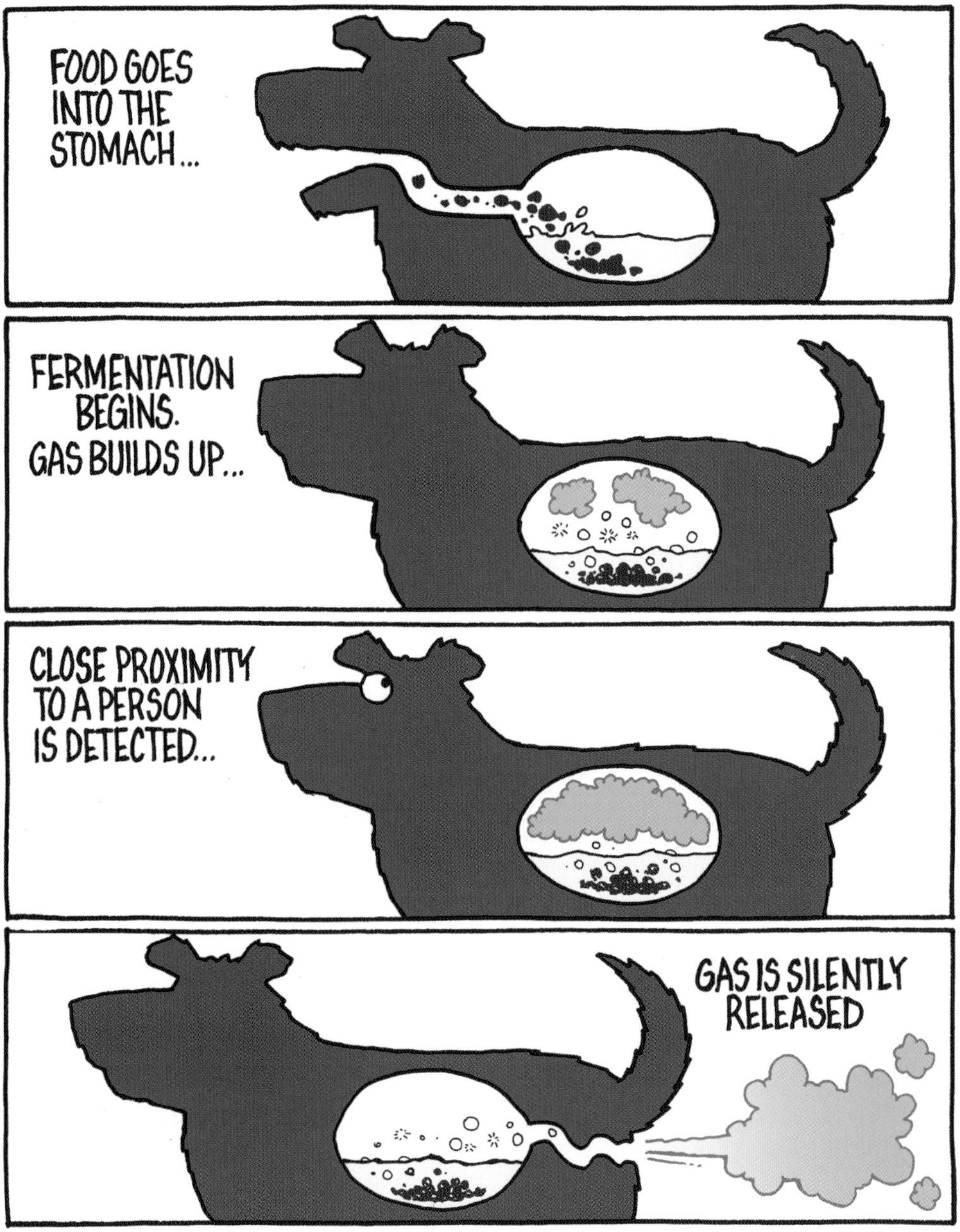
FOOD GOES INTO THE STOMACH...
FERMENTATION BEGINS. GAS BUILDS UP...
CLOSE PROXIMITY TO A PERSON IS DETECTED...
GAS IS SILENTLY RELEASED

Our sense of smell is thousands of times more sensitive than yours. However, by some quirk of nature, we are immune to our own farts.

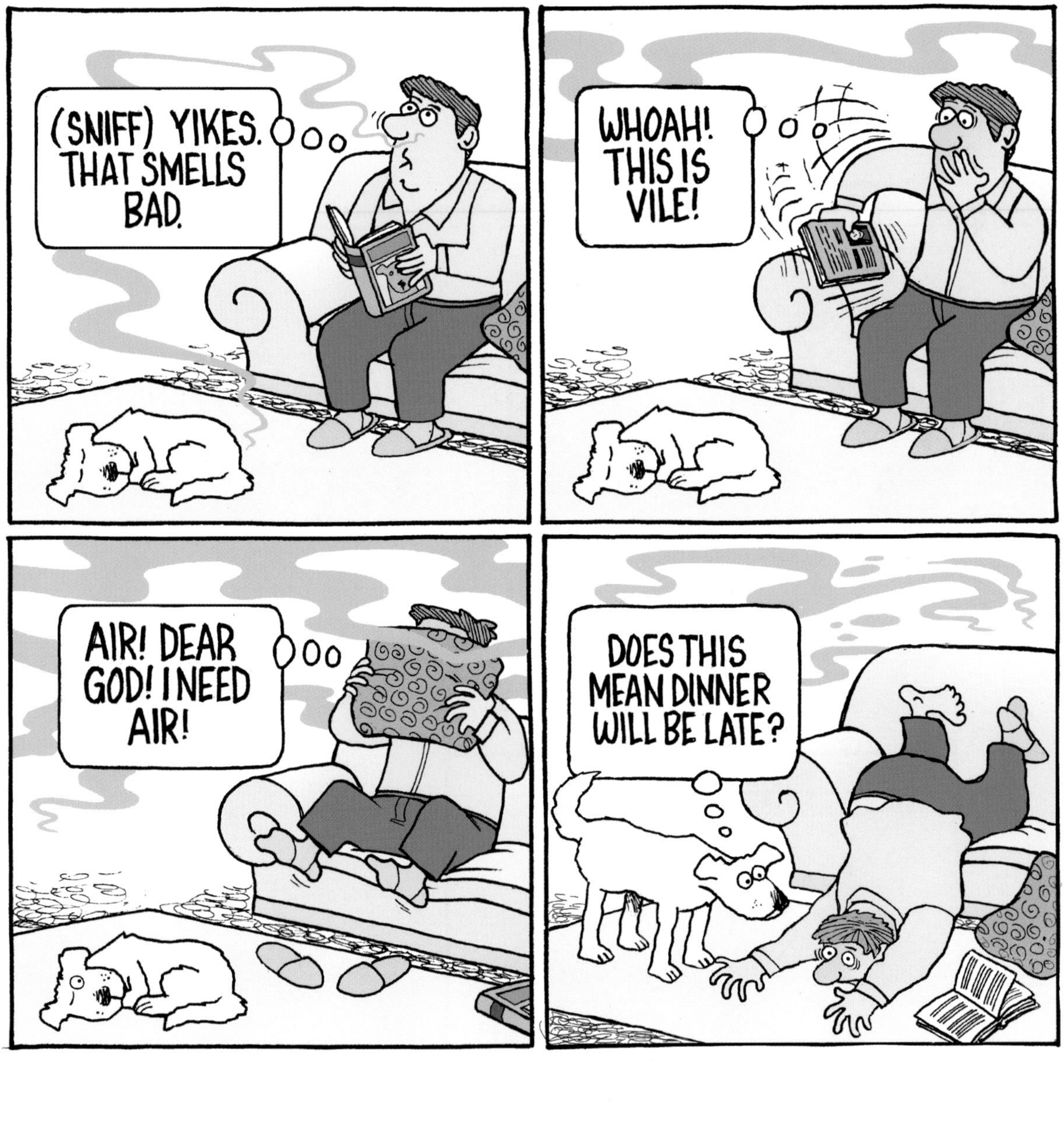
(SNIFF) YIKES. THAT SMELLS BAD.
WHOAH! THIS IS VILE!
AIR! DEAR GOD! I NEED AIR!
DOES THIS MEAN DINNER WILL BE LATE?

TO GIVE YOU THE FULL EFFECT OF OUR FARTS, WE PICK THE TIMING AND LOCATION CAREFULLY...

A COCKTAIL PARTY

A ROMANTIC EVENING

DINNER TIME

IN THE CAR, IN THE MIDDLE OF WINTER WITH THE WINDOWS FROZEN SHUT

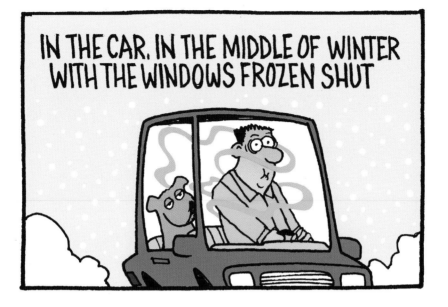

REVEALED!

WHERE DOG FARTS END UP

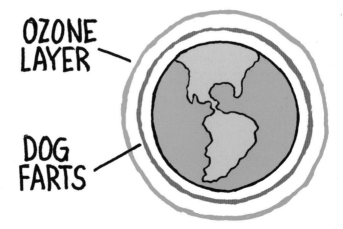

OZONE LAYER
DOG FARTS

Get to know our "we need to go outside" sounds.

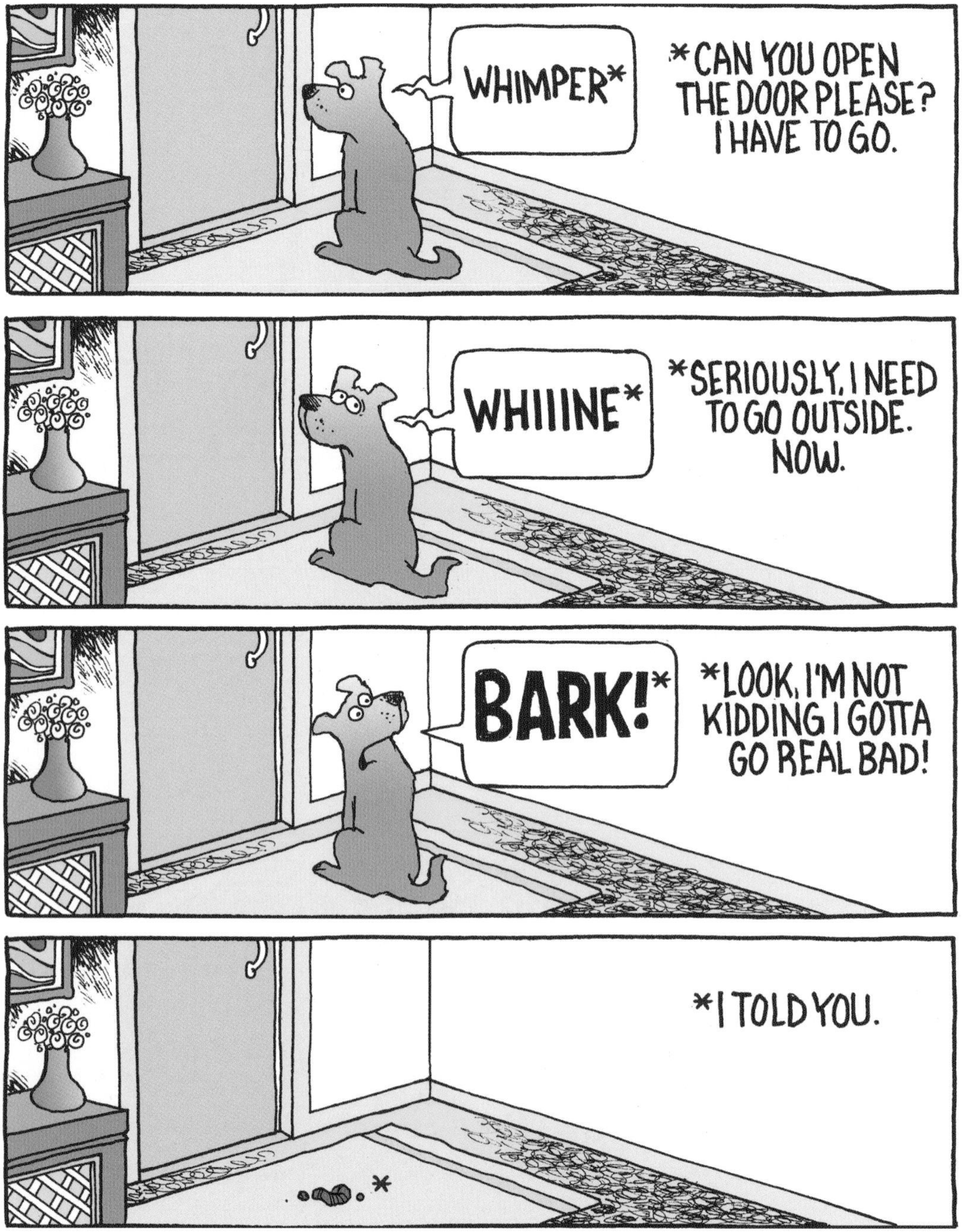

WHIMPER*
*CAN YOU OPEN THE DOOR PLEASE? I HAVE TO GO.
WHIIINE*
*SERIOUSLY, I NEED TO GO OUTSIDE. NOW.
BARK!*
*LOOK, I'M NOT KIDDING I GOTTA GO REAL BAD!
*I TOLD YOU.

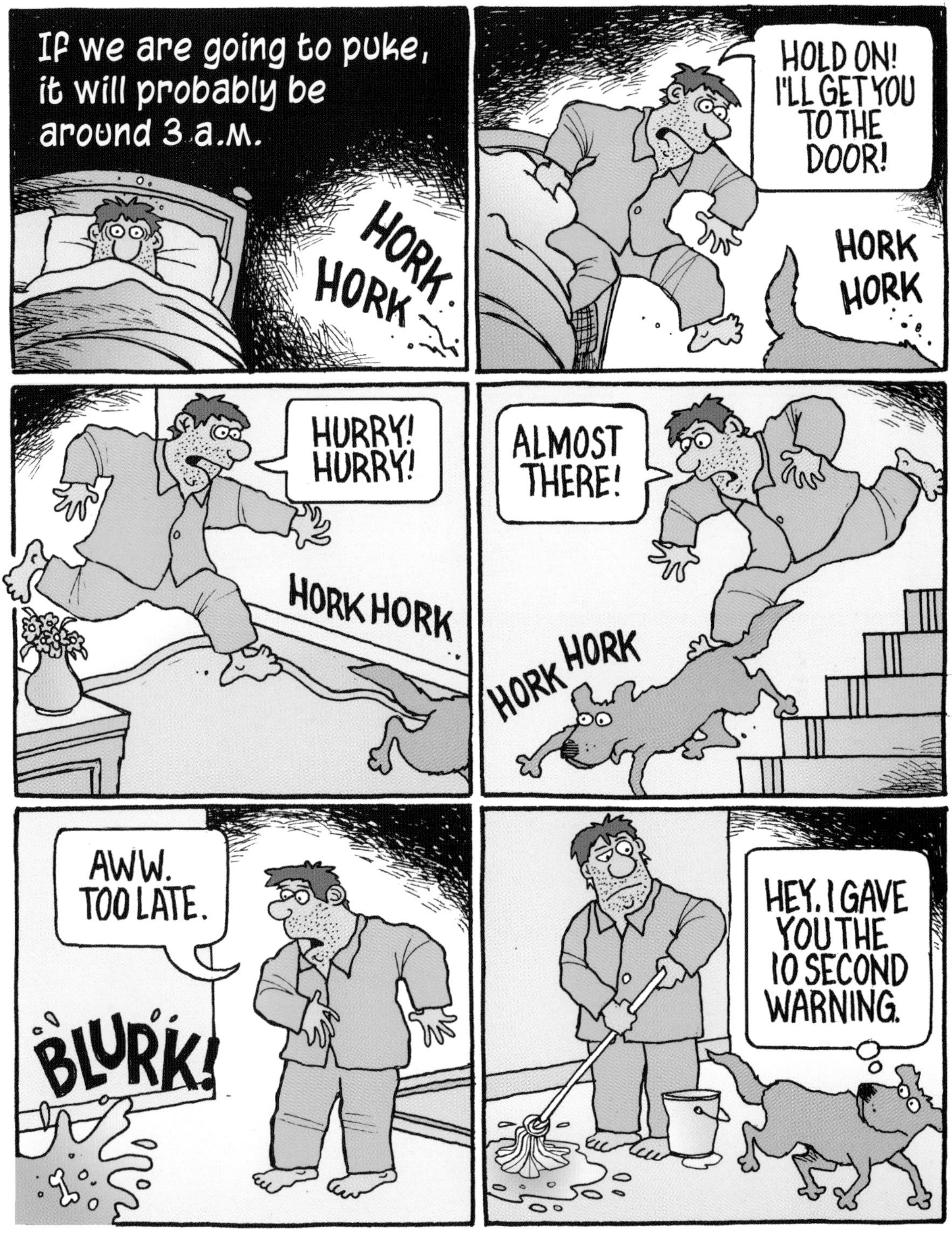

If we are going to puke, it will probably be around 3 a.m.
HORK HORK
HOLD ON! I'LL GET YOU TO THE DOOR!
HORK HORK
HURRY! HURRY!
HORK HORK
ALMOST THERE!
HORK HORK
AWW. TOO LATE.
BLURK!
HEY, I GAVE YOU THE 10 SECOND WARNING.

CHAPTER 7

EXERCISING

We used to run for miles chasing prey, but now we don't have to go much farther than the kitchen for a snack. However, if you haven't installed our own dog door it means you gotta take us out.

Besides bathroom breaks, which we don't consider exercise, we need to run. A simple race around the yard is okay, but we've sniffed everything out there, and if there are no other dogs peeing in the yard it's rather pointless after the second circuit.

So whether we're six inches or four feet tall, we love a long walk. But we will settle for a car ride, which is also a form of exercise from all the jumping and tail-chasing when we hear the car keys jingle. And if it's a car ride with a walk at the end of it, we're in heaven. If it's a car ride with a walk at the end of it and we're allowed to sit in the front seat next to you? Nirvana, baby!

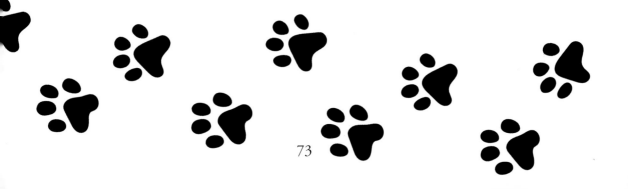

We may be couch potatoes but there is nothing we like better than a long walk and sniffing every tree, bush, fire hydrant and dog butt that we see. There is a right way and a wrong way to take us for a walk...

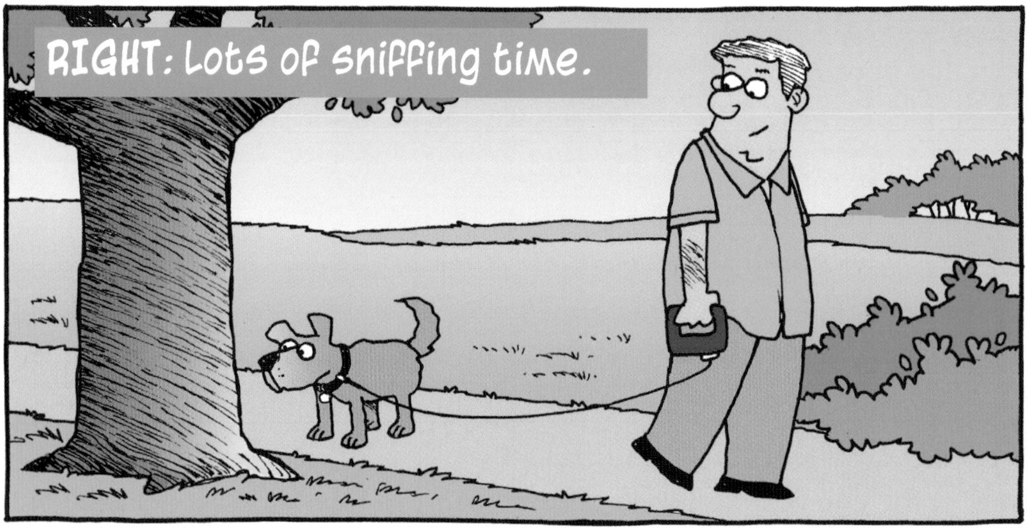
RIGHT: Lots of sniffing time.

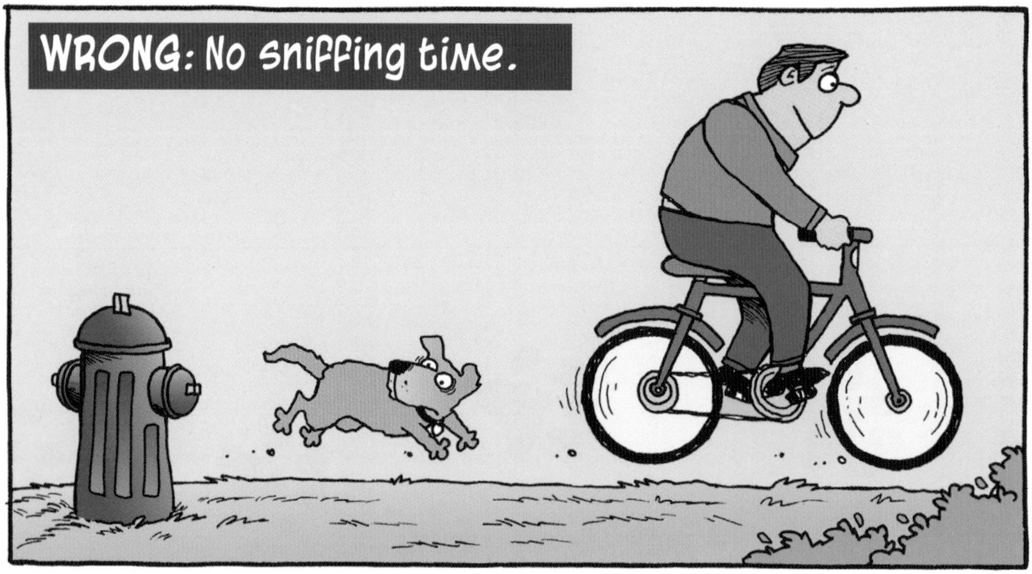
WRONG: No sniffing time.

Be aware, you are always under observation for signs of an impending walk.

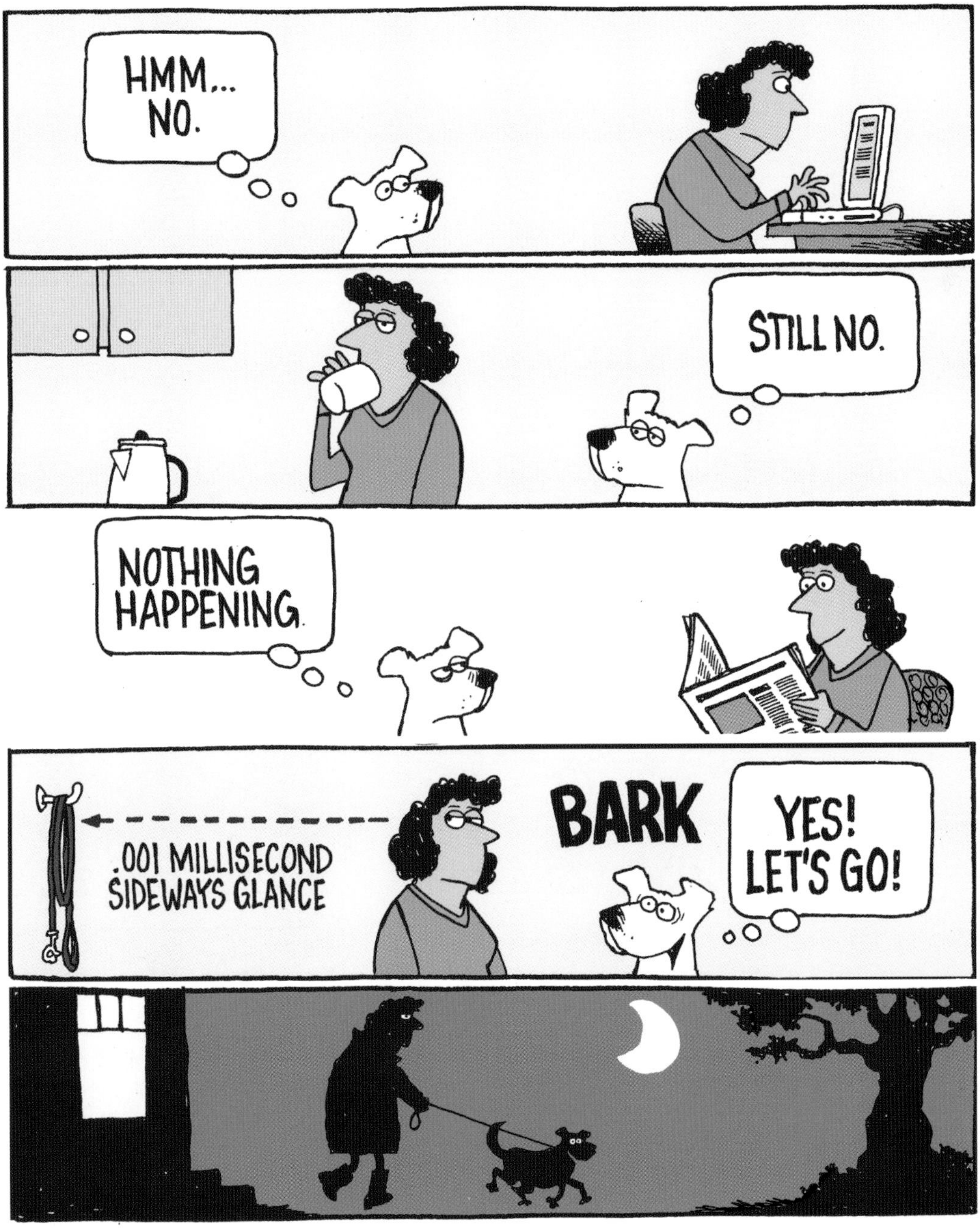
HMM... NO.
STILL NO.
NOTHING HAPPENING.
.001 MILLISECOND SIDEWAYS GLANCE
BARK
YES! LET'S GO!

A good walk is both a peaceful stroll and high drama.

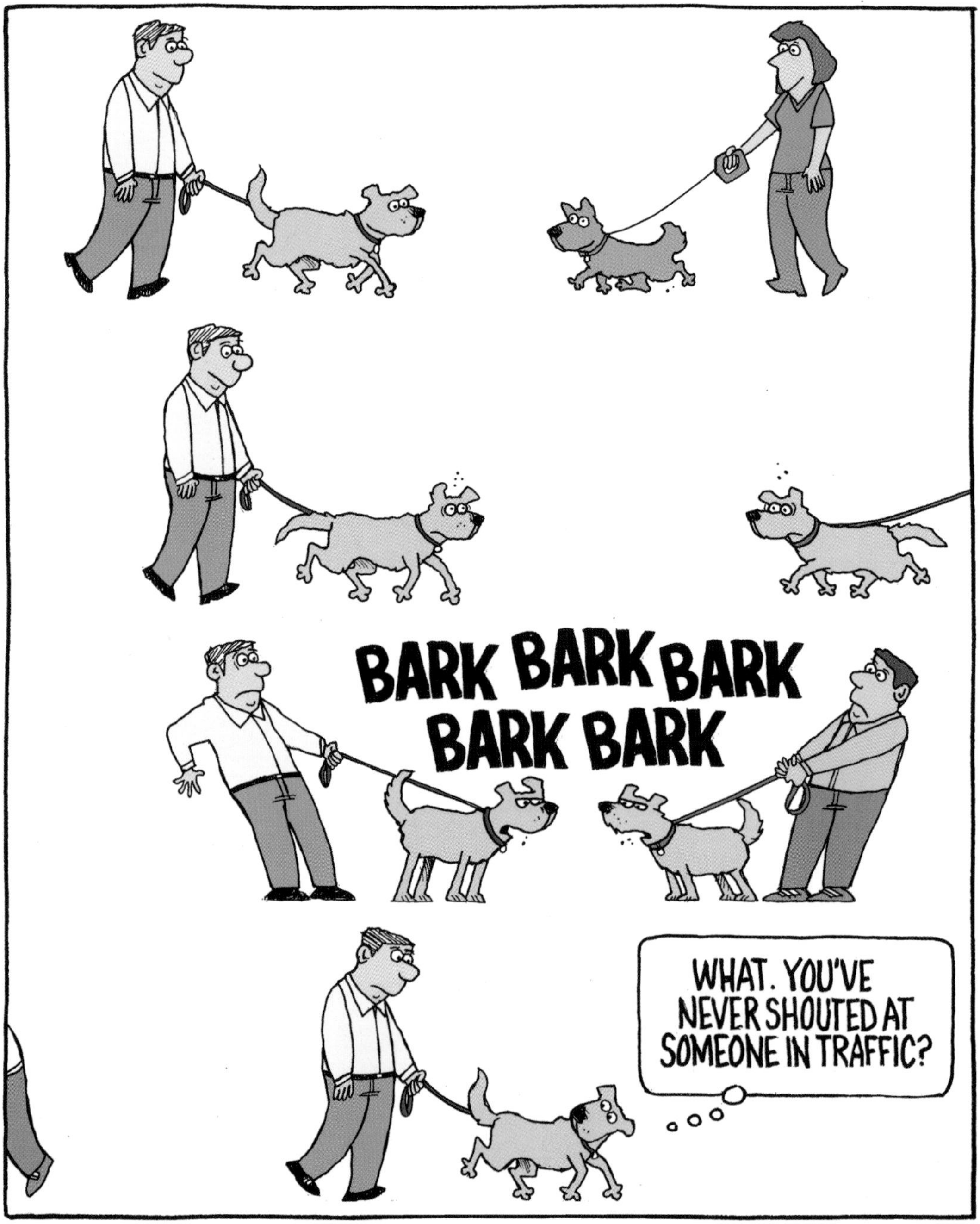
BARK BARK BARK
BARK BARK
WHAT. YOU'VE NEVER SHOUTED AT SOMEONE IN TRAFFIC?

REMINDER:
It's a walk, not an excuse to gossip.

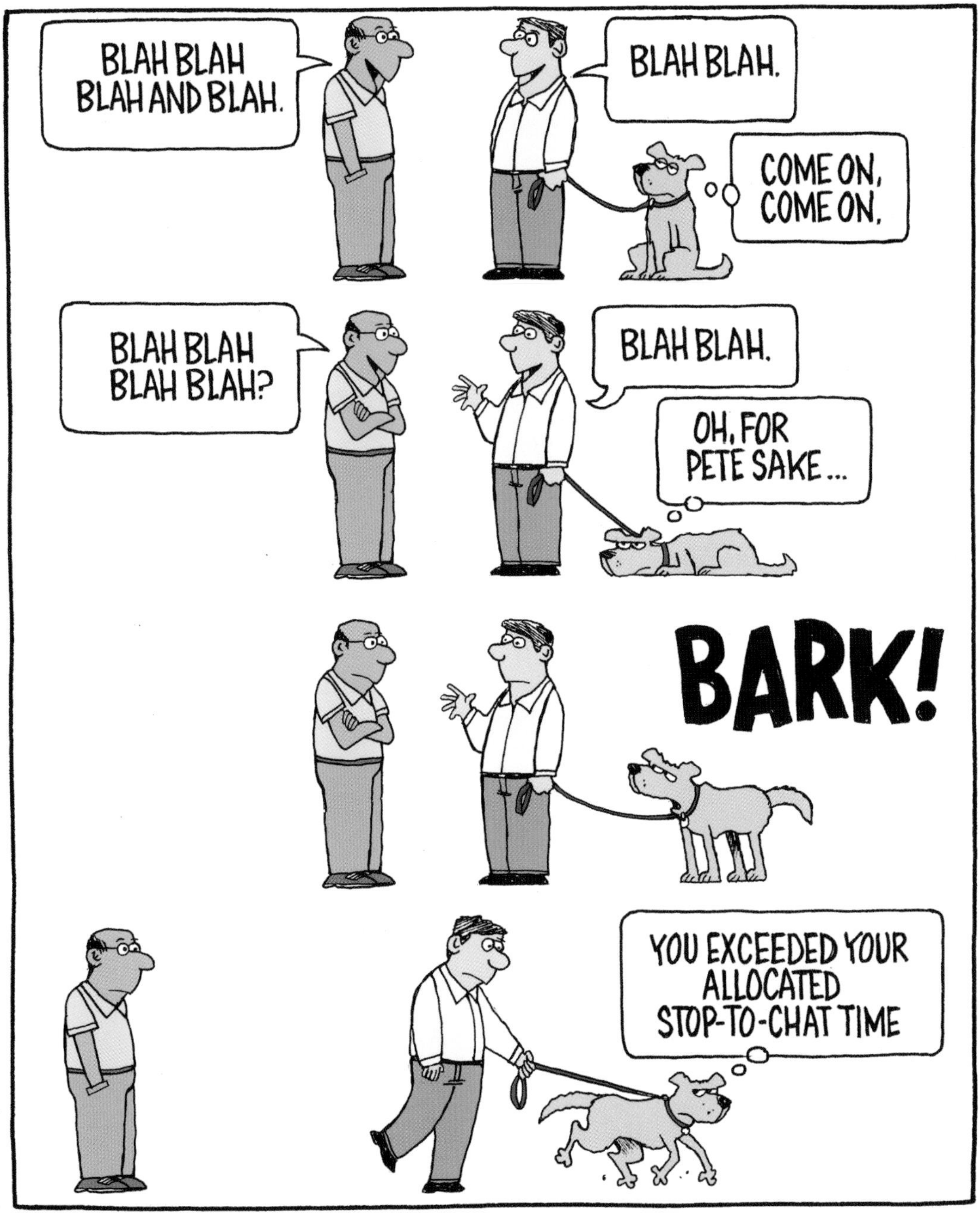
BLAH BLAH BLAH AND BLAH.
BLAH BLAH.
COME ON, COME ON.
BLAH BLAH BLAH BLAH?
BLAH BLAH.
OH, FOR PETE SAKE...
BARK!
YOU EXCEEDED YOUR ALLOCATED STOP-TO-CHAT TIME

DISSECTING THE PERFECT WALK

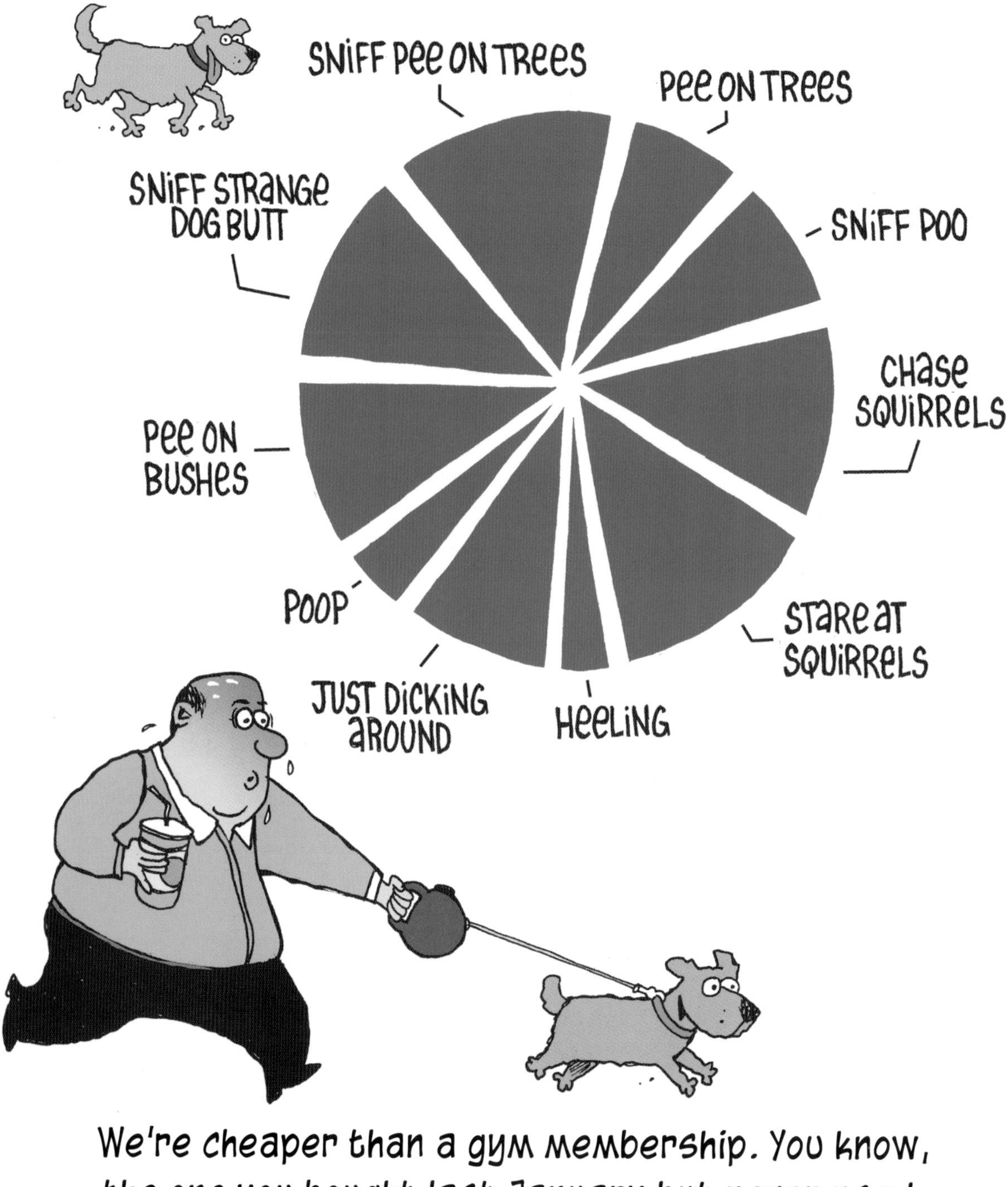
SNIFF PEE ON TREES
PEE ON TREES
SNIFF POO
CHASE SQUIRRELS
STARE AT SQUIRRELS
HEELING
JUST DICKING AROUND
POOP
PEE ON BUSHES
SNIFF STRANGE DOG BUTT

We're cheaper than a gym membership. You know, the one you bought last January but never used.

CHECKLIST FOR A SUCCESSFUL CAR RIDE

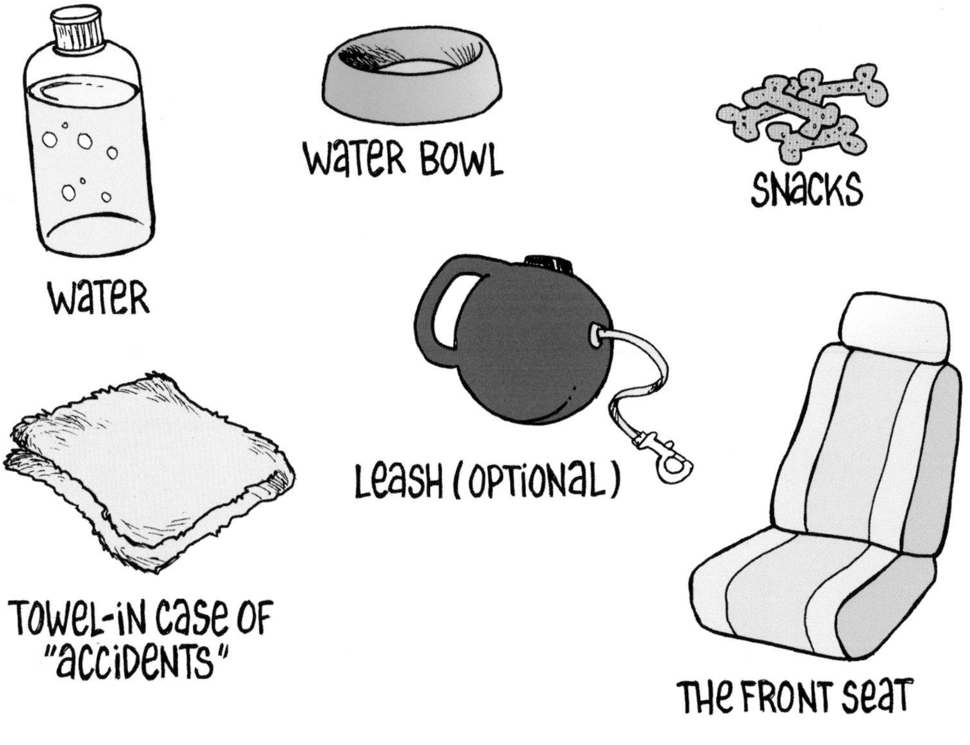
WATER
WATER BOWL
SNACKS
LEASH (OPTIONAL)
TOWEL-IN CASE OF "ACCIDENTS"
THE FRONT SEAT

DID YOU KNOW...?

All car keys have a unique jingle... we know them all.

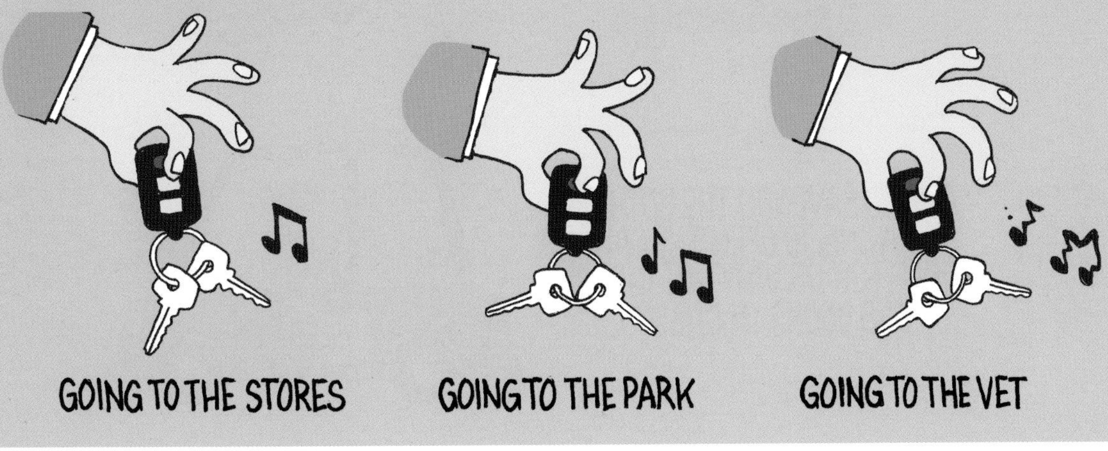
GOING TO THE STORES
GOING TO THE PARK
GOING TO THE VET

Why do we love car rides? To you, cars are a means of transportation. To us, they are much more exciting... cars are:

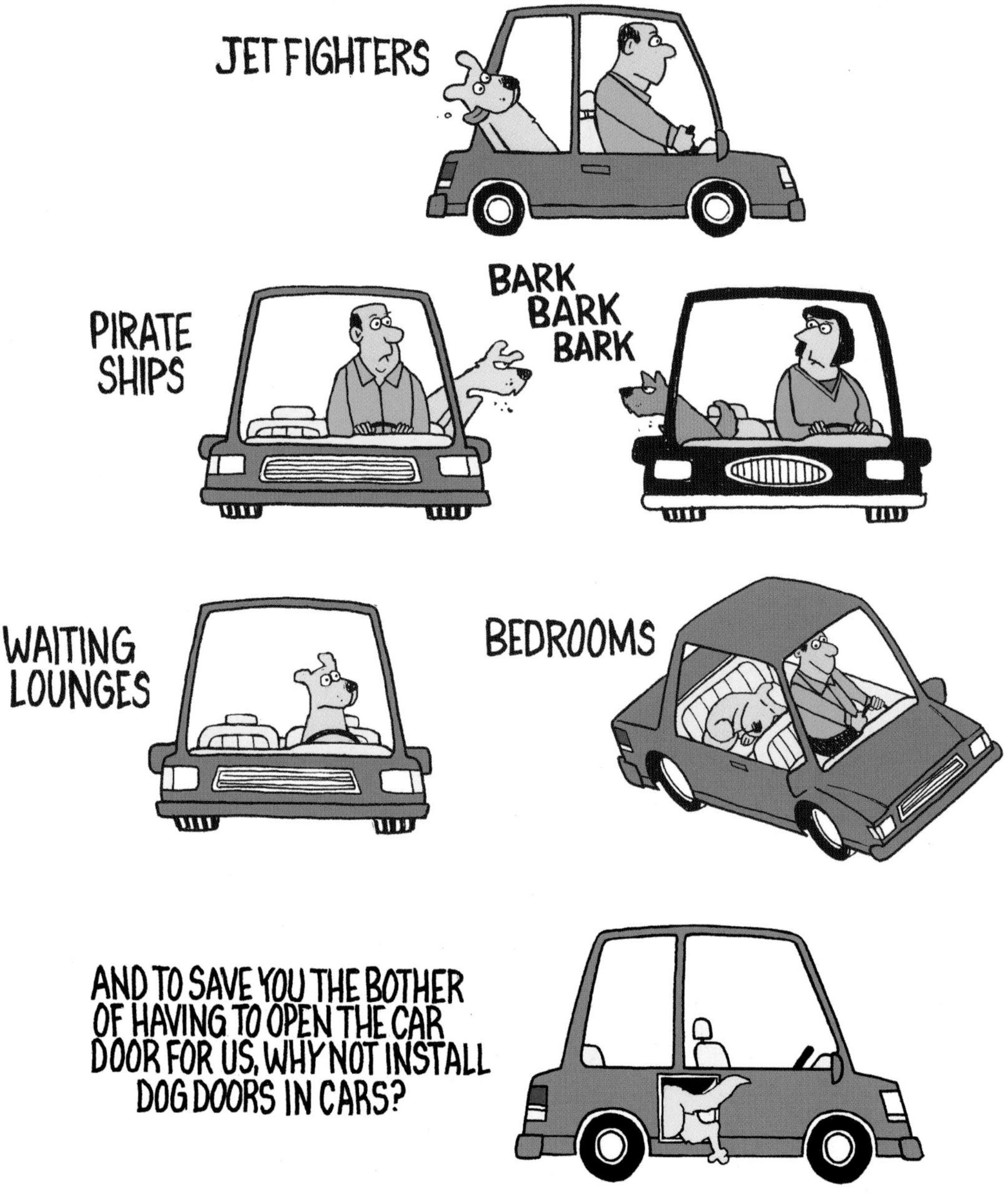
JET FIGHTERS
PIRATE SHIPS
BARK BARK BARK
WAITING LOUNGES
BEDROOMS
AND TO SAVE YOU THE BOTHER OF HAVING TO OPEN THE CAR DOOR FOR US, WHY NOT INSTALL DOG DOORS IN CARS?

Four reasons why we hop into the driver's seat when you leave us in the car:

THE SEAT IS WARM

IT'S THE POWER SEAT

BEST POSITION TO GUARD THE CAR

IT'S CLEANER THAN OUR SEAT

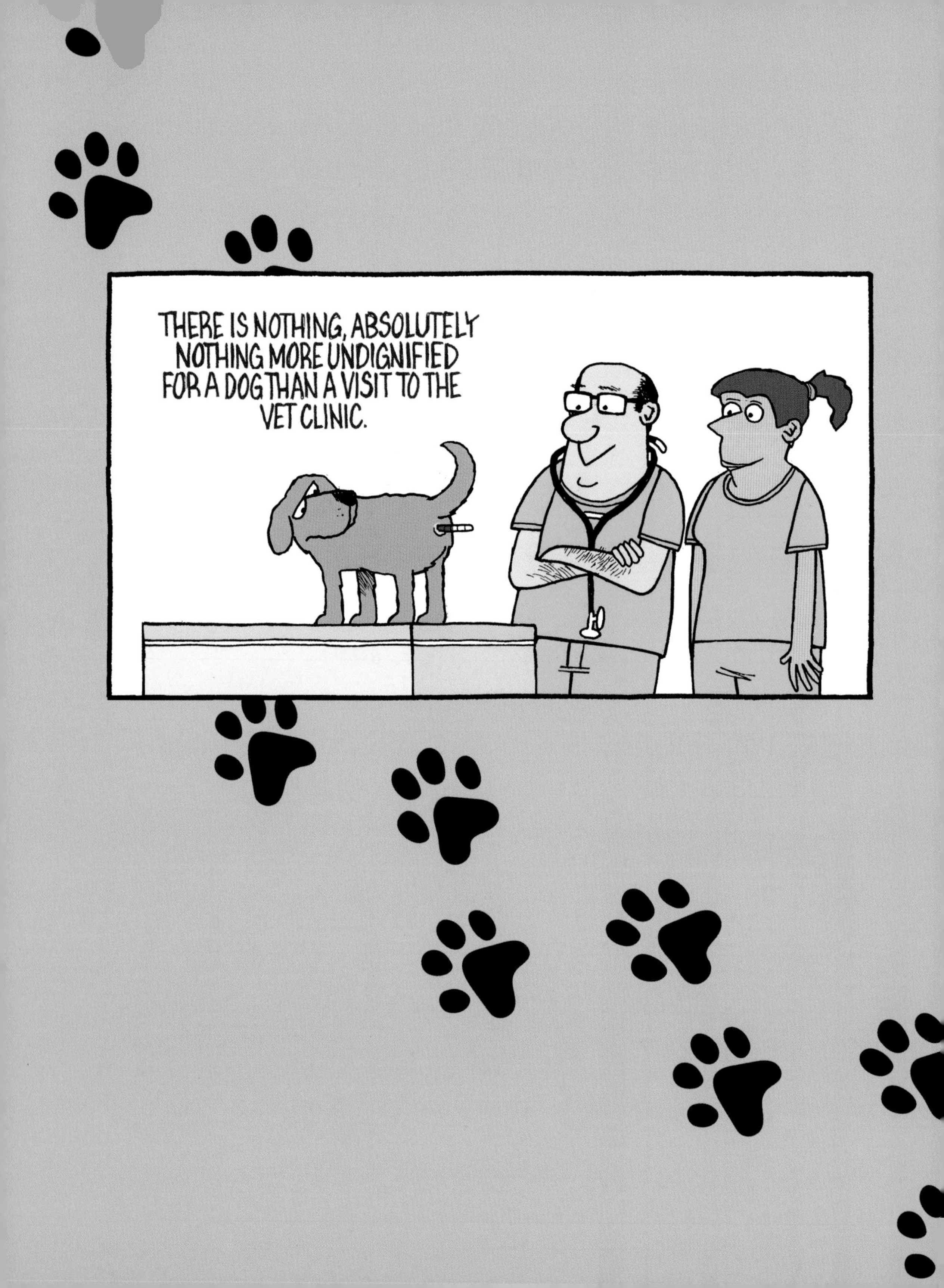
THERE IS NOTHING, ABSOLUTELY NOTHING MORE UNDIGNIFIED FOR A DOG THAN A VISIT TO THE VET CLINIC.

CHAPTER 8

REPAIRS AND MAINTENANCE

Dogs have two mortal enemies. The vacuum cleaner and the vet.

Like you, we get sick sometimes, although we tend to make less of a fuss than you do and prefer to suffer in silence. It goes back to that whole "weakest member of the pack gets eaten" thing.

We know you have a drawer full of pill bottles in the kitchen and it's up to us to avoid taking them. You can try to disguise that pill in a treat, but we will find it and spit it out. We can smell a Papillon's pee from a hundred metres; do you think we can't taste a pill in a chunk of cheese?

But pills are nothing compared to that yearly visit to the clinic where the vet will bring out the anal probe and basically strip us of our dignity. We get needles stuck in us, things squirted up our noses and, if we're lucky, maybe a small, dried liver treat afterwards. After what we've been through, the entire cow would be more appropriate.

To be fair to us, our deep-seated fear of vets (besides having things pushed up our wazoo) is from that first visit, when we came out of the clinic a little lighter than when we went in.

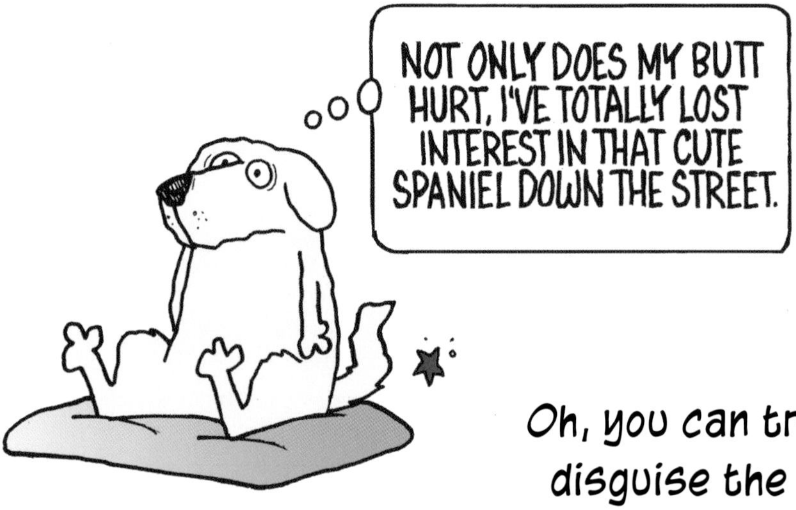
NOT ONLY DOES MY BUTT HURT, I'VE TOTALLY LOST INTEREST IN THAT CUTE SPANIEL DOWN THE STREET.

Oh, you can try and disguise the fact we were neutered by having prosthetic testicles inserted, but we know.

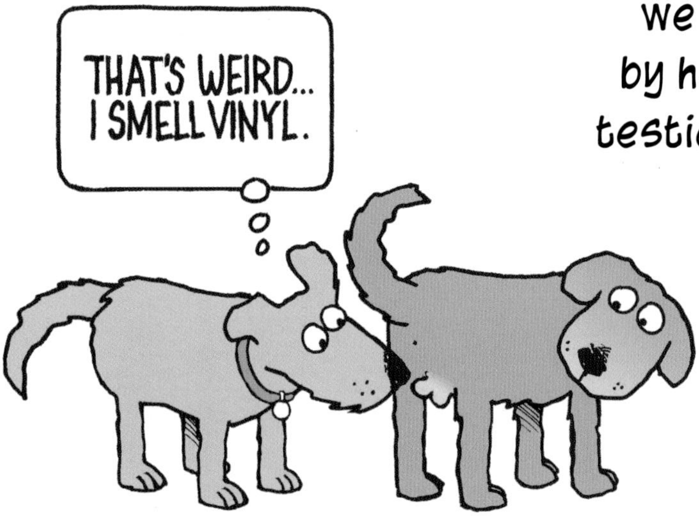
THAT'S WEIRD... I SMELL VINYL.

Then there are times when you will take us to the vet for our annual shots or a more serious ailment...

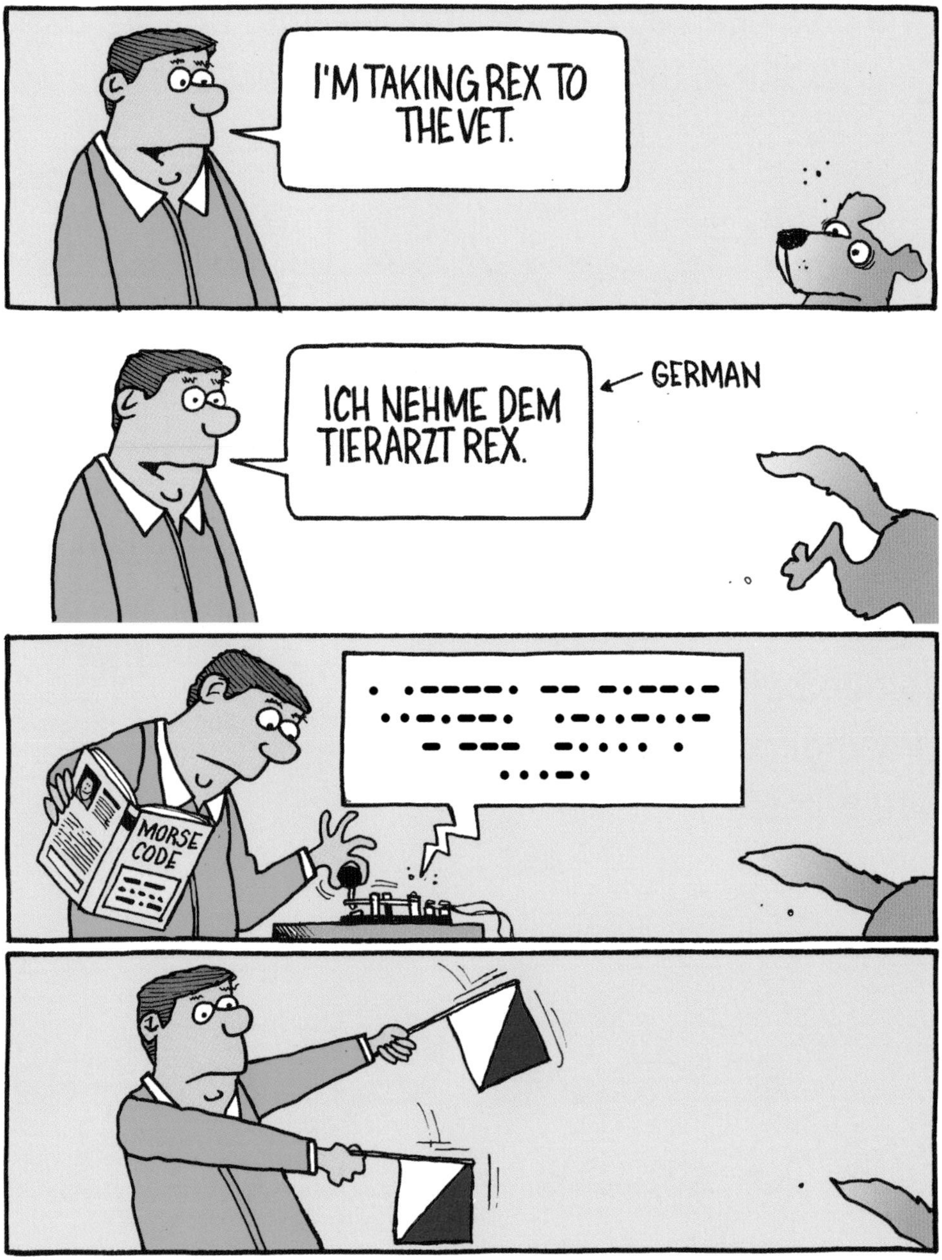
I'M TAKING REX TO THE VET.
ICH NEHME DEM TIERARZT REX.
GERMAN
MORSE CODE

... and on hearing the word "vet" we will make ourselves scarce. Don't bother using code words for "vet." We will quickly figure them out.

A visit to the vet can be unpleasant. But we can make it unpleasant for the vet, too.

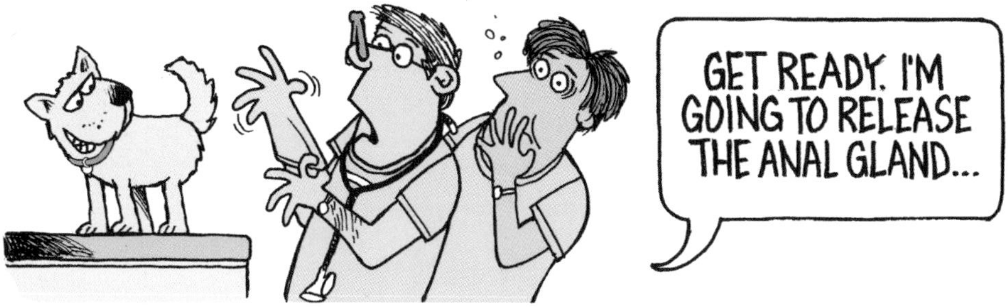
GET READY. I'M GOING TO RELEASE THE ANAL GLAND...

Besides being humiliating, cones cause a host of problems.

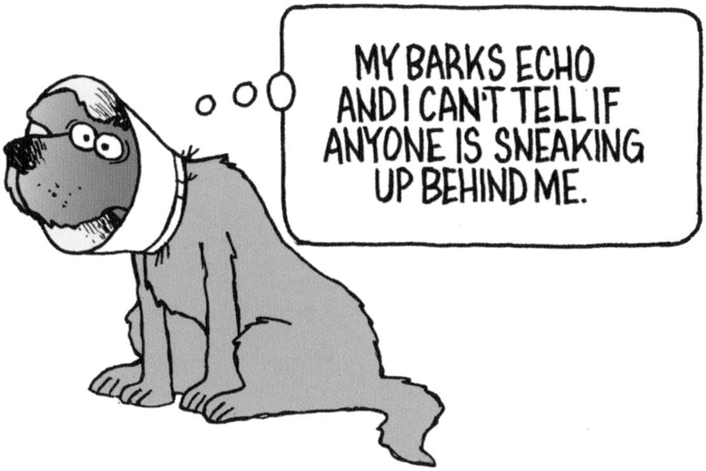
MY BARKS ECHO AND I CAN'T TELL IF ANYONE IS SNEAKING UP BEHIND ME.

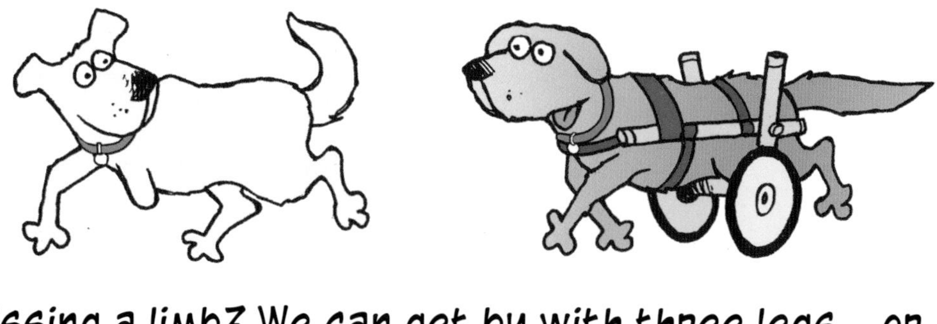

Missing a limb? We can get by with three legs... or two. We don't need your sympathy but could use a little help reaching up to the kitchen counter.

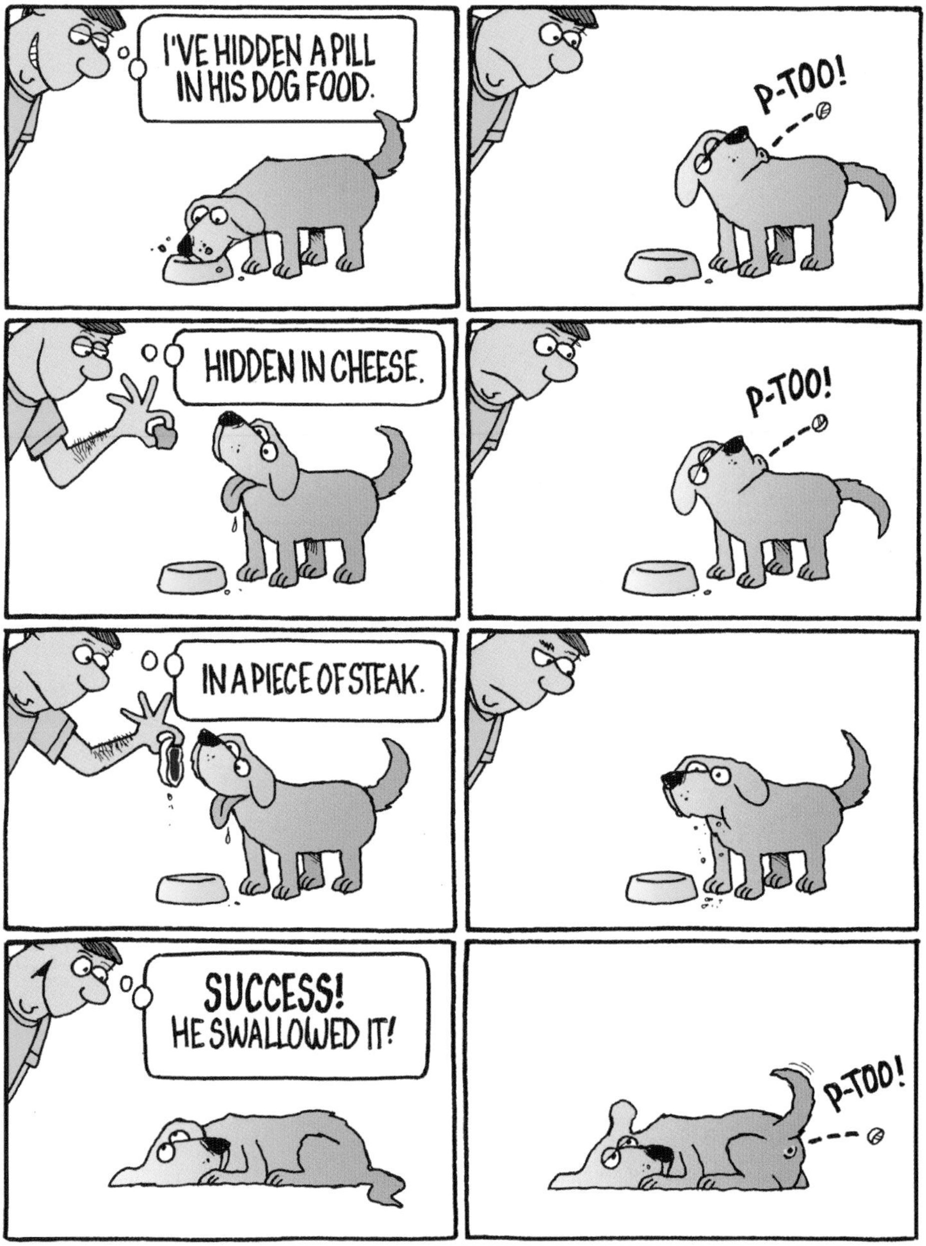
I'VE HIDDEN A PILL IN HIS DOG FOOD.
P-TOO!
HIDDEN IN CHEESE.
P-TOO!
IN A PIECE OF STEAK.
SUCCESS! HE SWALLOWED IT!
P-TOO!

No matter how crafty you think you are when it comes to getting us to take a pill, we are craftier.

Sure, we'll scarf down anything, but go easy on the treats.

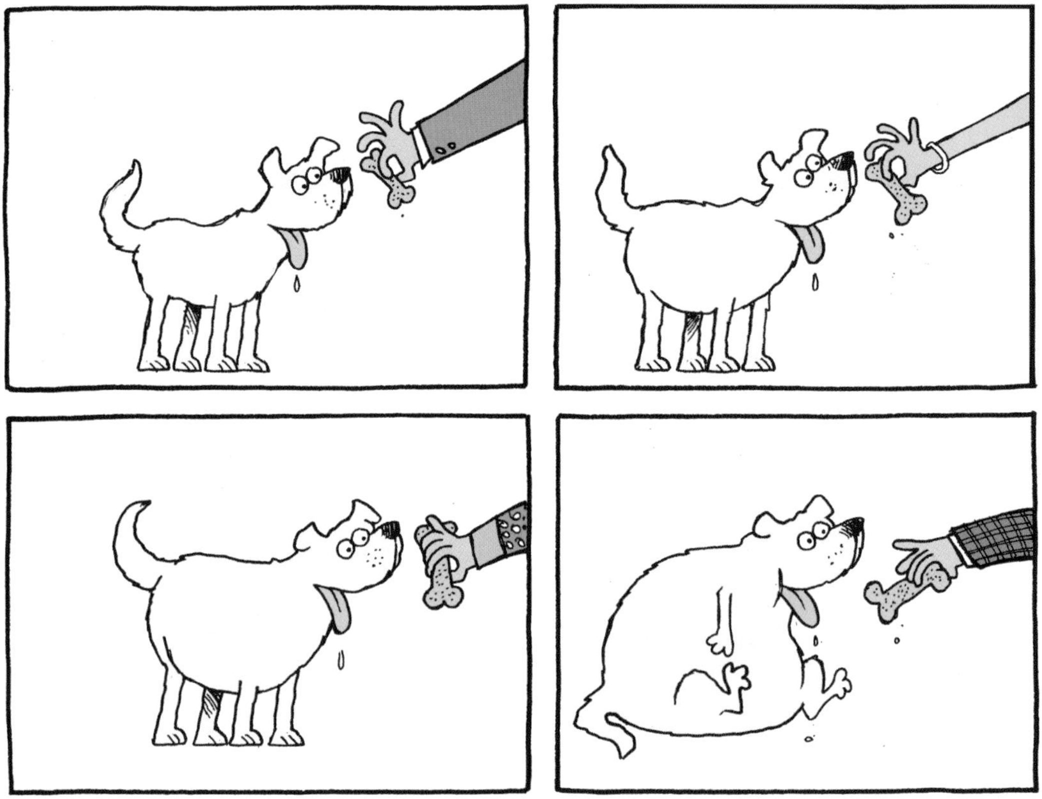

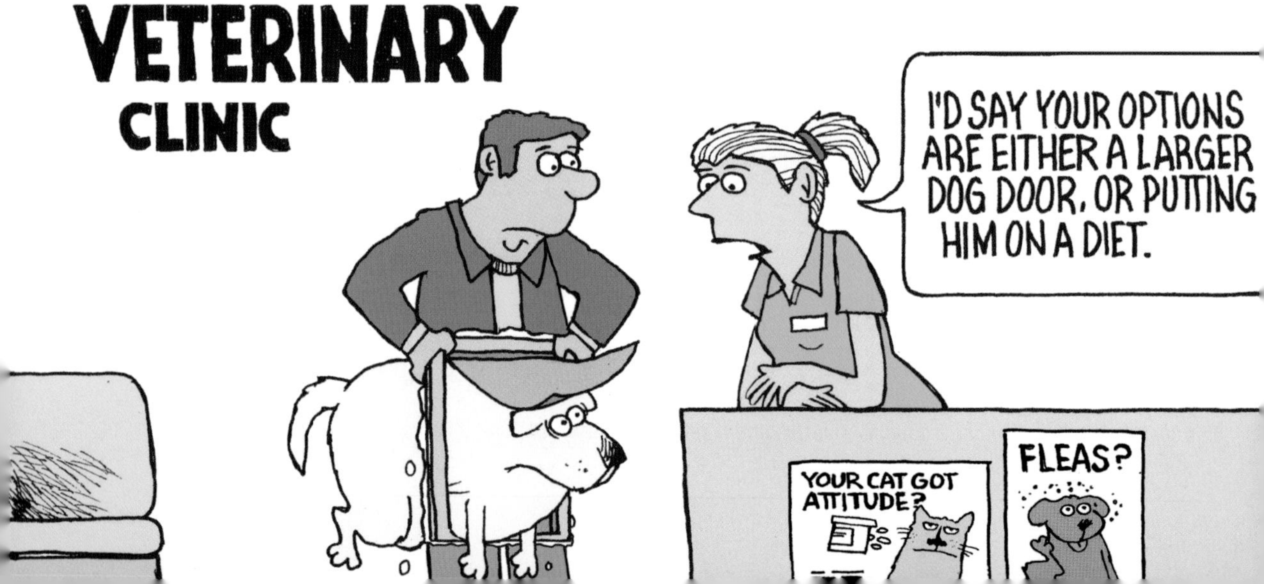
VETERINARY CLINIC
I'D SAY YOUR OPTIONS ARE EITHER A LARGER DOG DOOR, OR PUTTING HIM ON A DIET.
YOUR CAT GOT ATTITUDE?
FLEAS?

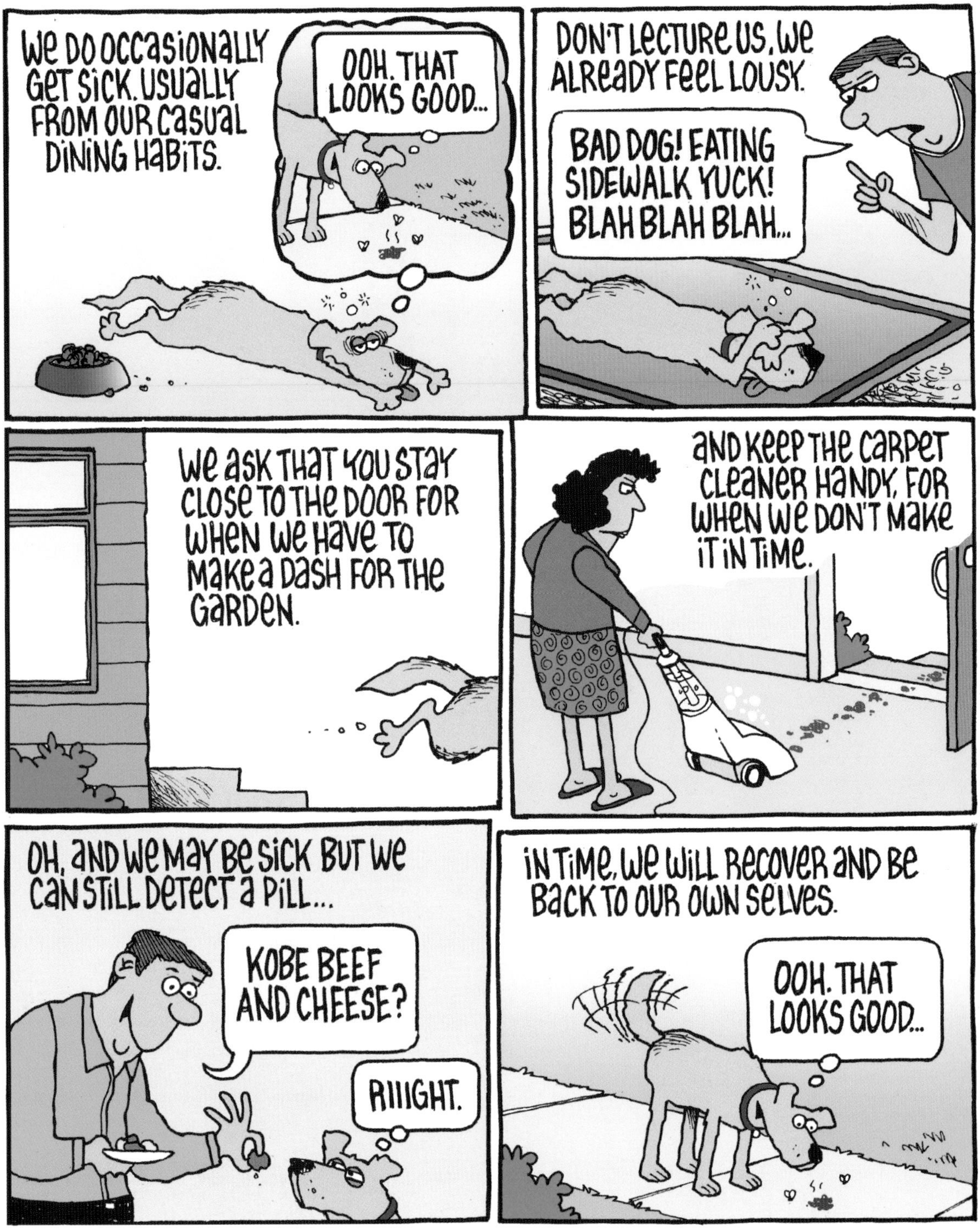

WE DO OCCASIONALLY GET SICK. USUALLY FROM OUR CASUAL DINING HABITS.
OOH. THAT LOOKS GOOD...
DON'T LECTURE US, WE ALREADY FEEL LOUSY.
BAD DOG! EATING SIDEWALK YUCK! BLAH BLAH BLAH...
WE ASK THAT YOU STAY CLOSE TO THE DOOR FOR WHEN WE HAVE TO MAKE A DASH FOR THE GARDEN.
AND KEEP THE CARPET CLEANER HANDY, FOR WHEN WE DON'T MAKE IT IN TIME.
OH, AND WE MAY BE SICK BUT WE CAN STILL DETECT A PILL...
KOBE BEEF AND CHEESE?
RIIIGHT.
IN TIME, WE WILL RECOVER AND BE BACK TO OUR OWN SELVES.
OOH. THAT LOOKS GOOD...

IF YOU DON'T WANT A HIGH VET BILL, OR WORSE, KEEP THE FOLLOWING FOODS OUT OF REACH OF OUR PAWS:

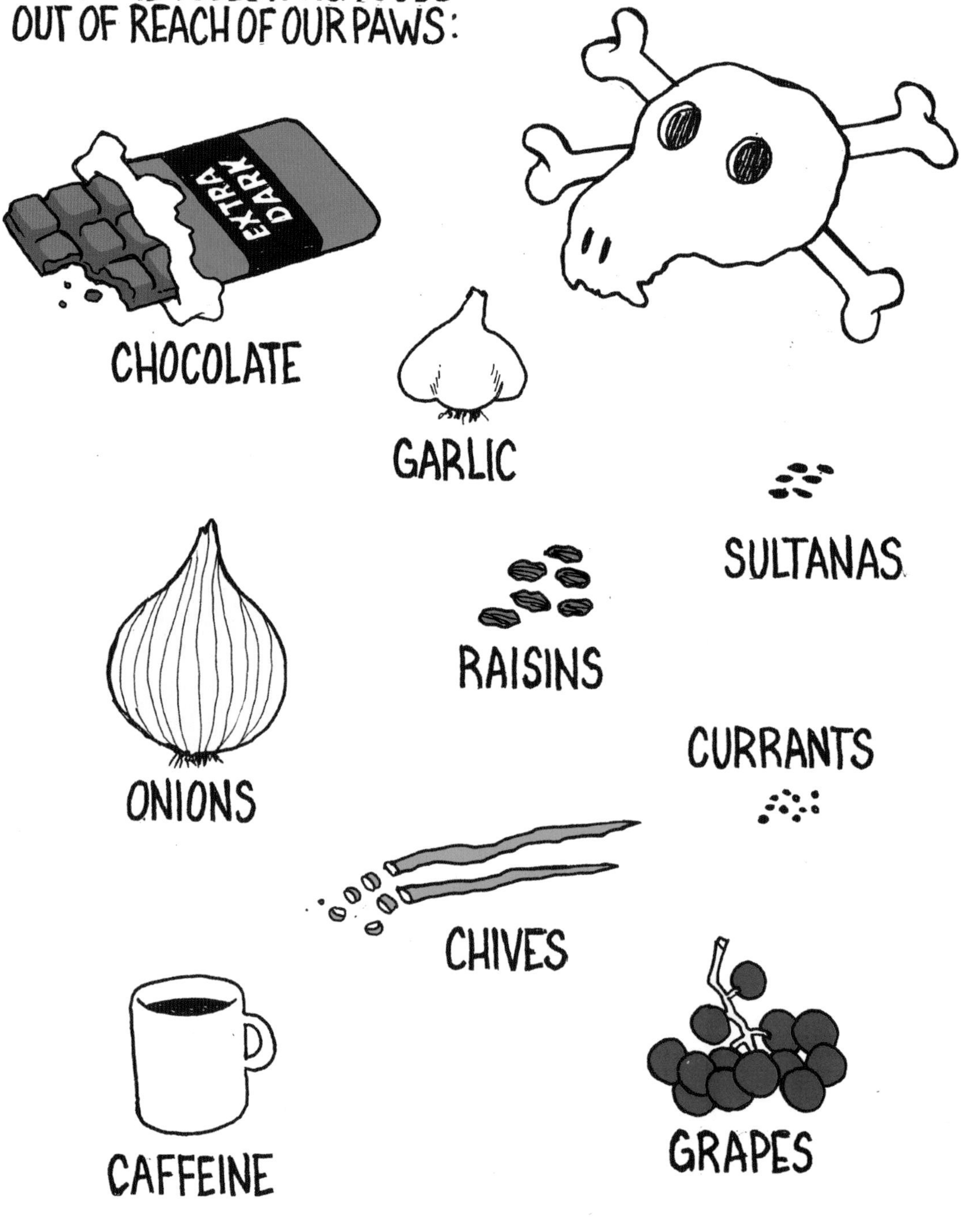
EXTRA DARK
CHOCOLATE
GARLIC
SULTANAS
RAISINS
ONIONS
CURRANTS
CHIVES
CAFFEINE
GRAPES

ALCOHOL

AVOCADO

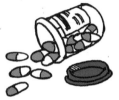

PRESCRIPTION DRUGS
(PEOPLE KIND)

CORN ON THE COB

MACADAMIA NUTS

ANY CANNABIS PRODUCTS

LEGO
BLOCKS

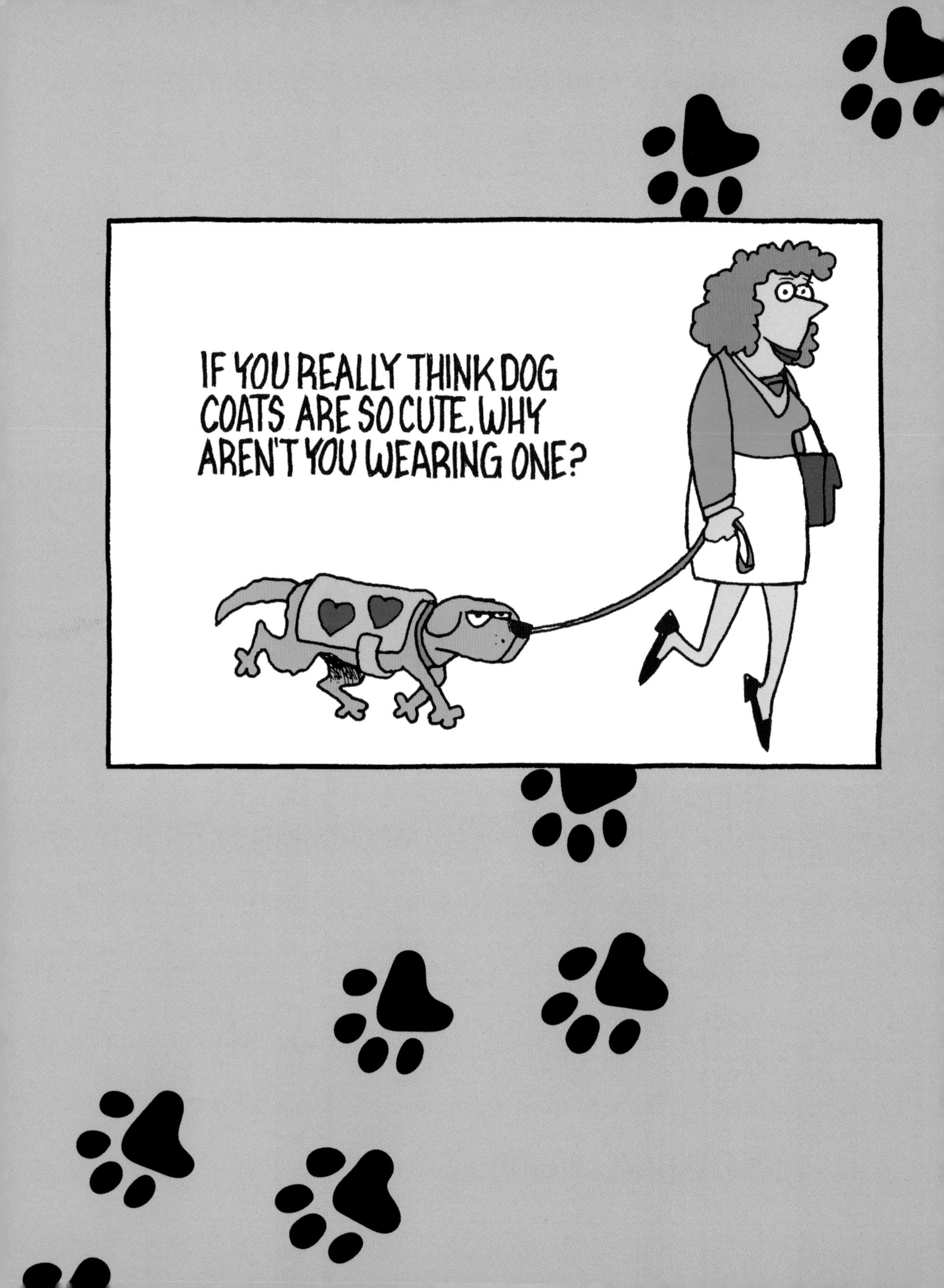
IF YOU REALLY THINK DOG COATS ARE SO CUTE, WHY AREN'T YOU WEARING ONE?

CHAPTER 9

ACCESSORIZING

Okay, we can put up with collars (not too tight!) and our tags—despite that annoying jingle that gives us away when we're trying to sneak out of the yard—and a dog coat can come in handy on a cold day. Yes, a cold day! Not the middle of summer! We have hair, we have our own built-in coats. Put a coat on us in summer and it's like a freaking sauna in there!

Speaking of which, what's with all the dogs that roast to death in cars on a hot summer day? You are smart enough to get a driver's licence, surely you can figure a hot car is no place for a dog. Maybe there should be a test before you get a dog licence…?

We know you look forward to holidays like Christmas, Easter, Valentine's Day and all the rest, and you like to put up cheesy decorations at those times, but seriously, do you have to decorate us too? You think we look cute wearing reindeer antlers that light up and play Christmas carols, but we think we look like giant dorks and all the other dogs laugh at us. Please, leave the decorations on the tree. And next time you are tempted to buy that to-die-for pink dog coat with matching rhinestone leash, why not just make a donation to an animal shelter instead?

Yeah, we get it. You like dressing up. But seriously, would you wear some of these outfits? Sure, we're colour blind(-ish) but we know when we look like a dork.

VERY HIP

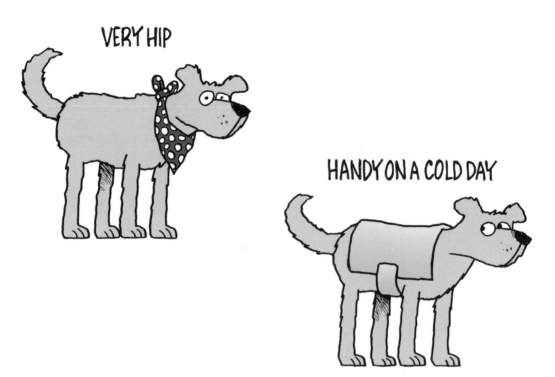

HANDY ON A COLD DAY

COULDN'T YOU JUST HAVE HAD KIDS INSTEAD?

If sayings on dog coats reflected what we were thinking:

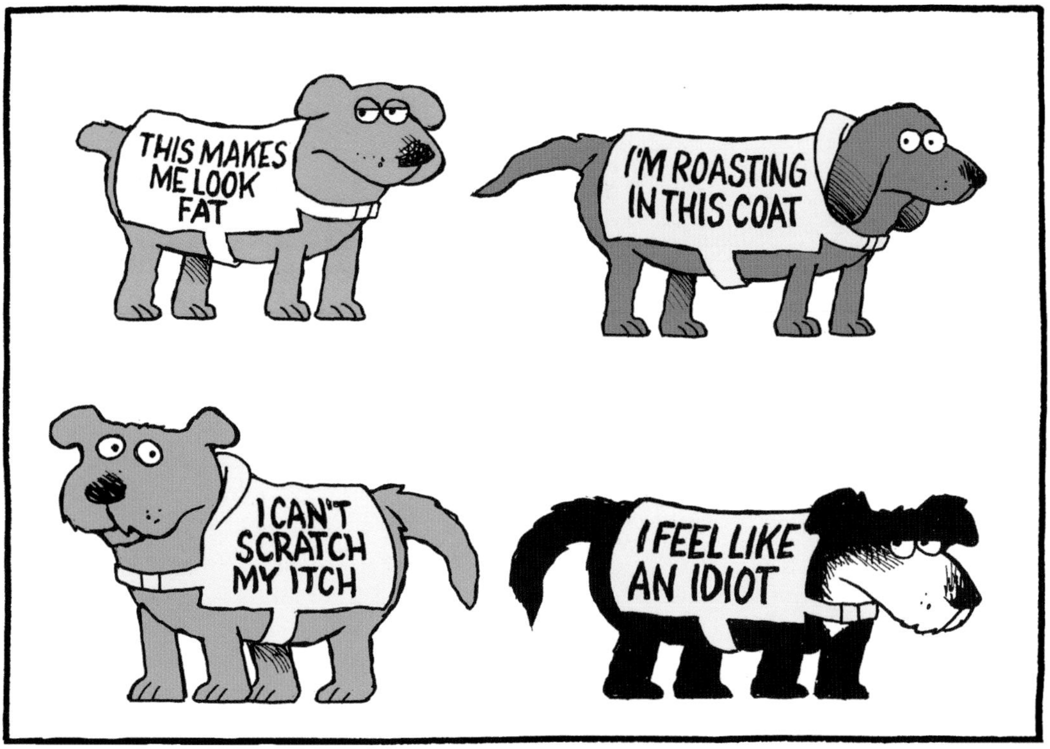
THIS MAKES ME LOOK FAT
I'M ROASTING IN THIS COAT
I CAN'T SCRATCH MY ITCH
I FEEL LIKE AN IDIOT

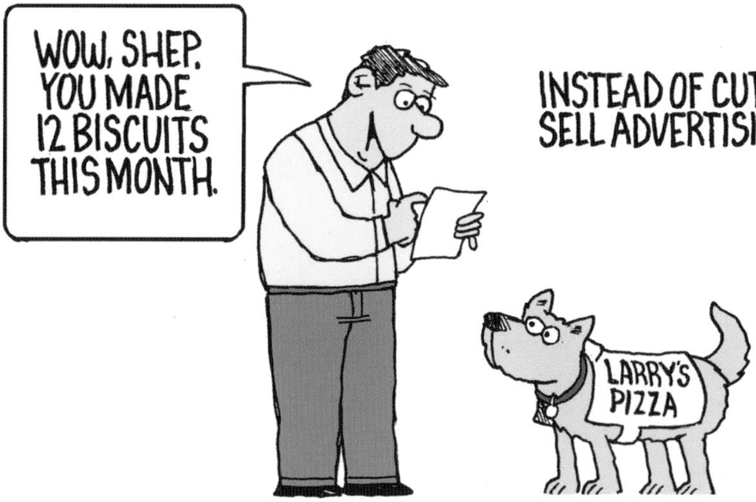
WOW, SHEP. YOU MADE 12 BISCUITS THIS MONTH.
LARRY'S PIZZA

INSTEAD OF CUTE SAYINGS, SELL ADVERTISING ON DOG COATS

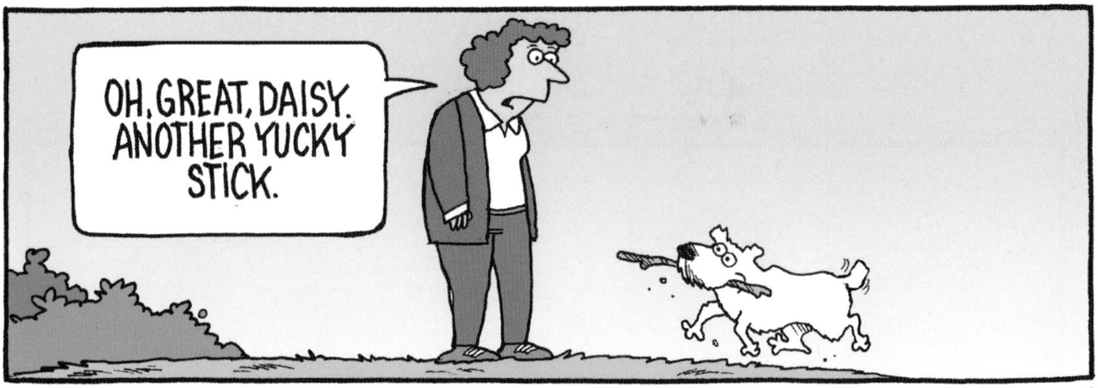
OH, GREAT, DAISY. ANOTHER YUCKY STICK.

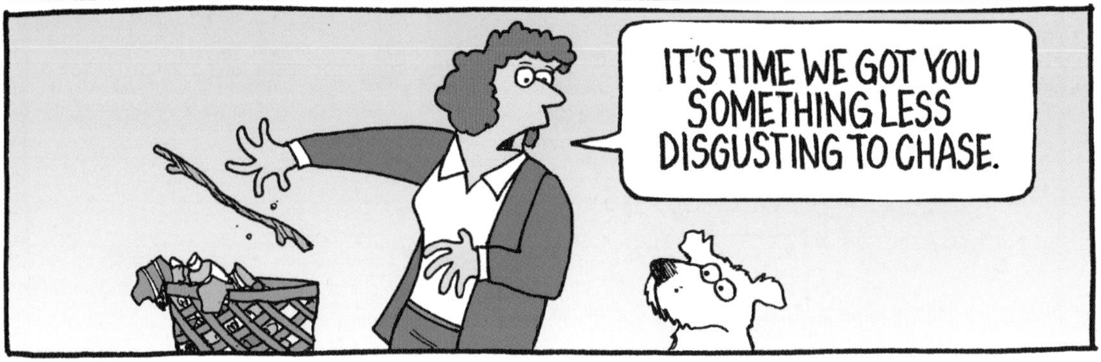
IT'S TIME WE GOT YOU SOMETHING LESS DISGUSTING TO CHASE.

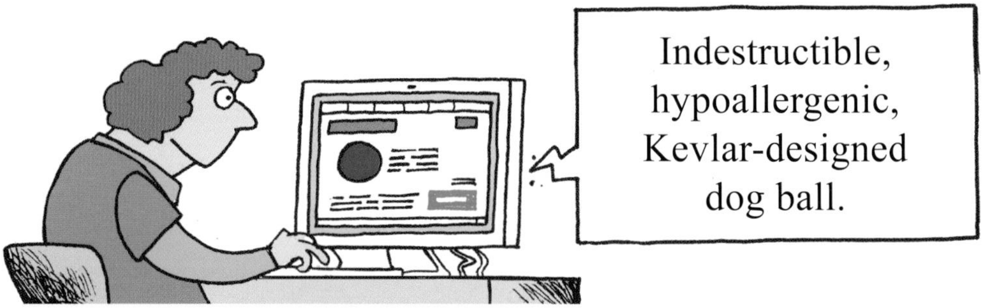
Indestructible, hypoallergenic, Kevlar-designed dog ball.

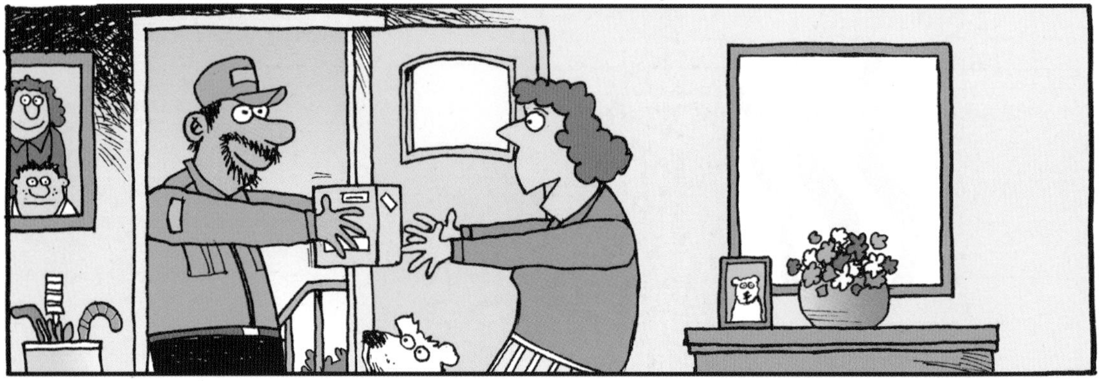

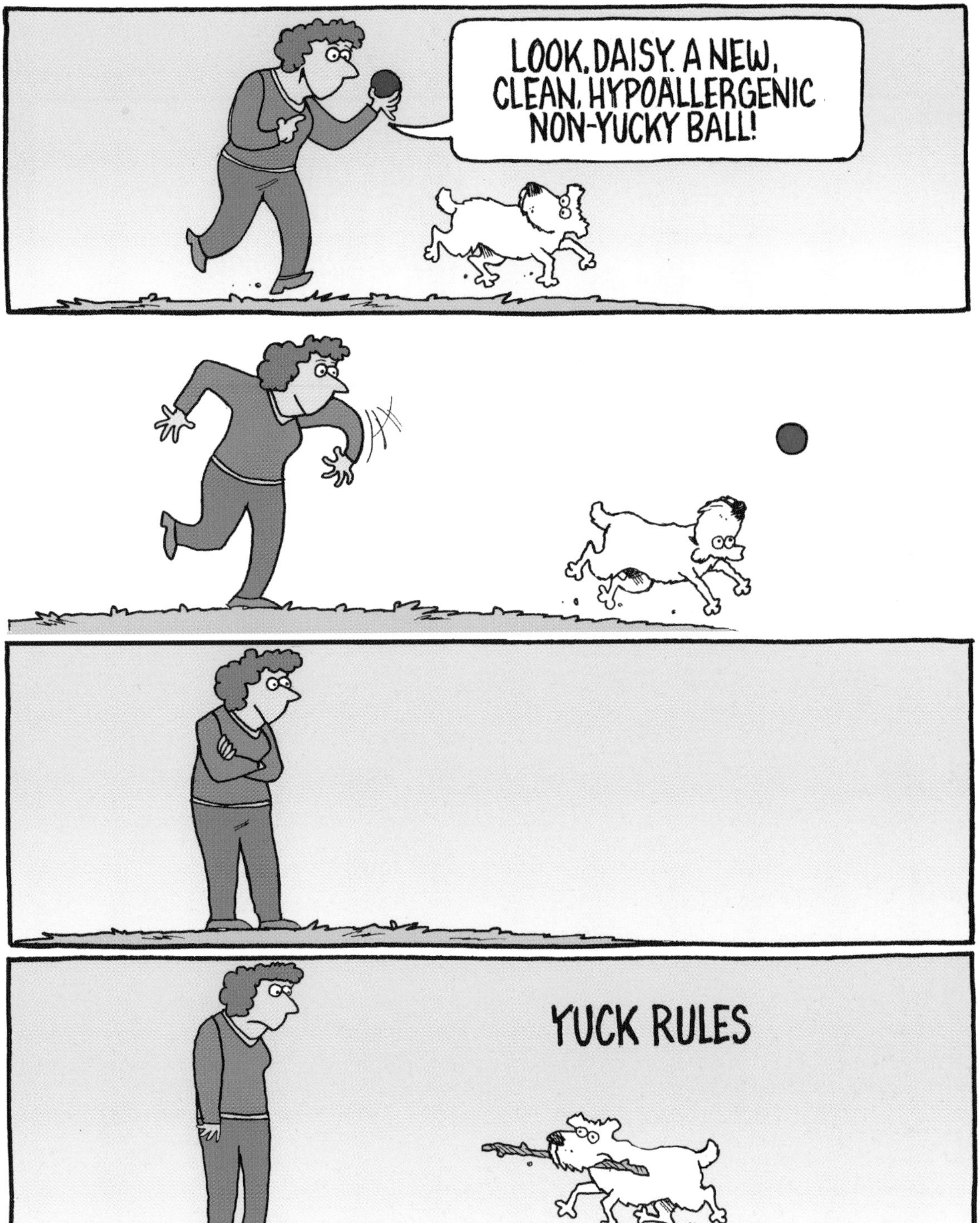
LOOK, DAISY. A NEW, CLEAN, HYPOALLERGENIC NON-YUCKY BALL!
YUCK RULES

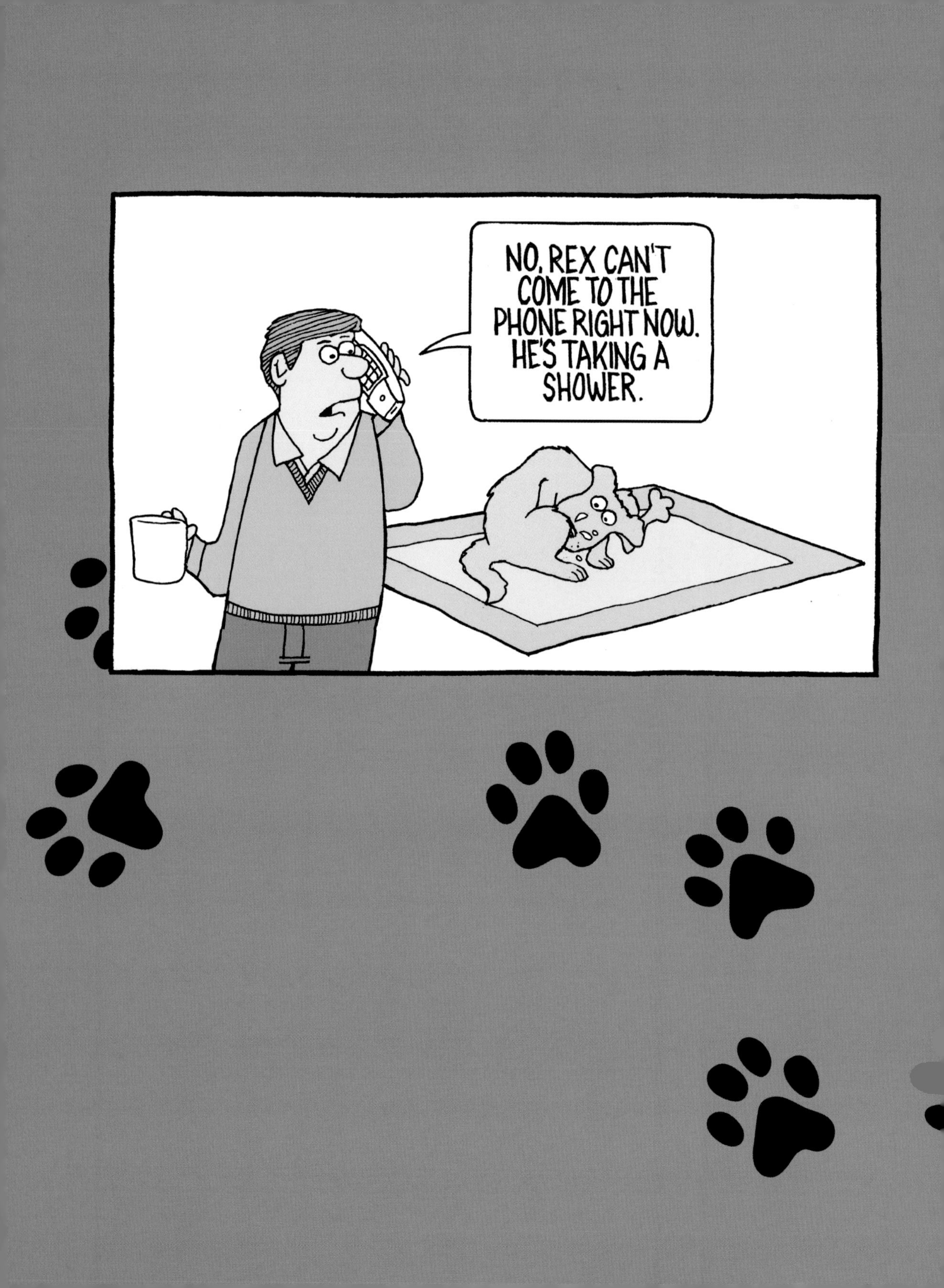
NO, REX CAN'T COME TO THE PHONE RIGHT NOW. HE'S TAKING A SHOWER.

CHAPTER 10

DOG BEHAVIOUR

You assume we're just sniffing, peeing, scrounging, pooping, couch-hogging, shedding quadrupeds.

In reality, we're highly evolved, complex, sniffing, peeing, scrounging, pooping, couch-hogging, shedding quadrupeds. For example, we know exactly what time (to the minute) our dinner is served. When you open the fridge door, we can tell the difference between a jar of pickles and left-over roast beef without even looking. Within seconds of meeting someone new we can tell if they are "dog people" and liable to have a treat in their pocket. We even know when you're coming home before you come home.

And think of all the amazing feats you've seen us do in movies or on agility courses. Okay, we do it for the biscuit, but still, pretty incredible stuff.

Even though we are superior to you in so many ways, there are some traits that people and dogs share...

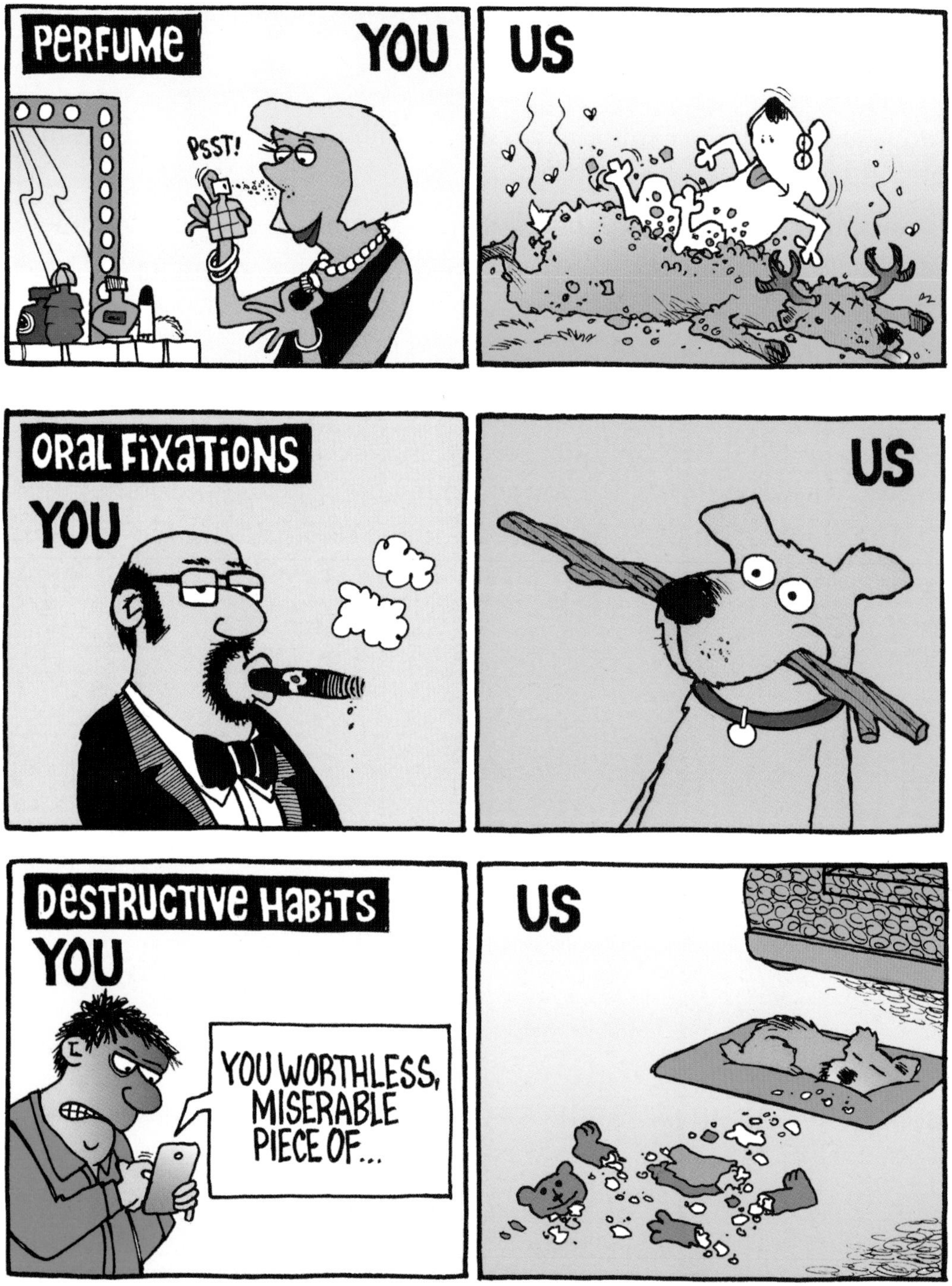
PERFUME
YOU
PSST!
US
ORAL FIXATIONS
YOU
US
DESTRUCTIVE HABITS
YOU
YOU WORTHLESS, MISERABLE PIECE OF...
US

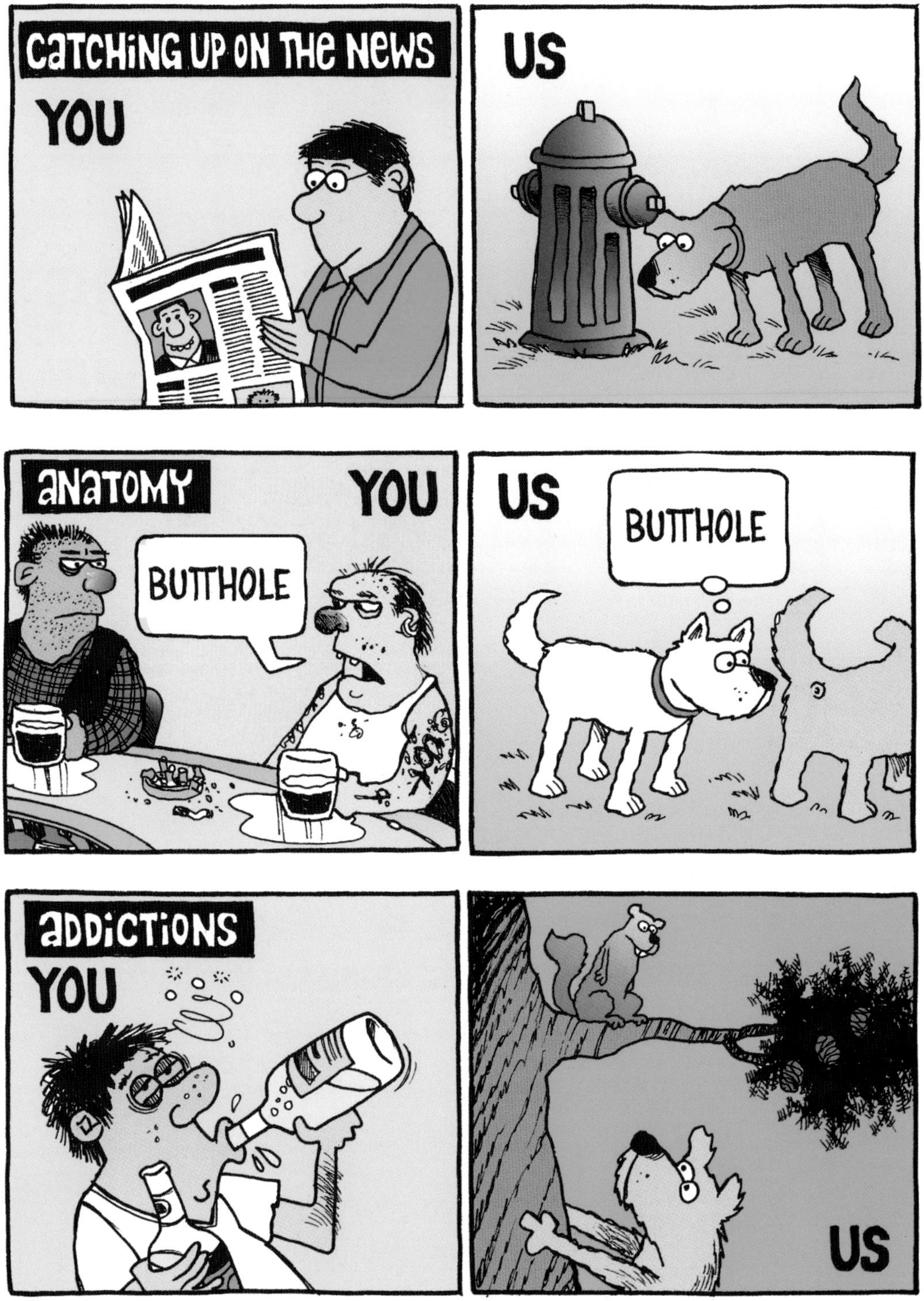
CATCHING UP ON THE NEWS
YOU
US
ANATOMY
YOU
BUTTHOLE
US
BUTTHOLE
ADDICTIONS
YOU
US

... but there is one important difference between us.

DRAMA & TRAGEDY | **YOU**

I BACKED THE CAR INTO A TREE.

YOU DID WHAAT?!

I BACKED THE CAR INTO A TREE.

US

I DON'T CARE, I STILL LOVE YOU.

DID YOU KNOW...?

When you see us fast asleep, leg twitching like crazy, you assume we're dreaming of chasing a squirrel, or rabbit... but we are actually processing very important information.

DON'T ASK US WHY. WE JUST DO IT.

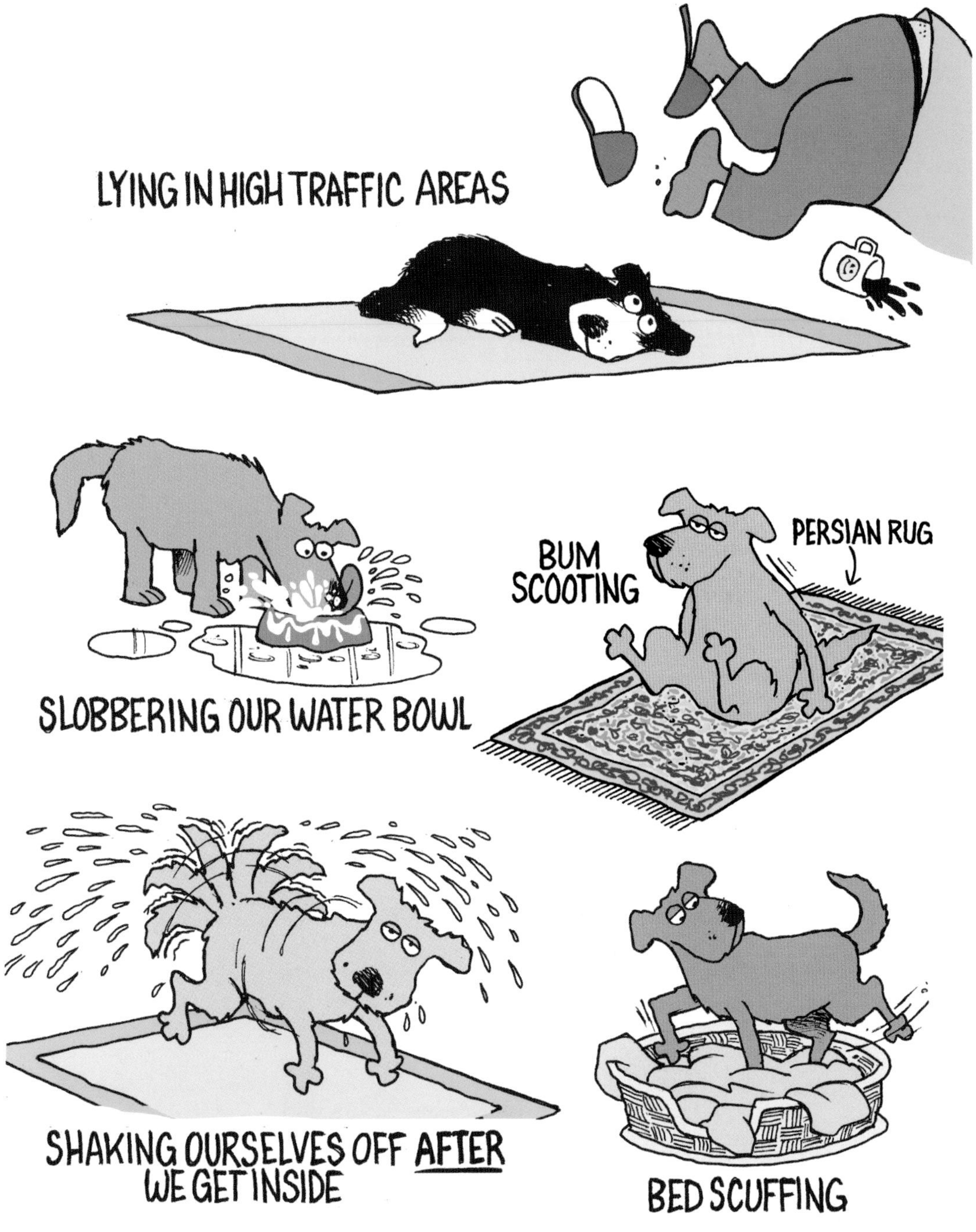
LYING IN HIGH TRAFFIC AREAS
SLOBBERING OUR WATER BOWL
BUM SCOOTING
PERSIAN RUG
SHAKING OURSELVES OFF AFTER WE GET INSIDE
BED SCUFFING

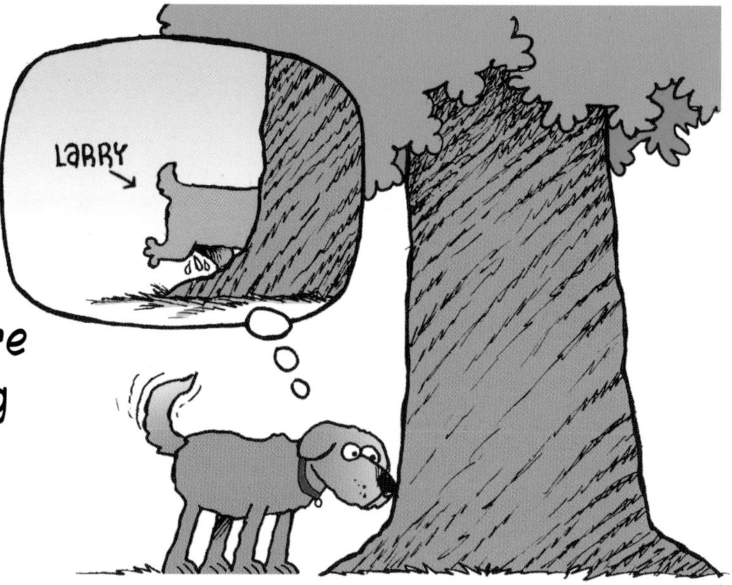
LARRY

You think all we're doing is sniffing another dog's pee.

In actual fact, by way of a complex formula, we can identify who the pee belongs to.

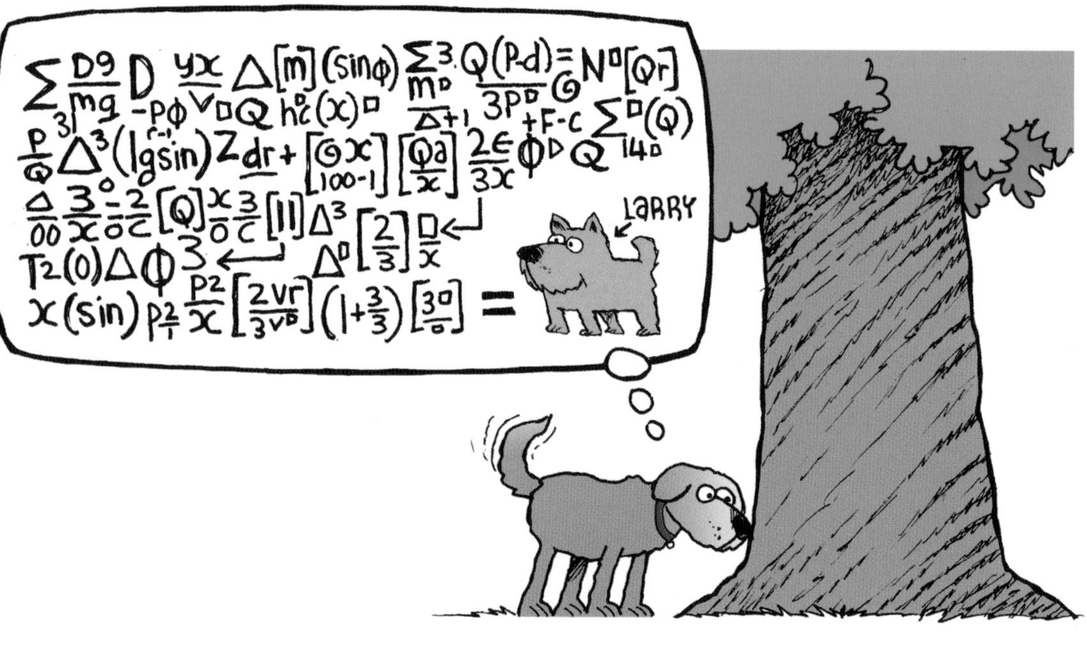
LARRY

Don't expect us to behave like the dogs you see on TV. They are just actors.

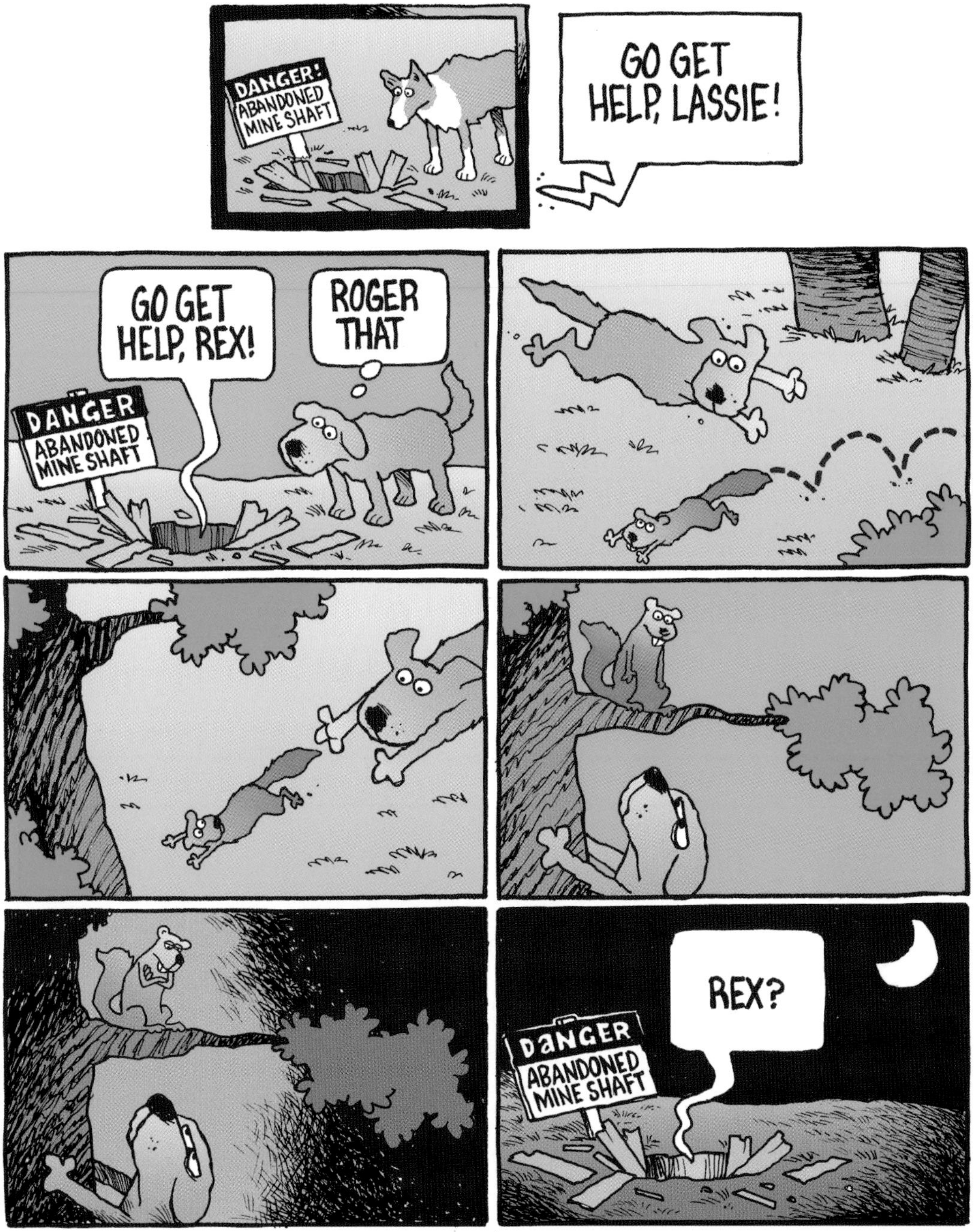
DANGER! ABANDONED MINE SHAFT
GO GET HELP, LASSIE!
GO GET HELP, REX!
ROGER THAT
DANGER ABANDONED MINE SHAFT
DANGER ABANDONED MINE SHAFT
REX?

We love our dog toys and can pick out individual toys from our collection. But be specific.

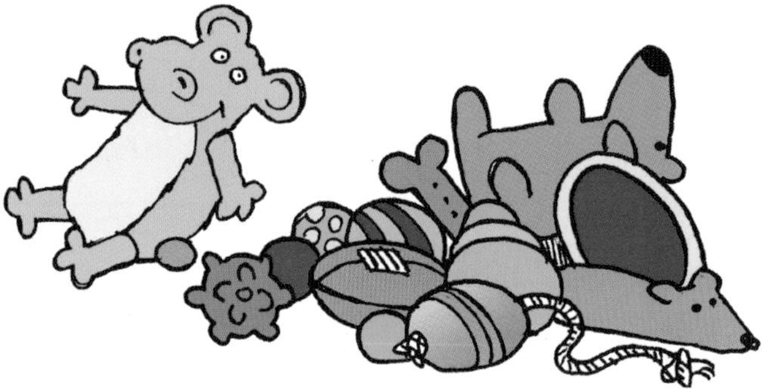

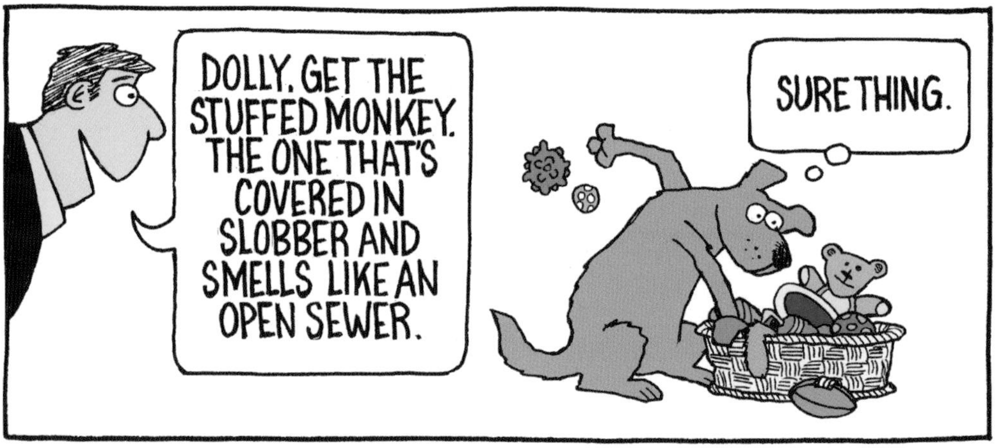
DOLLY, GET THE STUFFED MONKEY. THE ONE THAT'S COVERED IN SLOBBER AND SMELLS LIKE AN OPEN SEWER.
SURE THING.

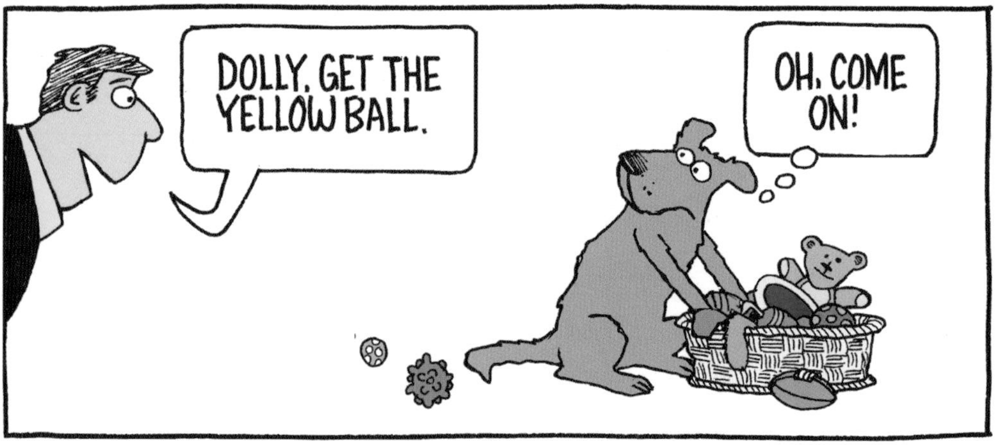
DOLLY, GET THE YELLOW BALL.
OH, COME ON!

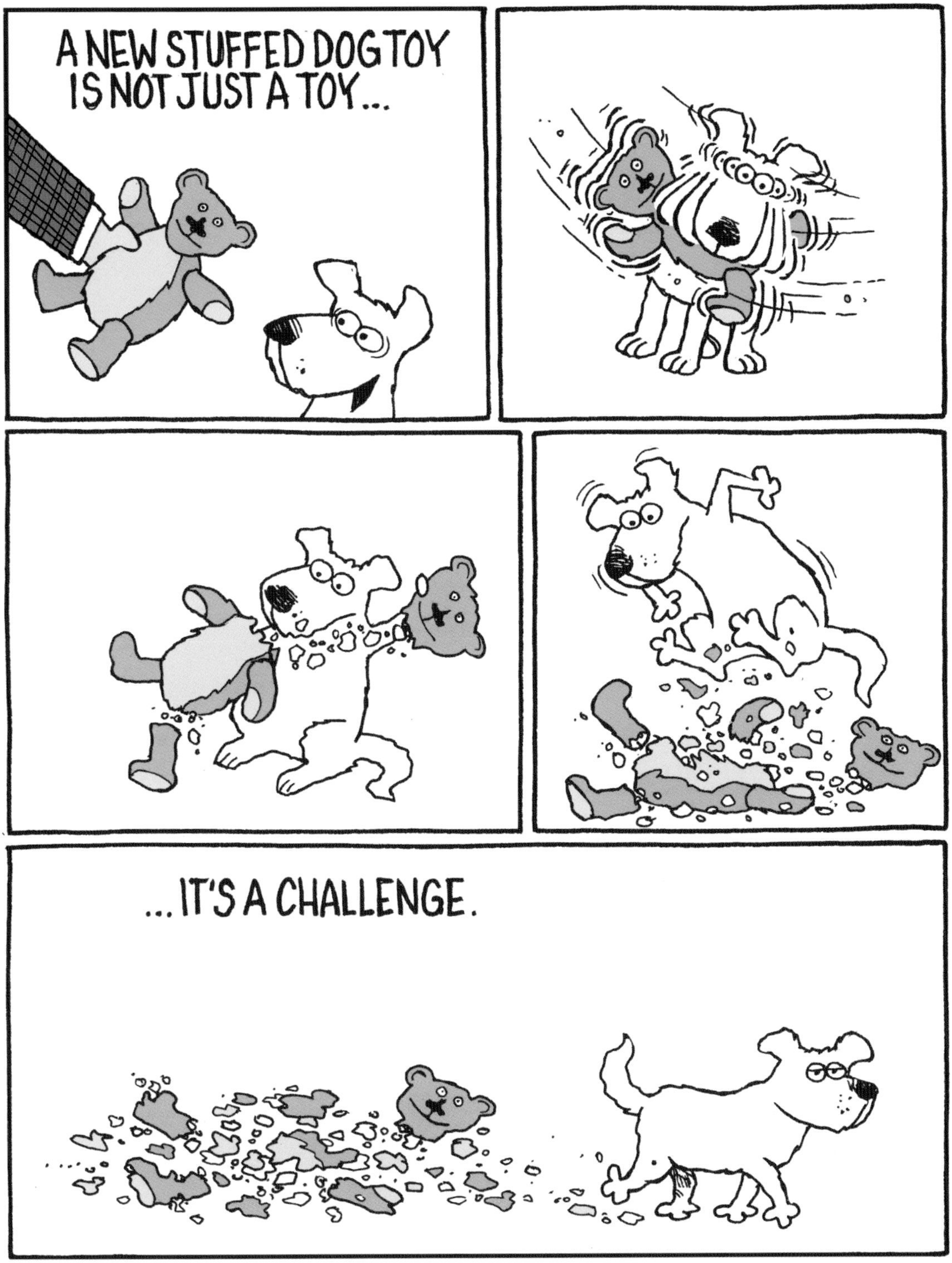
A NEW STUFFED DOG TOY IS NOT JUST A TOY...
...IT'S A CHALLENGE.

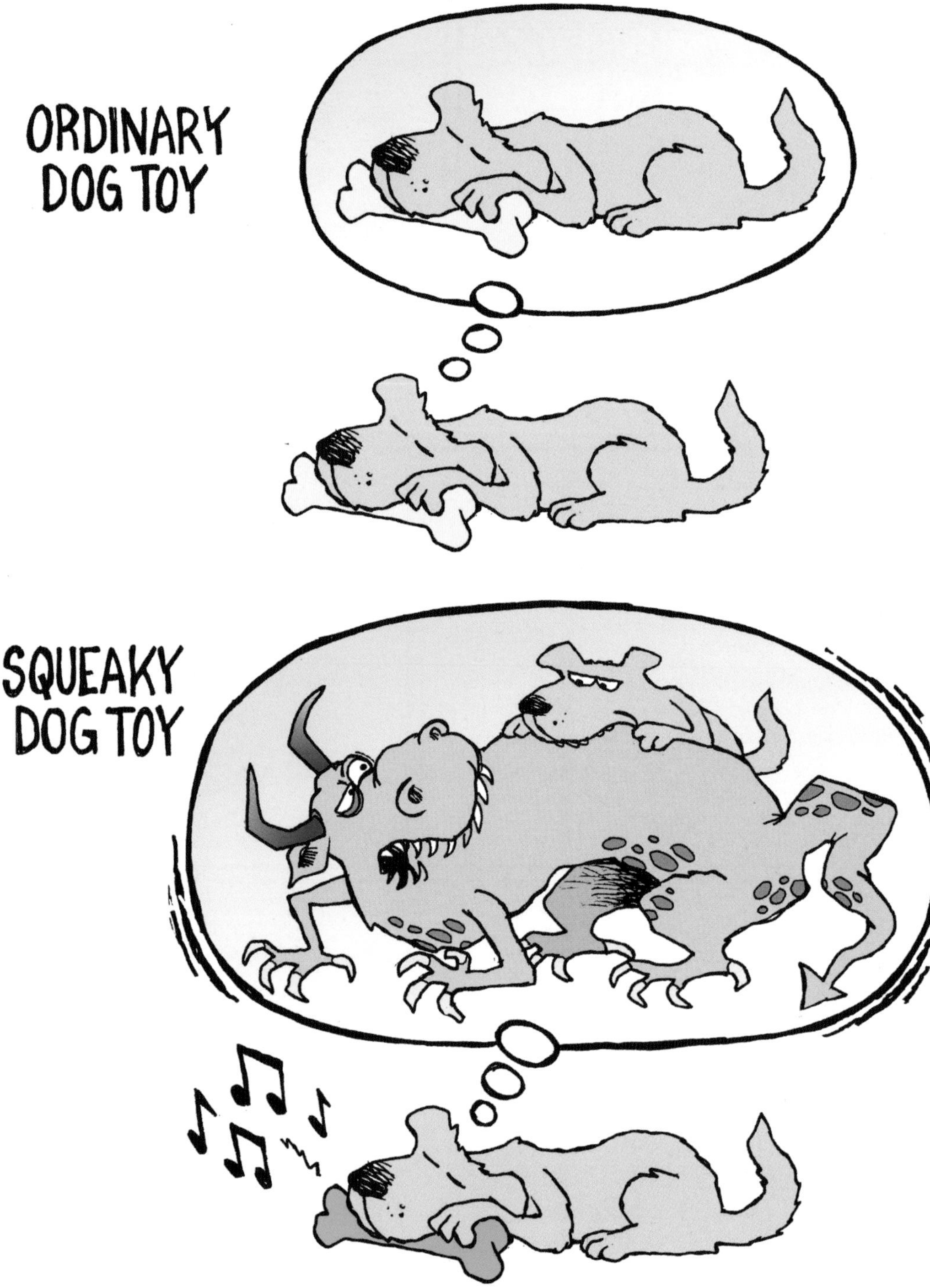
ORDINARY DOG TOY
SQUEAKY DOG TOY

Buy us all the fancy designer dog baskets you want.
As soon as you're out of the house,
we'll be warming the couch.

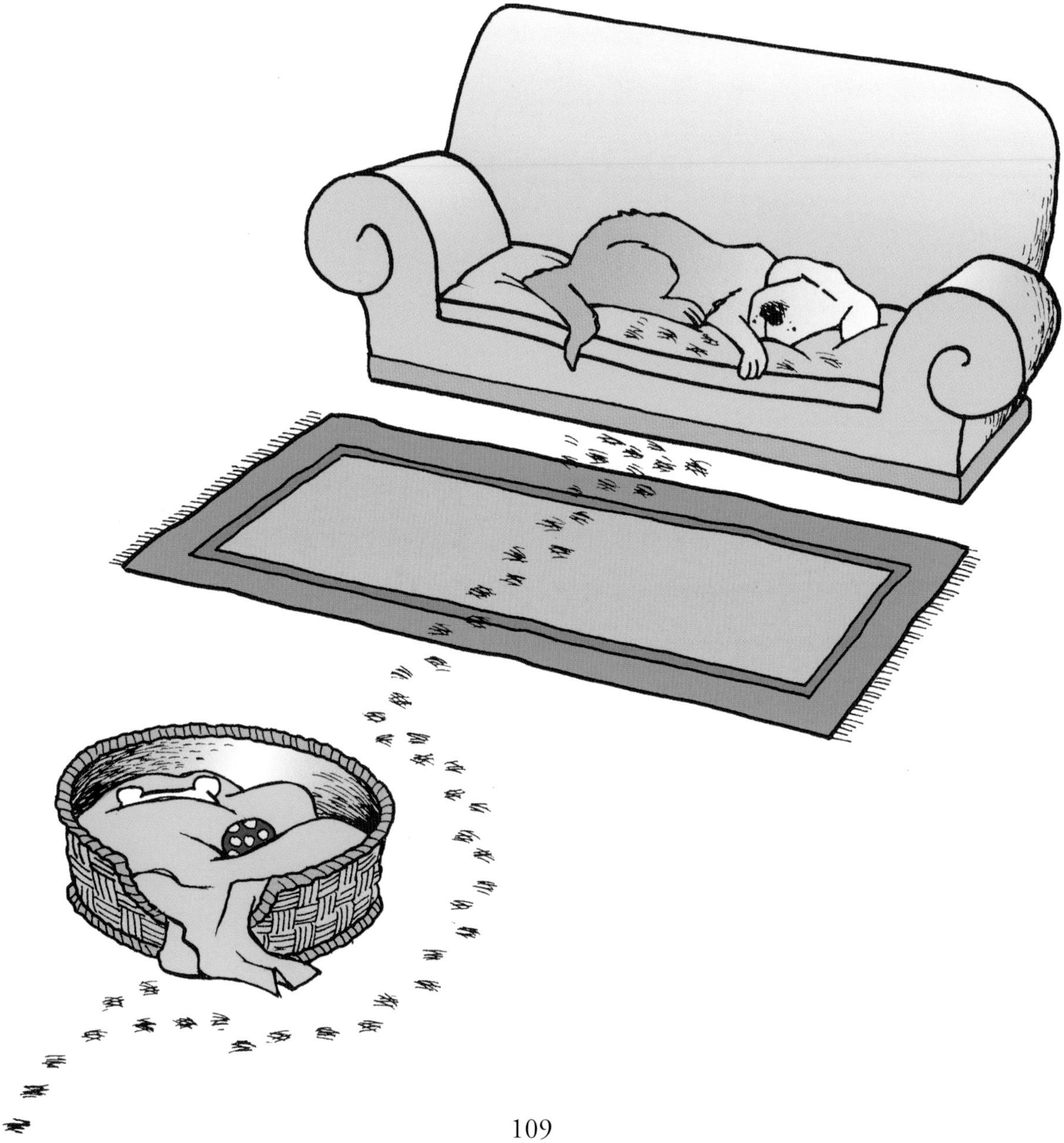

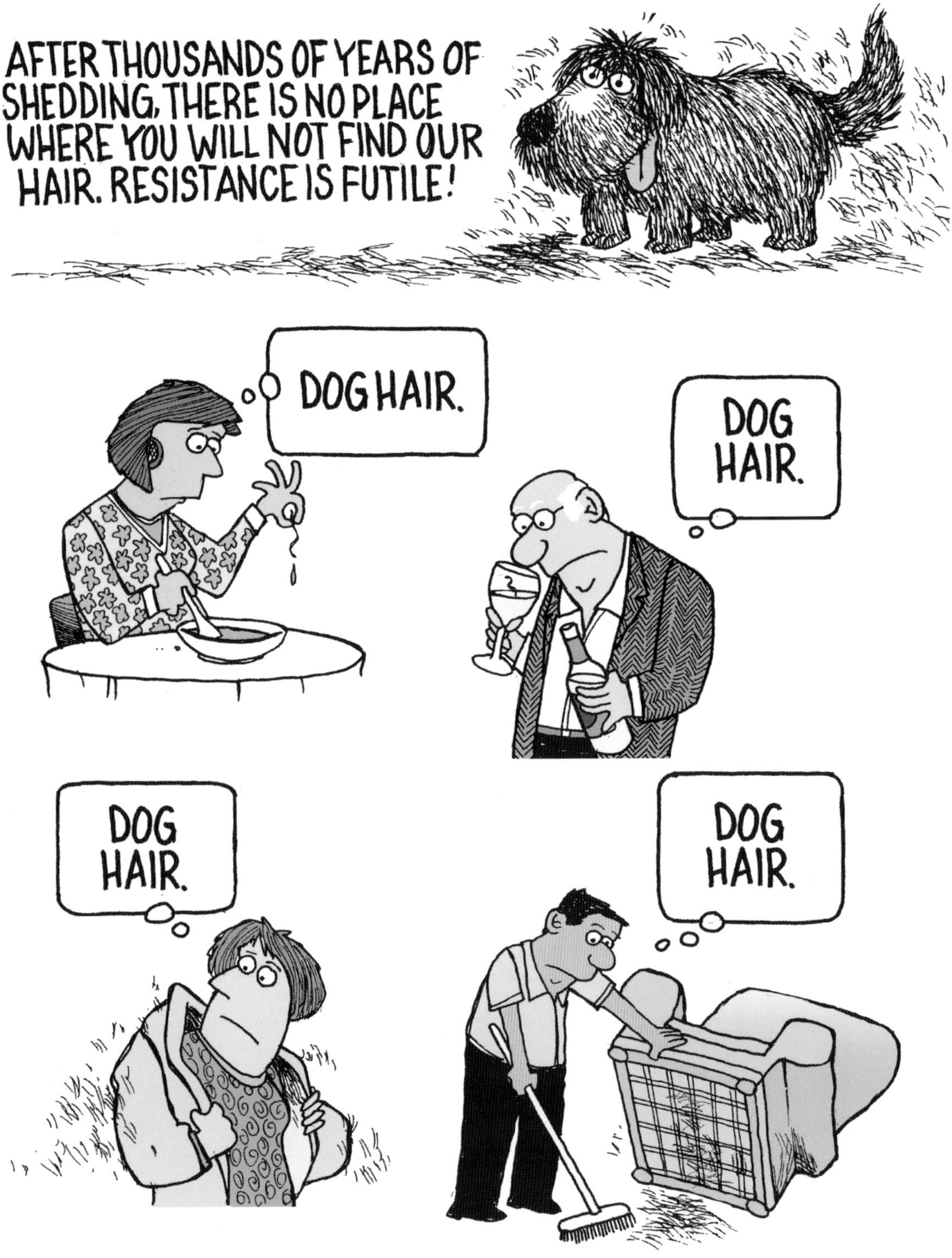
AFTER THOUSANDS OF YEARS OF SHEDDING, THERE IS NO PLACE WHERE YOU WILL NOT FIND OUR HAIR. RESISTANCE IS FUTILE!
DOG HAIR.
DOG HAIR.
DOG HAIR.
DOG HAIR.

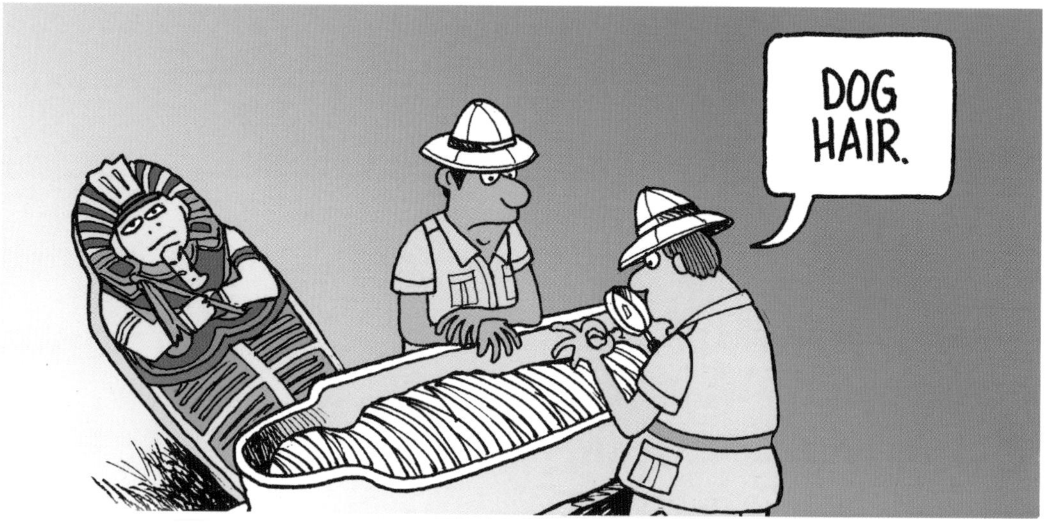
DOG HAIR.

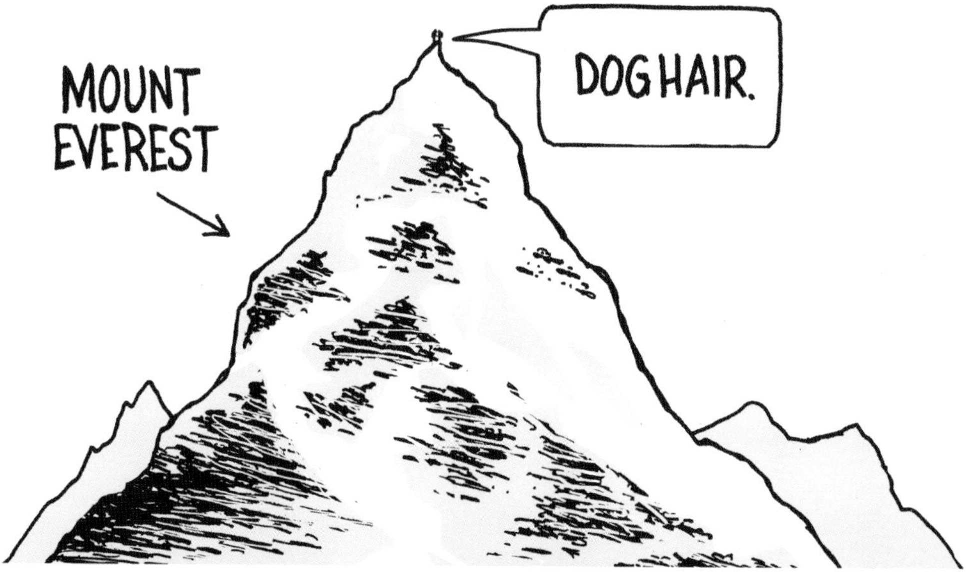
MOUNT EVEREST
DOG HAIR.

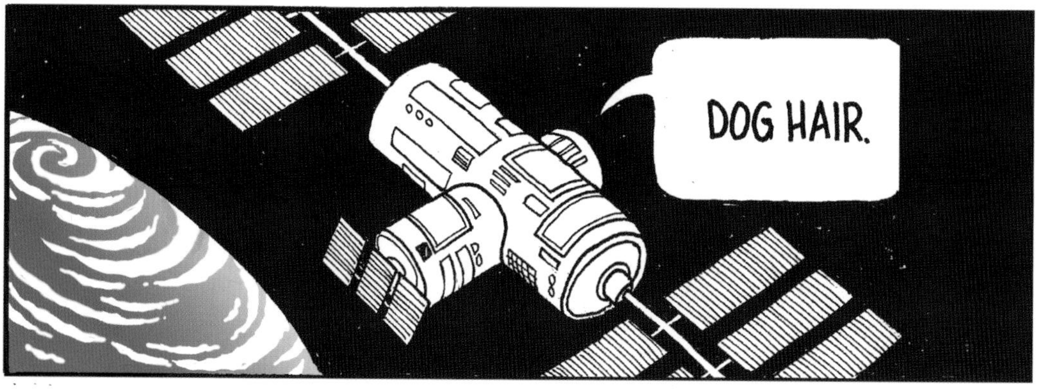
DOG HAIR.

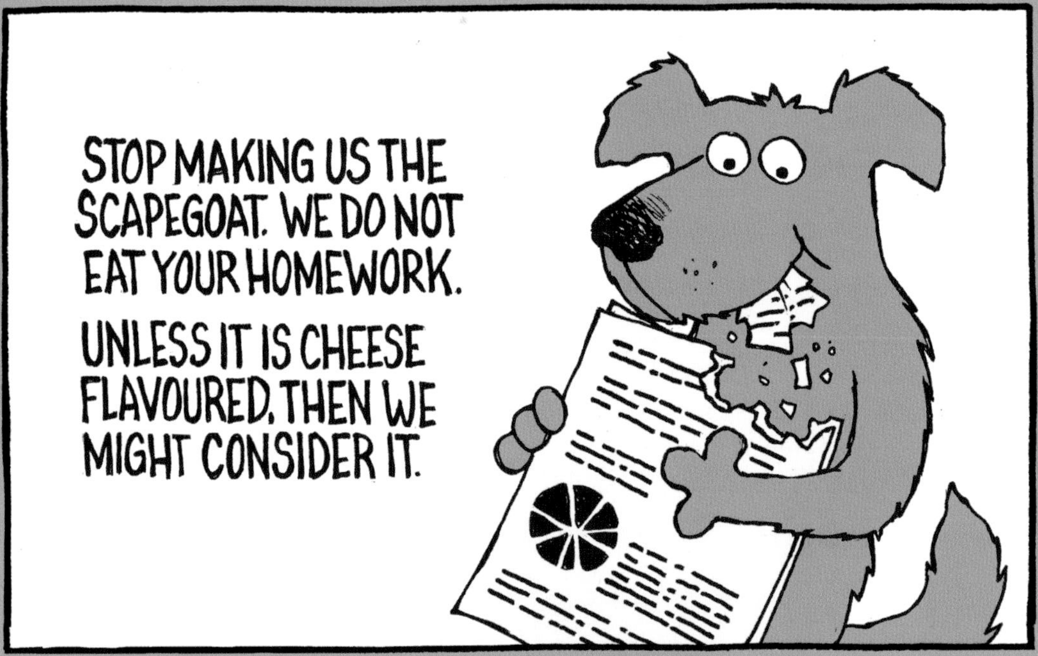
STOP MAKING US THE SCAPEGOAT. WE DO NOT EAT YOUR HOMEWORK.
UNLESS IT IS CHEESE FLAVOURED, THEN WE MIGHT CONSIDER IT.

CHAPTER  11

IT'S NOT FAIR!

We keep hearing the phrase, "You're part of the family." Oh really? There does seem to be a double standard when it comes to how four-legged family members are treated compared to the two-leggeds.

Do you put your kids in a crate when you go to bed? Can we sit up at the table instead of lying under it? (Although, being that close to the floor does make it easier to pounce on dropped food scraps.) And what's the deal with places that ban dogs. Okay, a grocery store might be off limits due to all the tempting treats at dog-height... but it's not fair to make beaches and parks off limits to us due to the possibility that we might foul them. Make them off limits to dog owners who don't pick up after us.

You buy yourselves all sorts of yummy food but then feed us the same old dried crap.

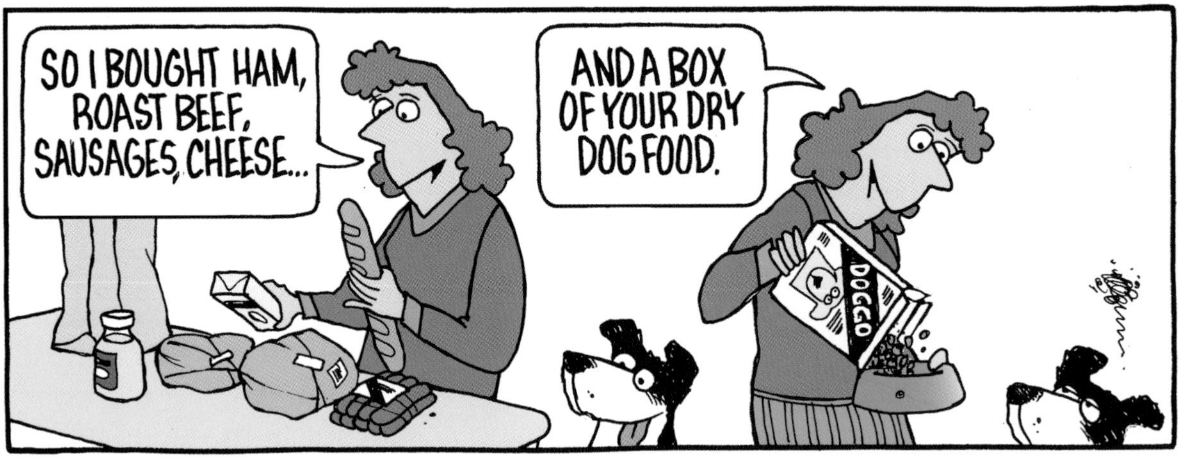
SO I BOUGHT HAM, ROAST BEEF, SAUSAGES, CHEESE...
AND A BOX OF YOUR DRY DOG FOOD.
DOGGO

We aren't allowed on some beaches in case we foul them...

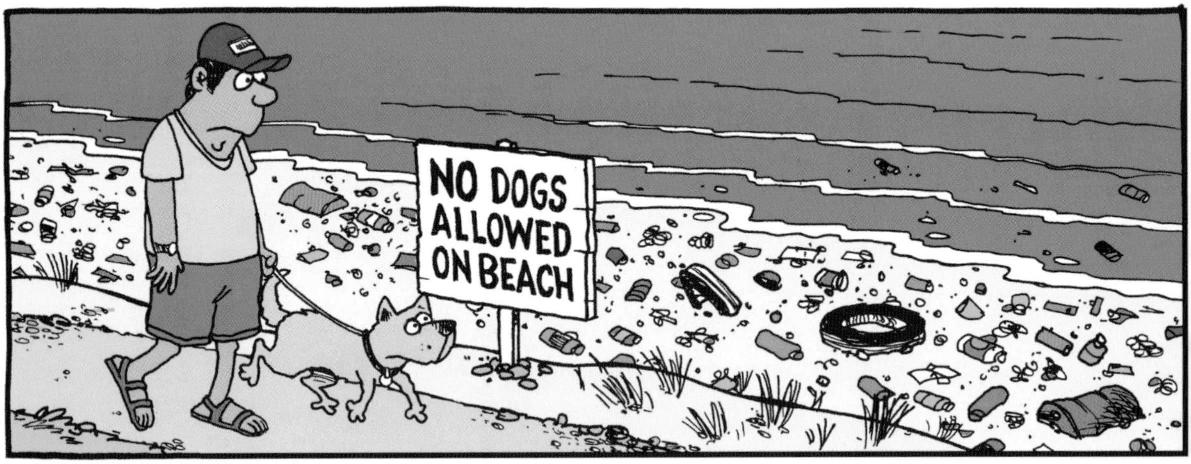
NO DOGS ALLOWED ON BEACH

... but you do a pretty good job of fouling beaches yourselves.

We know you have to go out and make a living so you can buy dog toys for us, but try to find a dog-friendly workplace. We won't bother you... and we probably smell better than the guy in the next cubicle.

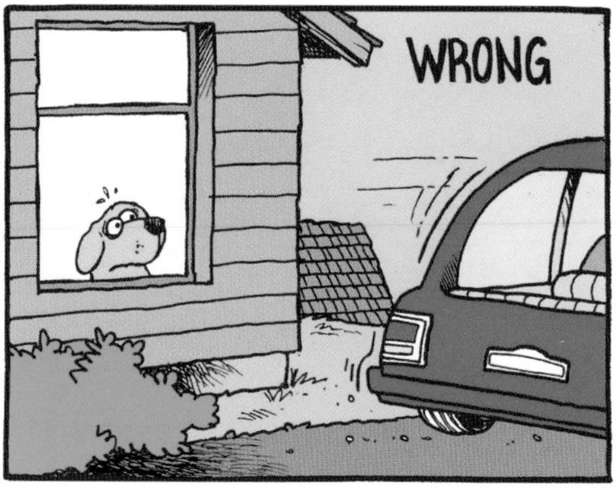
WRONG

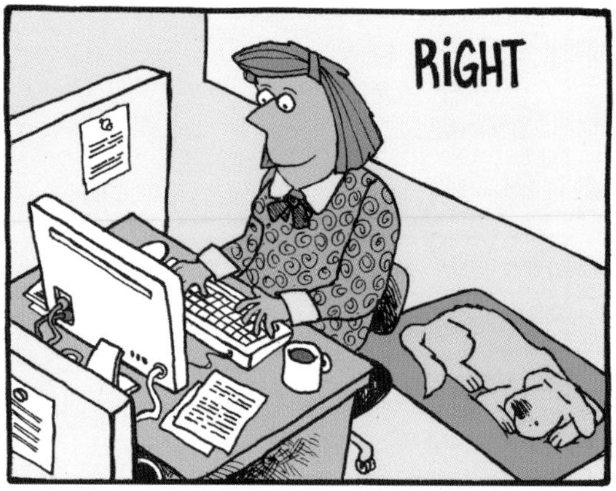
RIGHT

And while we're on the subject of going places... We've heard horror stories of dogs being left in locked vehicles on a hot day. So, please, next time you're running errands or distracted by your phone, remember: a car is a doggy death trap on a sunny day—okay?

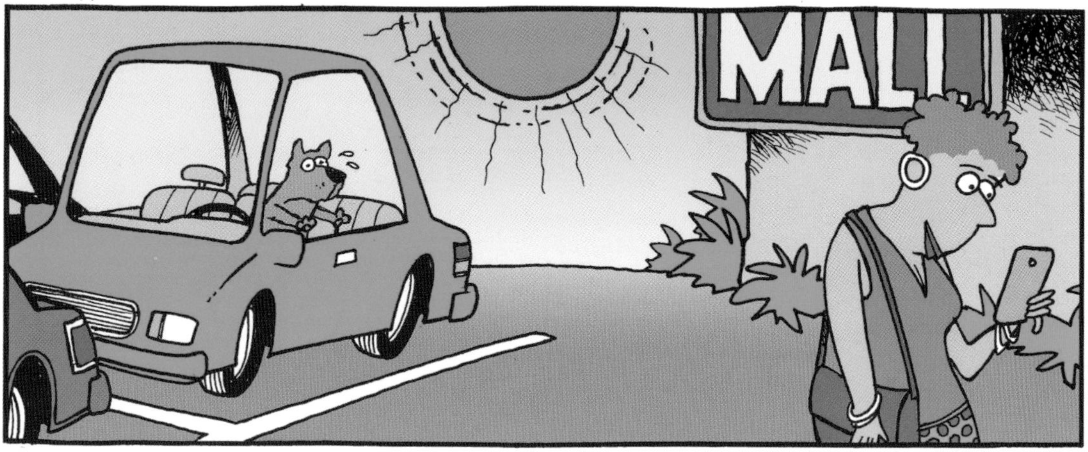
MALL

THINGS THAT PUZZLE US...

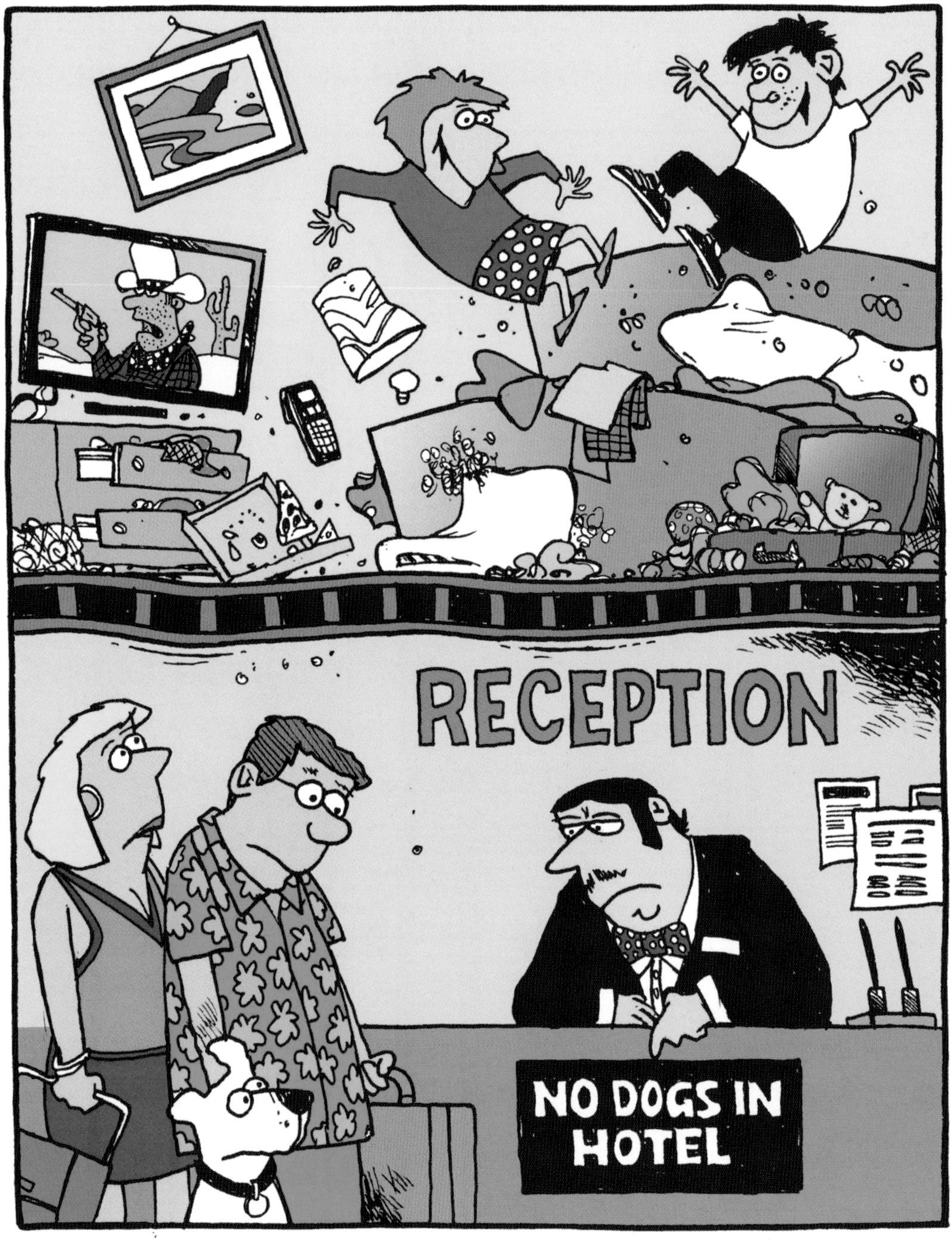
RECEPTION
NO DOGS IN HOTEL

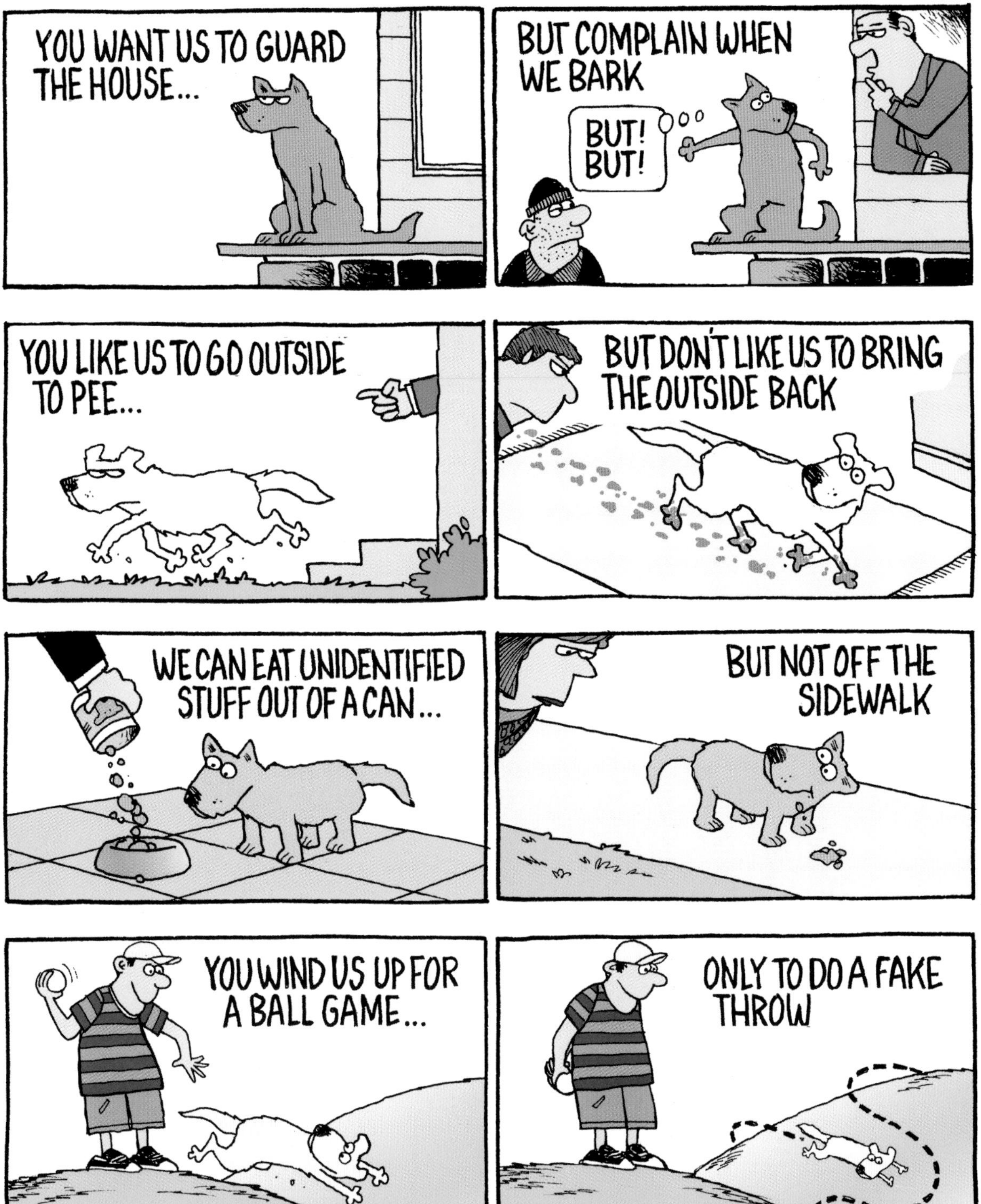
YOU WANT US TO GUARD THE HOUSE...
BUT COMPLAIN WHEN WE BARK
BUT! BUT!
YOU LIKE US TO GO OUTSIDE TO PEE...
BUT DON'T LIKE US TO BRING THE OUTSIDE BACK
WE CAN EAT UNIDENTIFIED STUFF OUT OF A CAN...
BUT NOT OFF THE SIDEWALK
YOU WIND US UP FOR A BALL GAME...
ONLY TO DO A FAKE THROW

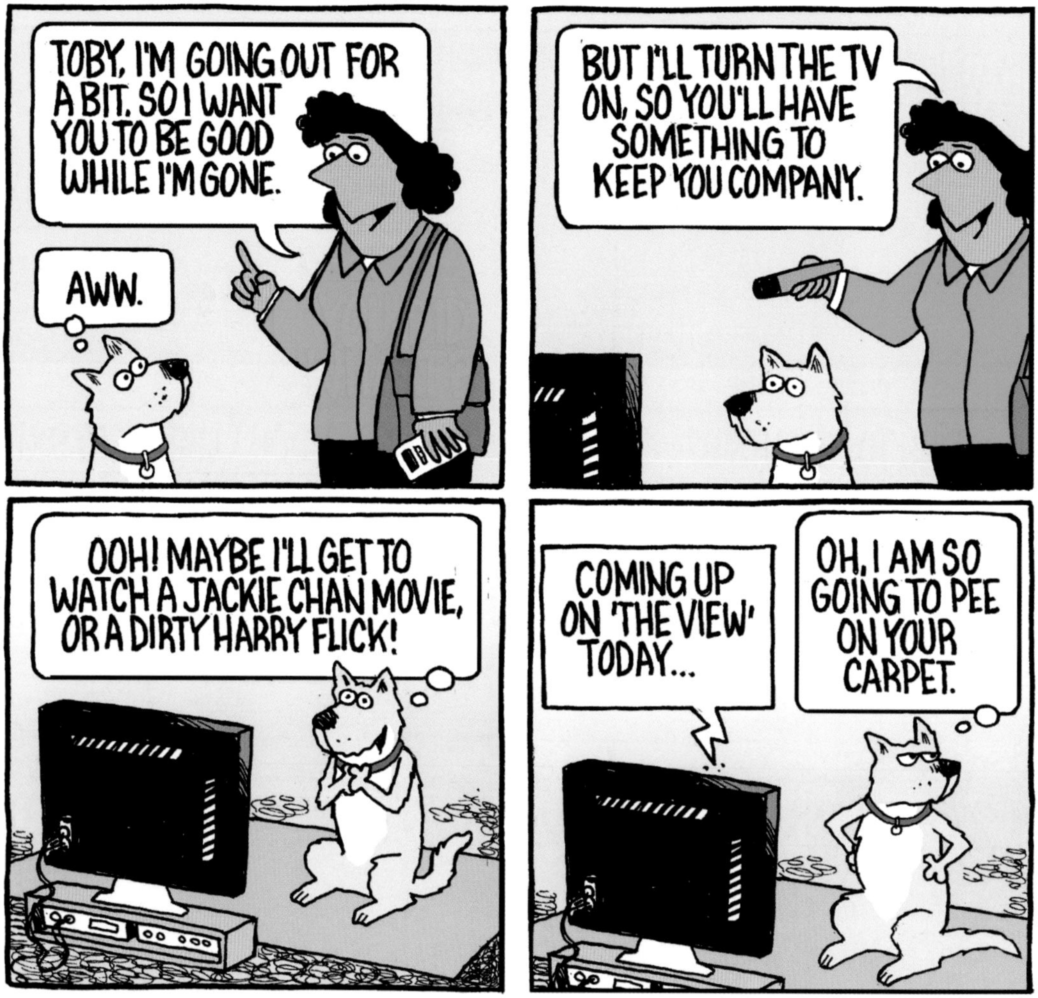
TOBY, I'M GOING OUT FOR A BIT. SO I WANT YOU TO BE GOOD WHILE I'M GONE.
AWW.
BUT I'LL TURN THE TV ON, SO YOU'LL HAVE SOMETHING TO KEEP YOU COMPANY.
OOH! MAYBE I'LL GET TO WATCH A JACKIE CHAN MOVIE, OR A DIRTY HARRY FLICK!
COMING UP ON 'THE VIEW' TODAY...
OH, I AM SO GOING TO PEE ON YOUR CARPET.

IF YOU'RE GOING TO LEAVE THE TV ON FOR US AT LEAST SUBSCRIBE TO A CHANNEL WE CAN WATCH.

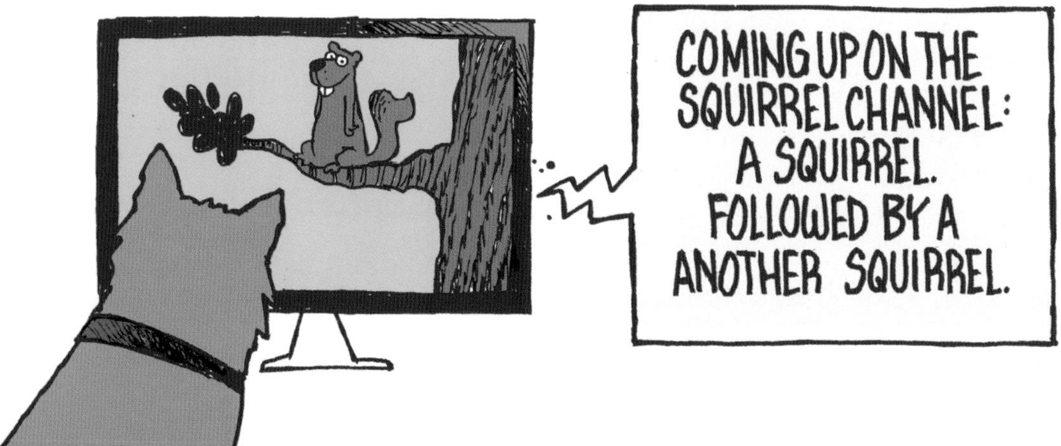
COMING UP ON THE SQUIRREL CHANNEL: A SQUIRREL. FOLLOWED BY A ANOTHER SQUIRREL.

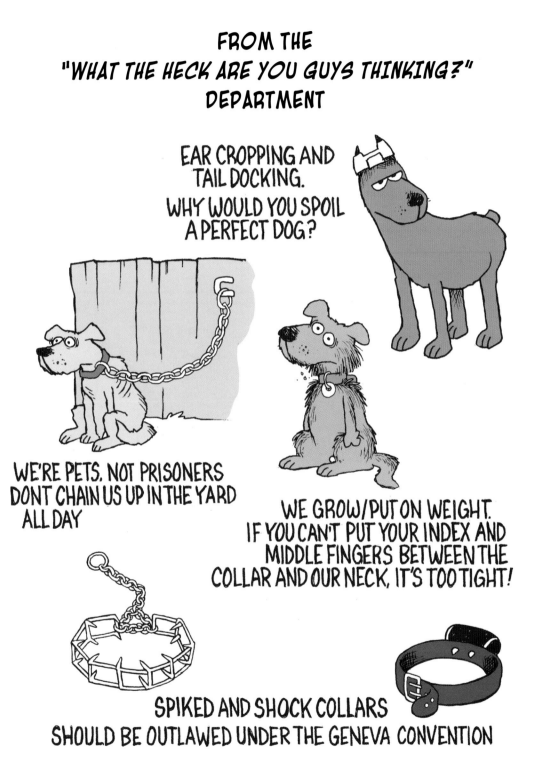

FROM THE *"WHAT THE HECK ARE YOU GUYS THINKING?"* DEPARTMENT

EAR CROPPING AND TAIL DOCKING.
WHY WOULD YOU SPOIL A PERFECT DOG?

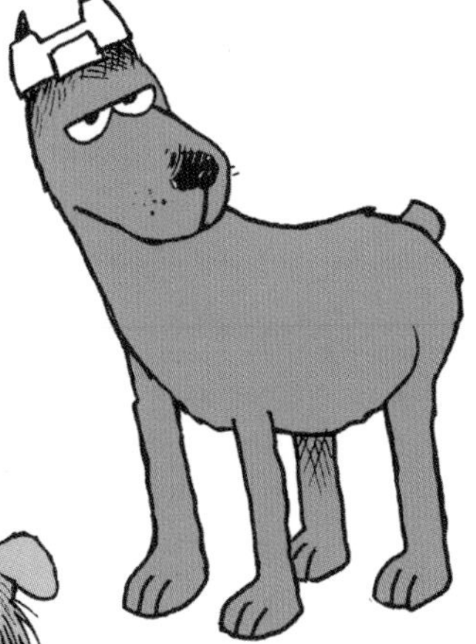

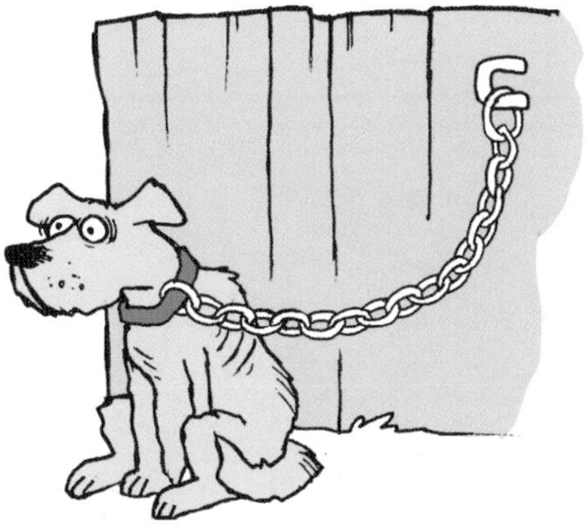

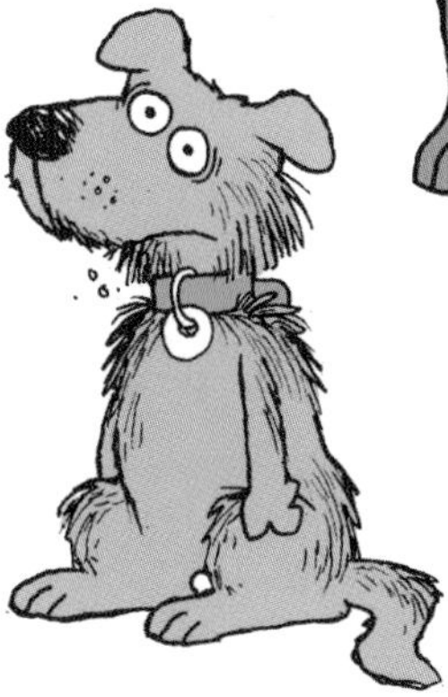

WE'RE PETS. NOT PRISONERS
DONT CHAIN US UP IN THE YARD ALL DAY

WE GROW/PUT ON WEIGHT.
IF YOU CAN'T PUT YOUR INDEX AND MIDDLE FINGERS BETWEEN THE COLLAR AND OUR NECK, IT'S TOO TIGHT!

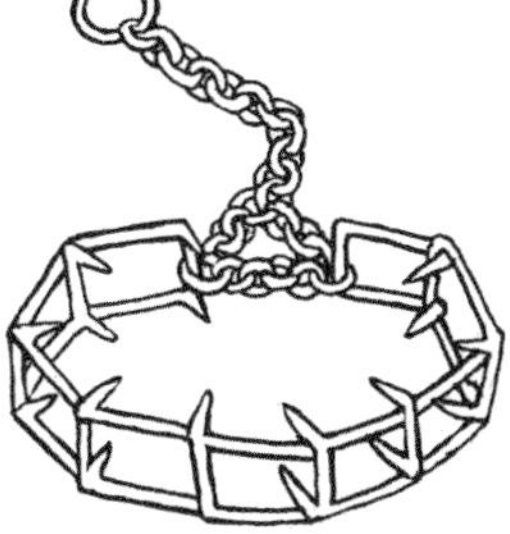

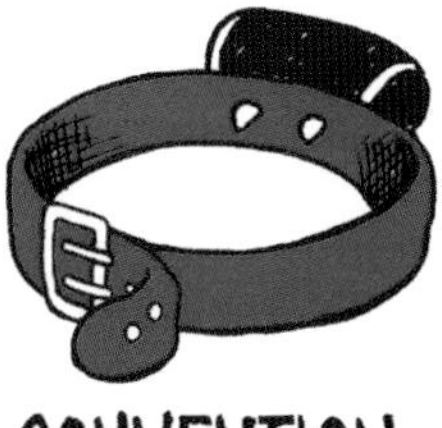

SPIKED AND SHOCK COLLARS
SHOULD BE OUTLAWED UNDER THE GENEVA CONVENTION

CAT CAFÉS? Why not dog cafés?

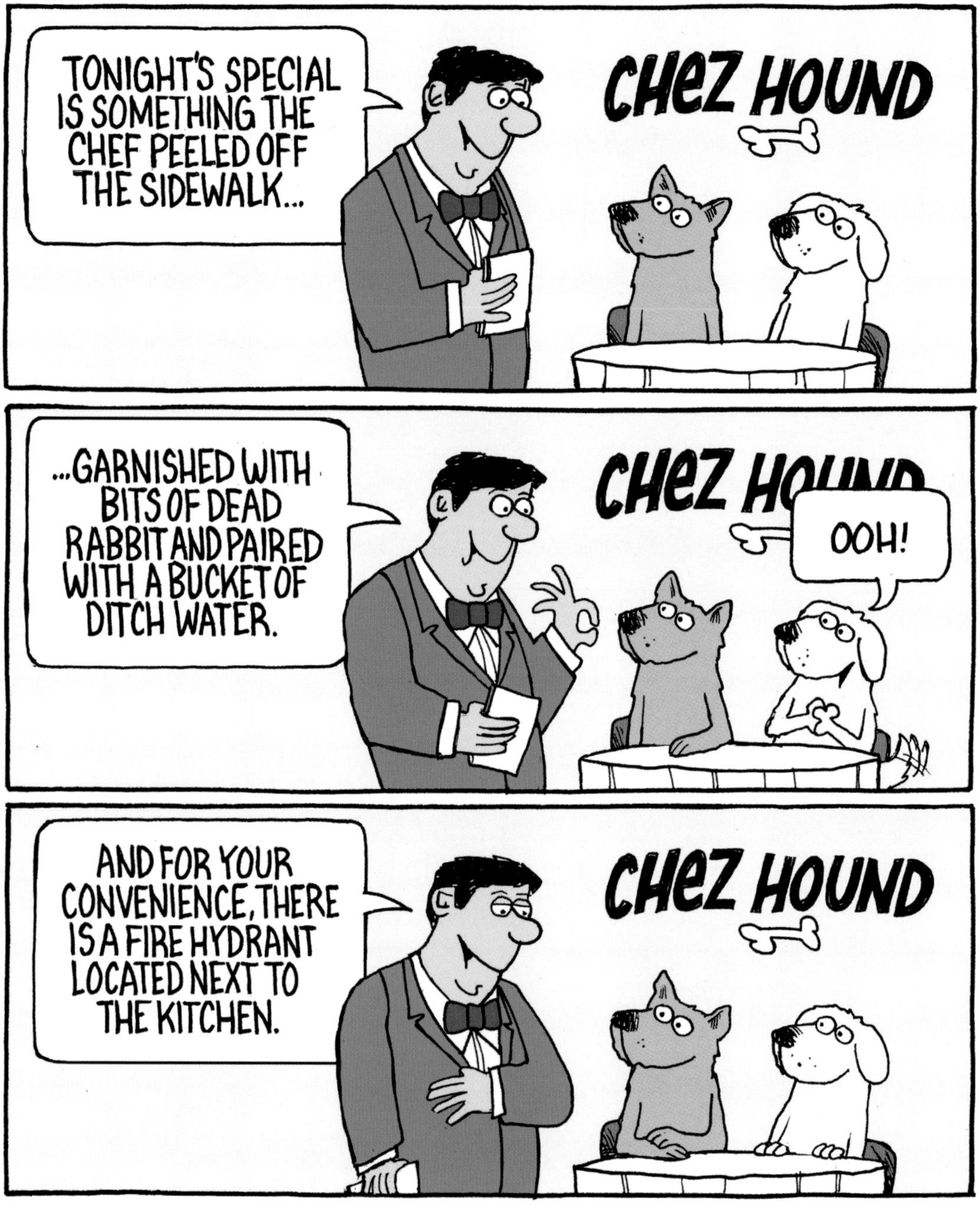
TONIGHT'S SPECIAL IS SOMETHING THE CHEF PEELED OFF THE SIDEWALK...
CHEZ HOUND
...GARNISHED WITH BITS OF DEAD RABBIT AND PAIRED WITH A BUCKET OF DITCH WATER.
OOH!
AND FOR YOUR CONVENIENCE, THERE IS A FIRE HYDRANT LOCATED NEXT TO THE KITCHEN.
CHEZ HOUND

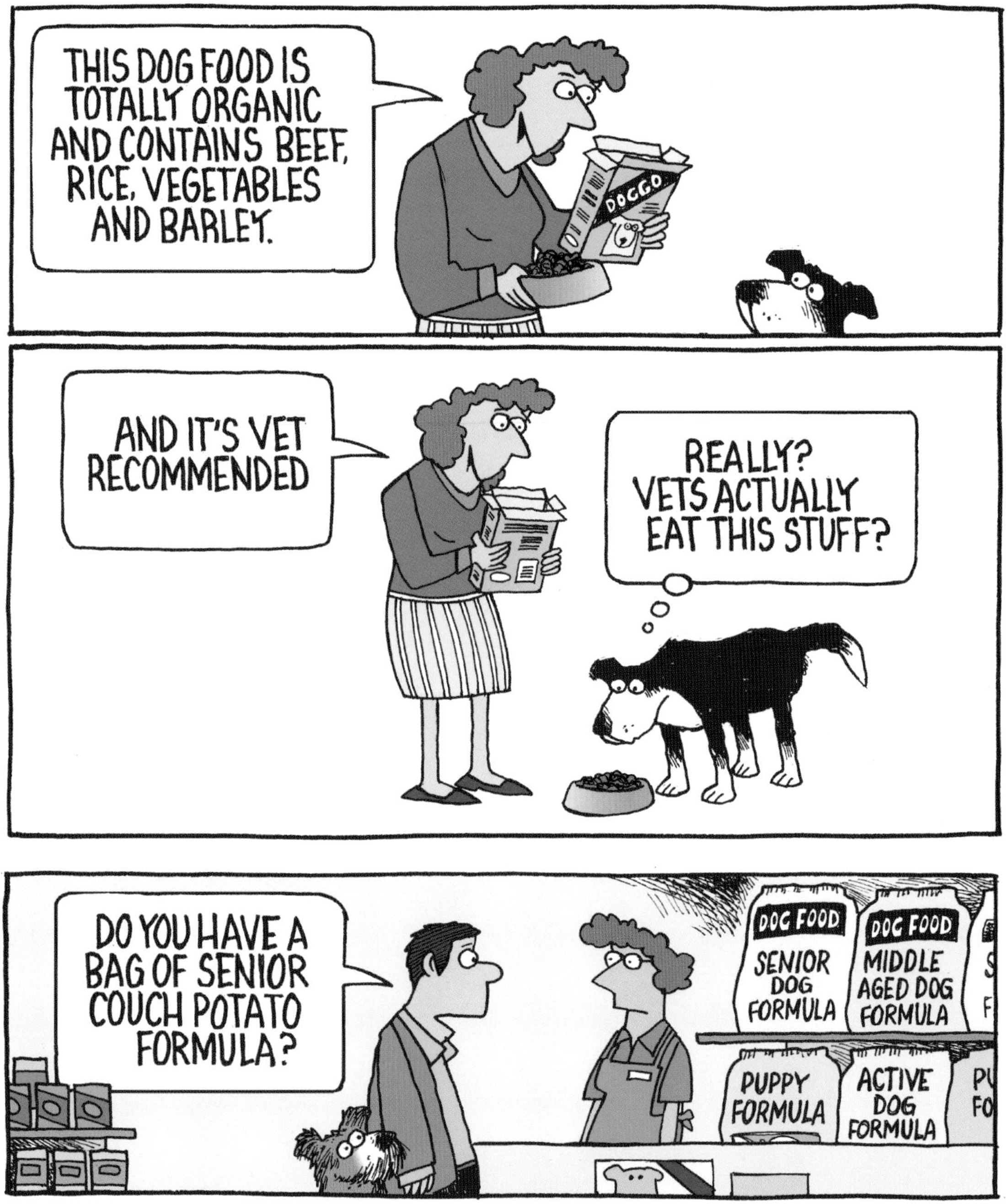
THIS DOG FOOD IS TOTALLY ORGANIC AND CONTAINS BEEF, RICE, VEGETABLES AND BARLEY.
DOGGO
AND IT'S VET RECOMMENDED
REALLY? VETS ACTUALLY EAT THIS STUFF?
DO YOU HAVE A BAG OF SENIOR COUCH POTATO FORMULA?
DOG FOOD
SENIOR DOG FORMULA
DOG FOOD
MIDDLE AGED DOG FORMULA
PUPPY FORMULA
ACTIVE DOG FORMULA

If you don't eat it, how can you tell us it's good for us?

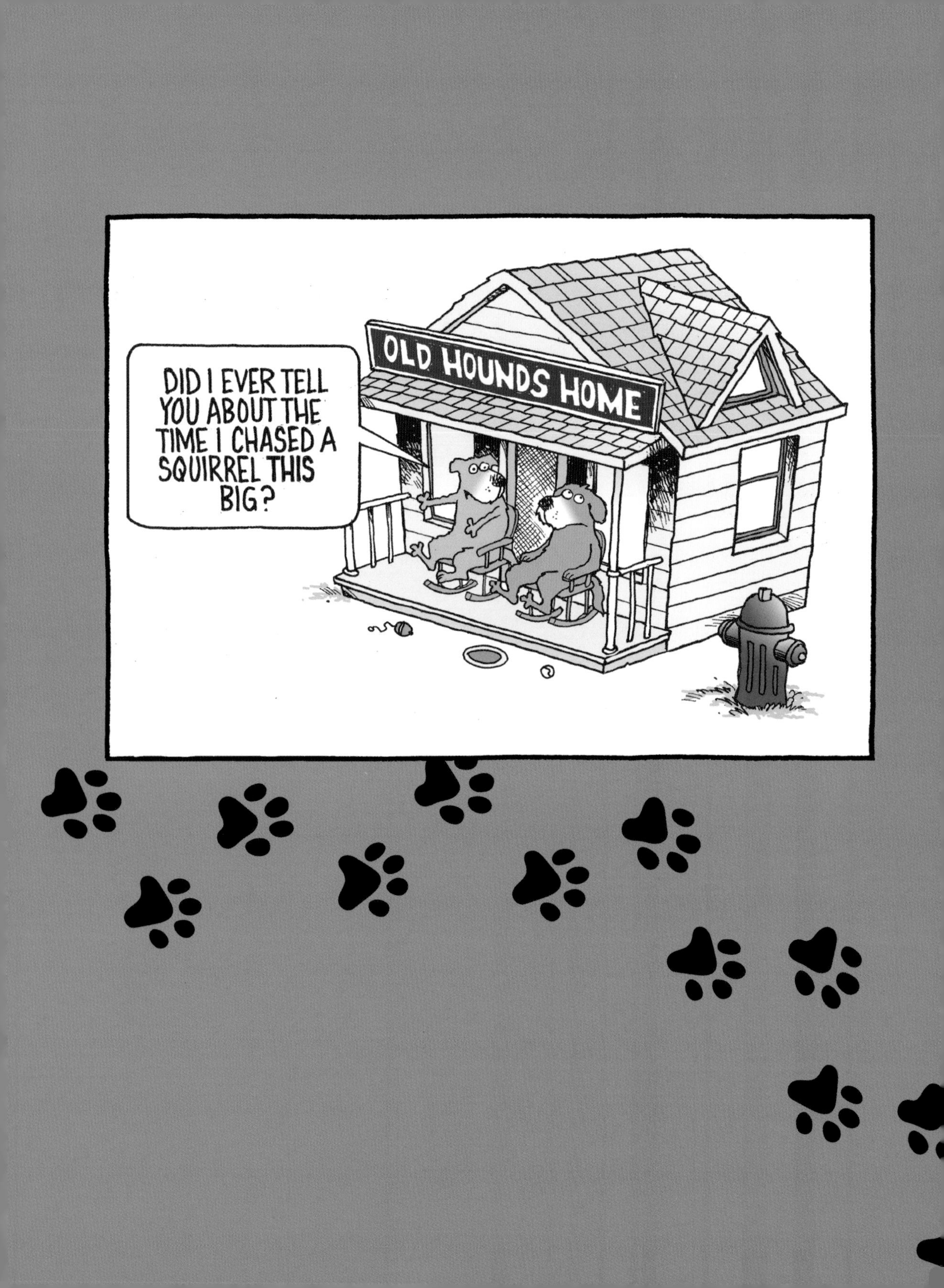
DID I EVER TELL YOU ABOUT THE TIME I CHASED A SQUIRREL THIS BIG?
OLD HOUNDS HOME

CHAPTER 12

THE LAST FACE LICK

It's something none of us want to talk about; however, when you picked us up from the shelter/breeder, you may not have realized it during all the excitement, but in doing so, you made a pact to be there with us all the way to the end. Which will inevitably happen, as we age differently than you do.

Of course, we fit a lot more into our short years. For example, how many steps do we take on a walk compared to you? And ten minutes for us in a dog park is like a half marathon to you. So yes, we wear out faster, which means there will come a time when we have to leave you and make our journey to the Rainbow Bridge.

All we ask is for you to know how we are feeling and not to let us suffer. Don't mourn us; remember the good times—the walks, the couch snuggles, the ball games. We will always be with you in your hearts. And in the future, if we ever slip your mind, you will find a strand of dog hair in the most unexpected place to remind you.

There is nothing sadder than an empty, well-worn collar.

It's an unhappy fact of life: we don't live as long as you do. I guess it's because we pack so much into our short lives, we wear out faster.

There are some signs that indicate we're aging...

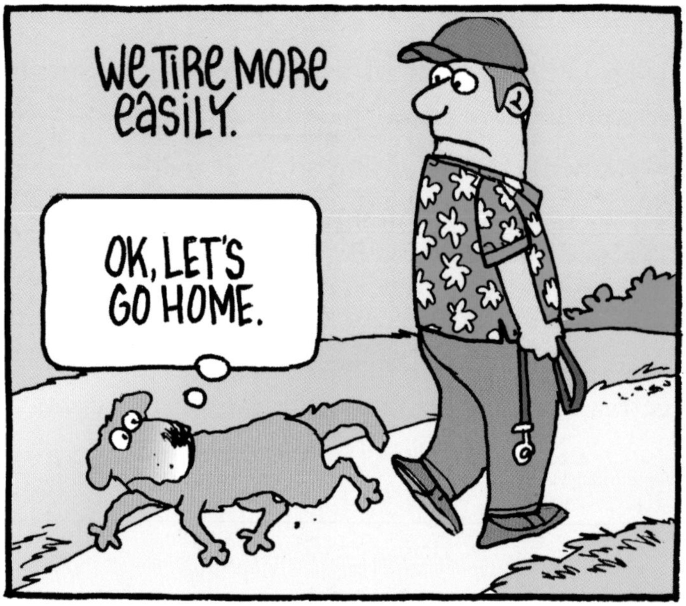
WE TIRE MORE EASILY.
OK, LET'S GO HOME.

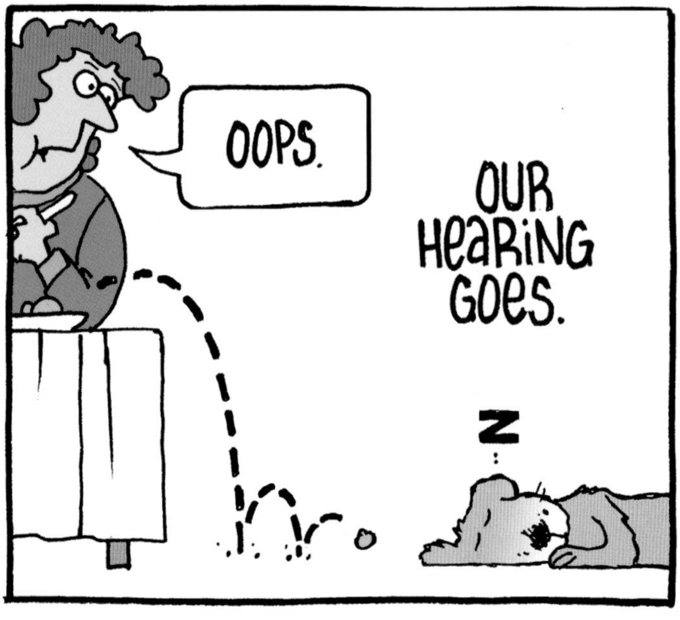
OOPS.
OUR HEARING GOES.
Z

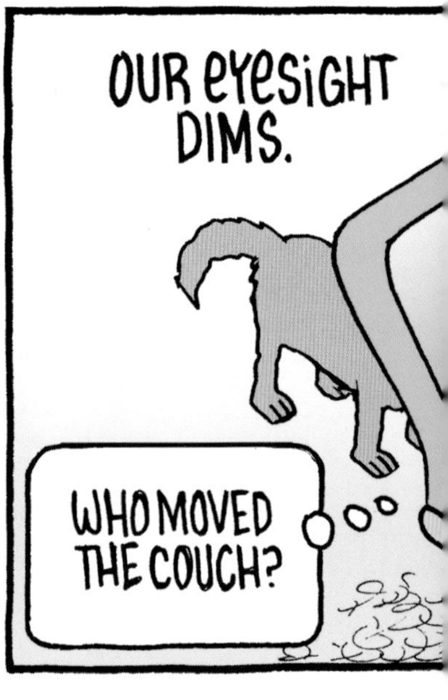
OUR EYESIGHT DIMS.
WHO MOVED THE COUCH?

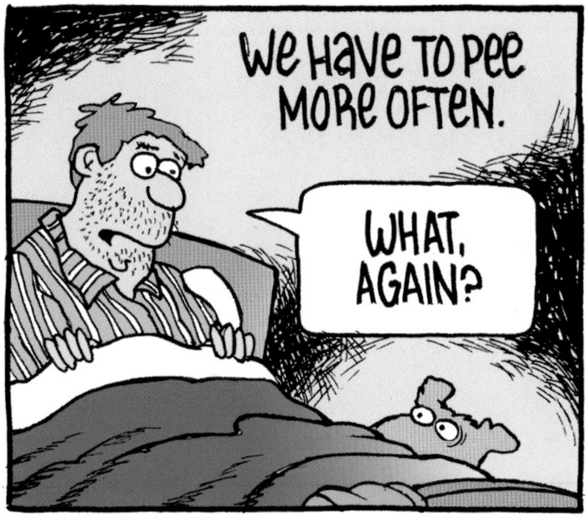
WE HAVE TO PEE MORE OFTEN.
WHAT, AGAIN?

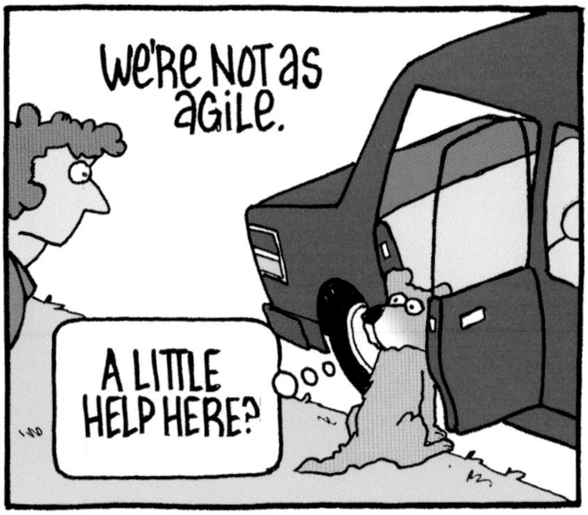
WE'RE NOT AS AGILE.
A LITTLE HELP HERE?

BUT THE AFFECTION WE SHOW YOU NEVER CHANGES.

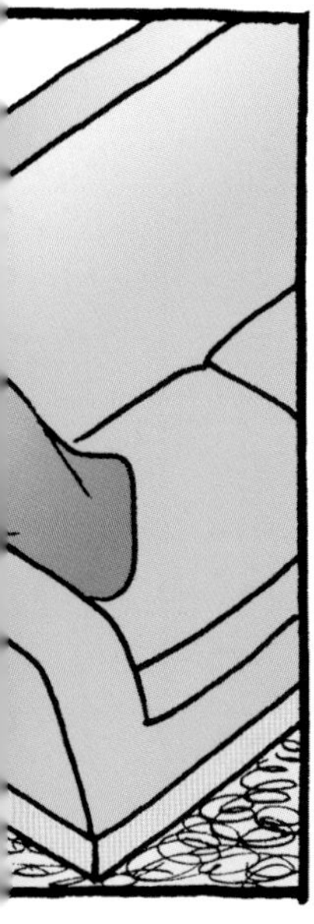

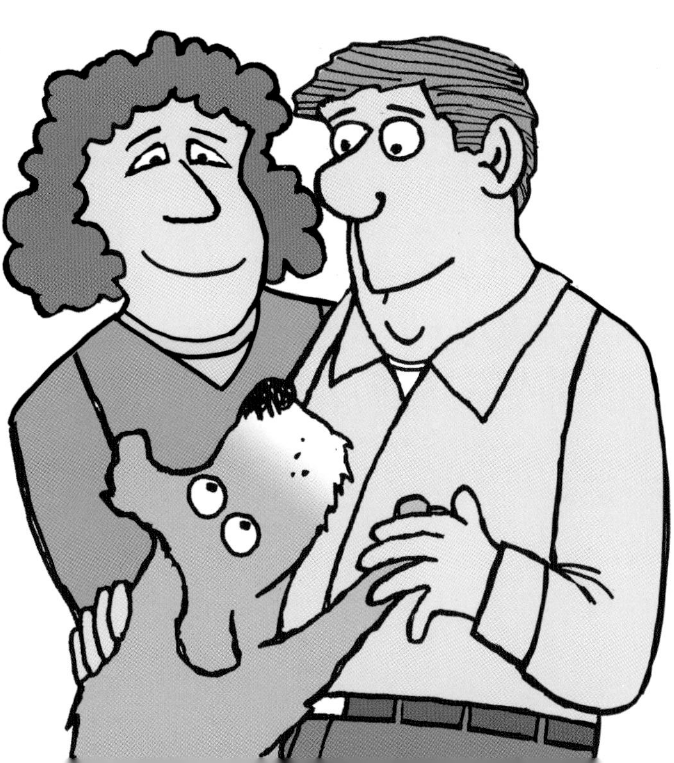

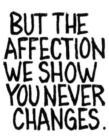

We know the day you come back from the vet alone will be hard on you.

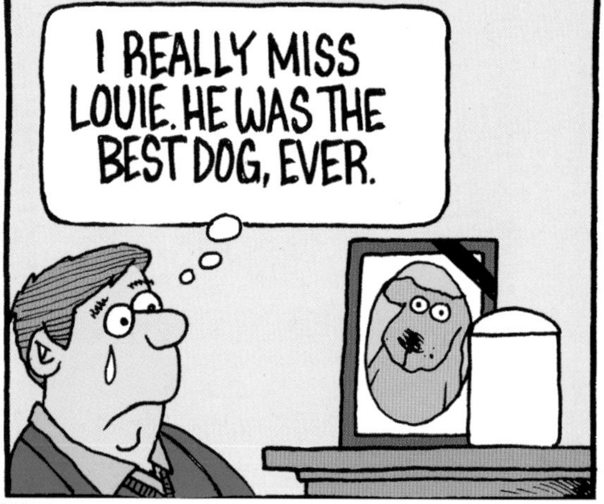
I REALLY MISS LOUIE. HE WAS THE BEST DOG, EVER.

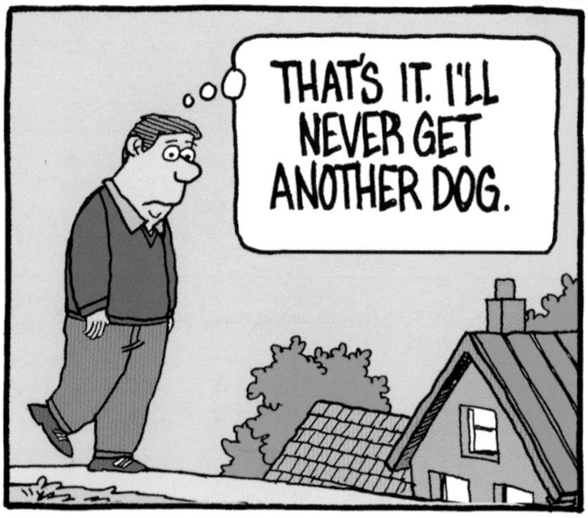
THAT'S IT. I'LL NEVER GET ANOTHER DOG.

Cherish the memories of the time we spent together...

... but there are more doggy memories to be made out there.

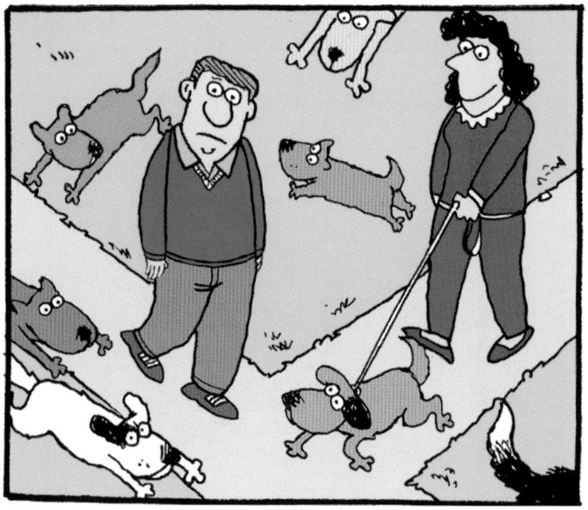

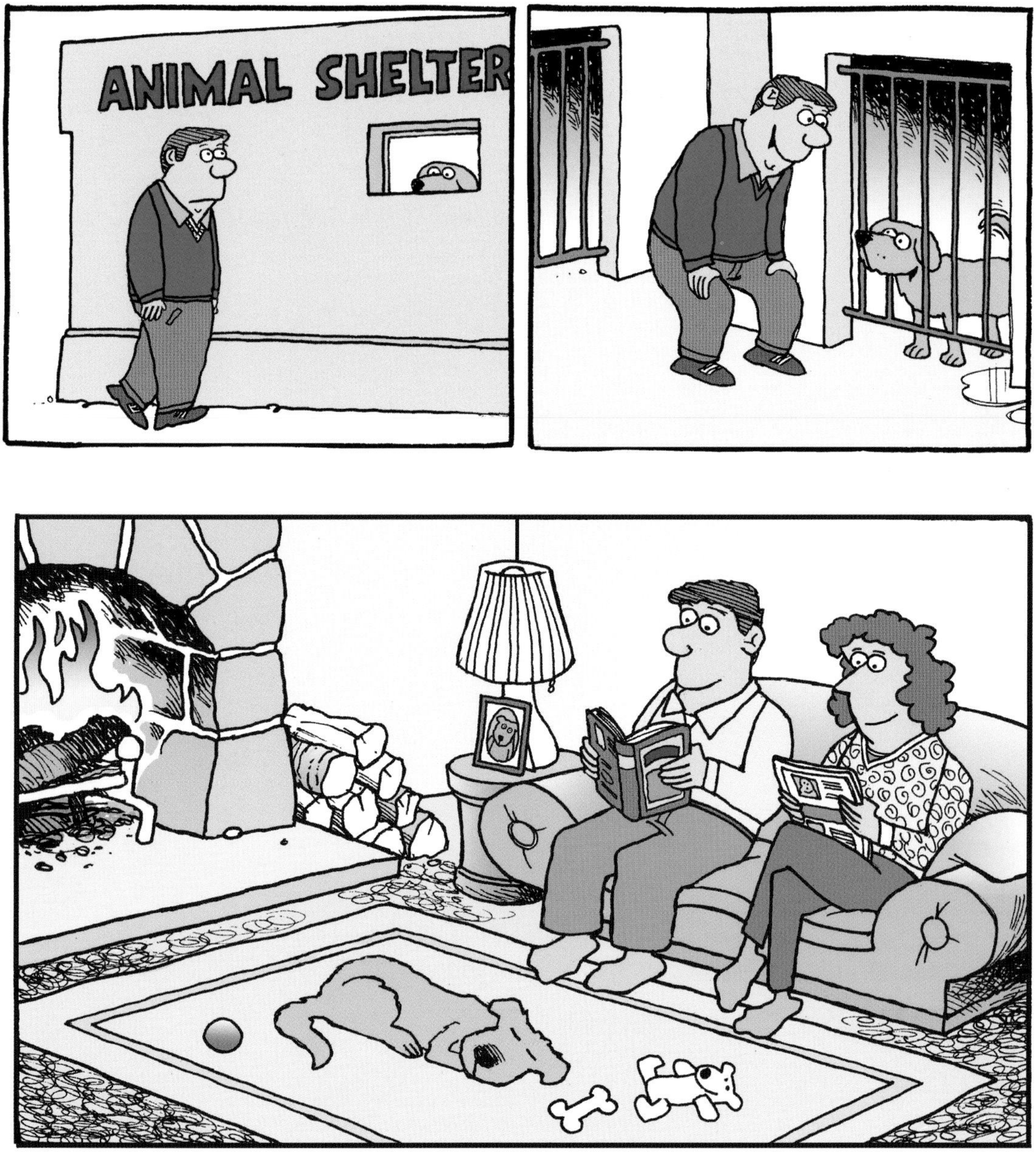
ANIMAL SHELTER

Besides, it would be a shame to waste a perfectly good dog person.

Check out this guy's other books about man's best friend, and other hilarious things...

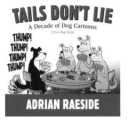

TAILS DON'T LIE
A Decade of Dog Cartoons
THUMP!
THUMP!
THUMP!
THUMP!
ADRIAN RAESIDE

TAILS DON'T LIE
A Decade of Dog Cartoons (70 in Dog Years)

ISBN: 9781550175998
Paperback / 8″× 8″/ 128 pp

TAILS DON'T LIE 2
A Pack of Dog Cartoons
ADRIAN RAESIDE

TAILS DON'T LIE 2
A Pack of Dog Cartoons

ISBN: 9781550177930
Paperback / 8″× 8″/ 128 pp

ADRIAN RAESIDE
THE
RAINBOW
BRIDGE
A Visit to Pet Paradise

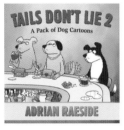

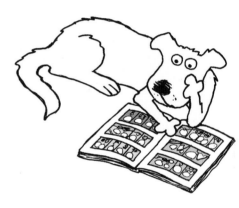

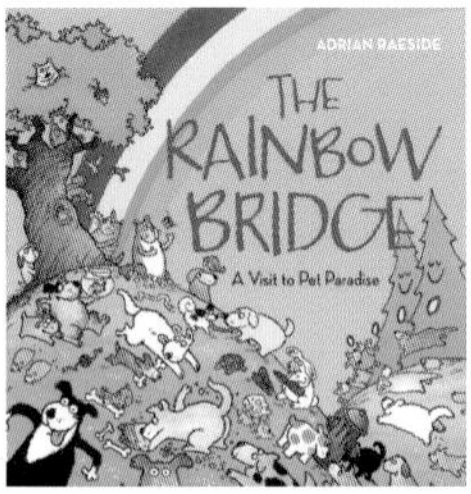

THE RAINBOW BRIDGE
A Visit to Pet Paradise

ISBN: 9781550175844
Paperback / 8″× 8″/ 32 pp

ISBN: 9781550179422
Hardcover / 8″× 8″/ 32 pp

INK
A TREASURY OF BC CARTOONS
THE BEST OF
ADRIAN RAESIDE

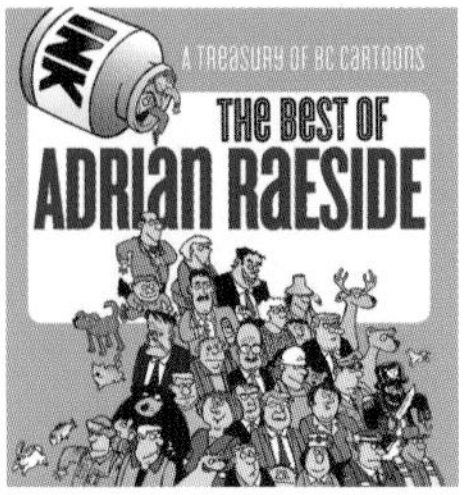

THE BEST OF ADRIAN RAESIDE
A Treasury of BC Cartoons

ISBN: 9781550176315
Paperback / 8″× 8″/ 192 pp

30 YEARS OF BC FERRIES CARTOONS
NO SAILING WAITS
and Other Ferry Tales
ADRIAN RAESIDE

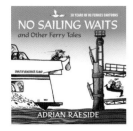

NO SAILING WAITS AND OTHER FERRY TALES
30 Years of BC Ferries Cartoons

ISBN: 9781550175967
Paperback / 8″× 8″/ 128 pp

For more laughs visit Adrian Raeside's website: www.raesidecartoon.com